REFORMING THEOLOGICAL ANTHROPOLOGY

··

*After the Philosophical Turn
to Relationality*

F. LeRon Shults

William B. Eerdmans Publishing Company
Grand Rapids, Michigan / Cambridge, U.K.

© 2003 Wm. B. Eerdmans Publishing Co.

Wm. B. Eerdmans Publishing Co.
255 Jefferson Ave. S.E., Grand Rapids, Michigan 49503 /
P.O. Box 163, Cambridge CB3 9PU U.K.

Printed in the United States of America

08 07 06 05 04 03   7 6 5 4 3 2 1

Library of Congress Cataloging-in-Publication Data

Shults, F. LeRon.
   Reforming theological anthropology: after the philosophical turn
   to relationality / F. LeRon Shults.
      p.   cm.
   Includes bibliographical references and index.
   ISBN 0-8028-4887-7 (pbk.: alk. paper)
   1. Man (Theology)   I. Title.

BT701.3.S48   2003
233 — dc21
                                                2002192537

www.eerdmans.com

REFORMING
THEOLOGICAL
ANTHROPOLOGY

To my children
Sara Elizabeth, Lee Michael, and Laura Anne

Contents

II. THEOLOGY, ANTHROPOLOGY, AND RELATIONALITY

Abbreviations

ANF	Ante-Nicene Fathers
ATP	Wolfhart Pannenberg, *Anthropology in Theological Perspective*, trans. Matthew J. O'Connell. Philadelphia: Westminster, 1985
CD	Karl Barth, *Church Dogmatics*, ed. G. W. Bromiley and T. F. Torrance, trans. G. W. Bromiley et al. 4 vols. Edinburgh: T&T Clark, 1936-69
CF	Friedrich Schleiermacher, *The Christian Faith*, trans. H. R. Mackintosh and J. S. Stewart. 1928. Reprint Edinburgh: T&T Clark, 1989
EvQ	Evangelical Quarterly
GOTR	*Greek Orthodox Theological Review*
Inst.	John Calvin, *Institutes of the Christian Religion*, ed. John T. McNeill, trans. Ford Lewis Battles. Philadelphia: Westminster, 1960
JAAR	*Journal of the American Academy of Religion*
JTS	*Journal of Theological Studies*
LCC	Library of Christian Classics
LW	Luther's Works, ed. Jaroslav Pelikan and Helmut T. Lehmann, trans. Pelikan, et al. St. Louis: Concordia; Philadelphia: Fortress, 1958-86
NPNF	Nicene and Post-Nicene Fathers, Series 1 and 2
NZST	*Neue Zeitschrift für systematischer Theologie*
PG	*Patrologia graeca*, ed. J.-P. Migne, 162 vols. Paris, 1857-86
PL	*Patrologia latina*, ed. J.-P. Migne, 217 vols. Paris, 1844-64
ST	Wolfhart Pannenberg, *Systematic Theology*, trans. G. W. Bromiley. 3 vols. Grand Rapids: Eerdmans, 1991-98
SumTh	Thomas Aquinas, *Summa Theologiae*
SVTQ	*St. Vladimir's Theological Quarterly*
TS	*Theological Studies*
TZ	*Theologische Zeitschrift*

Preface

I had originally intended to write a single book that would explore the implications of the turn to relationality in philosophy and science for both the Christian doctrine of anthropology and the doctrine of God. The reciprocal relation between our ideas of God and our self-understanding naturally suggested such a course. However, these themes shape not only each other but every Christian doctrine; as a result, I found myself pulled toward the implications of late modern relational categories for Christology, Pneumatology, soteriology, ecclesiology, eschatology, and just about everything else. Finally, I decided to limit myself in this book by focusing on the traditional loci of theological anthropology (human nature, sin, *imago Dei*), observing the transversal hermeneutical interplay across various Christian doctrines and identifying the most promising directions for reforming the presentation of these themes in dialogue with contemporary culture. Anthropology provides a heuristic lens and hermeneutical horizon for other doctrines, and vice versa; the following chapters often make explicit this reciprocity. Because a full constructive proposal for theological anthropology would have to include a treatment of all these interrelations, I have limited myself in *Reforming Theological Anthropology* to a programmatic outline of the most promising opportunities for reconstructing the doctrines of human nature, sin, and the image of God in light of the challenges of late modernity.

The reformative impetus and thematic organization of the chapters are explained in the Introduction, but it will be helpful here to note the relation of this book to other works, some of which resulted from the dissection of my original intention and others that are still in process. Naturally my own intuitions about the doctrine of God are operative in my reflections on anthropology in the chapters that follow. While I occasionally make these explicit, I often refer the reader to an essay in which I have provided the basic contours of a doctrine of God: "Sharing in the Divine Nature: Transformation, *Koinōnia* and the Doctrine of God," in Todd Speidell, ed., *On Being Christian . . . and Human: Essays in Celebration of Ray S. Anderson* (Eugene, Ore.: Wipf and Stock, 2002), 87-127. In particular, I trace there the retrieval of divine infinity, the revival of trinitarian doctrine, and the renewal of eschatological reflection in twentieth-century systematic theology. I am currently working on a manuscript that will further explicate these developments and their implications for the doctrine of God.

Our soteriological and ecclesiological views are also saturated by and embedded within our anthropological doctrinal formulations. Knowing, acting, and being *in community* are essential aspects of human existence, and a full anthropology would need to deal with the political issues of race, gender, and class. Because I have dealt with these dynamics in the context of another book (with psychologist Steven J. Sandage), *The Faces of Forgiveness: Searching for Wholeness and Salvation* (Grand Rapids: Baker Academic, 2003), I only touch on them here and refer the reader to the relevant sections. My proposal in part III below is correlated with my argument in *Faces of Forgiveness,* that salvation involves finding personal identity in Jesus Christ, dying to sin with Jesus Christ, and conforming to the image of Jesus Christ. I am also working on a project that will further explore directions for articulating a presentation of Christology in dialogue with the plausibility structures of late modern philosophy and contemporary science.

For the most part, I refer the reader to the most common and easily accessible English translations of classical and contemporary texts. Occasionally, however, for the sake of the argument, I provide my own amended or new translations from the original languages; this is explained in the relevant footnotes. Translations of the Hebrew Bible and the New Testament come from the New Revised Standard Version, unless otherwise noted.

Thanks goes to the editors of the various journals in which some of the material contained in parts I and II previously appeared. They graciously provided me permission to include revised and altered parts of the following articles in this book: "*Holding On* to the Theology-

Psychology Relationship: The Underlying Fiduciary Structures of Interdisciplinary Method," *Journal of Psychology and Theology* 25, no. 3 (Fall 1997): 329-40; "Pedagogy of the Repressed: What Keeps Seminarians from Transformational Learning?" *Theological Education* 36, no. 1 (Fall 1999): 157-69; "One Spirit with the Lord: Insights from James Loder's Theological Anthropology," *Princeton Theological Review* 7, no. 3 (Summer 2000): 17-26; "Schleiermacher's *Reciprocal Relationality:* The Regulative Principle of His Theological Method," in *Schleiermacher on the Workings of the Knowing Mind,* ed. Ruth Drucilla Richardson (Lewiston, N.Y.: Edwin Mellen Press, 1998): 177-96; "Constitutive Relationality in Anthropology and Trinity: The Shaping of the *Imago Dei* Doctrine in Barth and Pannenberg," *Neue Zeitschrift für systematische Theologie und Religionsphilosophie* 39 (December 1997): 304-22; and "A Dubious Christological Formula: From Leontius of Byzantium to Karl Barth," *Theological Studies* 57 (September 1996): 431-46.

I am also thankful for a 2001 sabbatical made available by the Bethel Seminary community, which allowed me to carve out time for reading and writing. An award from the Center for Theology and Natural Science for my course, "Theology and Science," made it possible to extend this sabbatical. I am particularly grateful to colleagues who read all or part of the manuscript at different stages, including Niels-Henrik Gregersen, Jan-Olav Henricksen, Ivica Novakovic, Shane Oborn, Alan Padgett, Ken Reynhout, J. Wentzel van Huyssteen, and James Wilson. In addition, conversations with several of my Bethel colleagues, especially David Clark, Robert Rakestraw, and Steve Sandage, helped me to focus my presentation. Special thanks to Leland Eliason and Greg Bourgond, whose administrative work and personal friendship have provided space for scholarship. Thanks also to Bill Eerdmans, Jr., for his personal encouragement, and to Chuck Van Hof, Jenny Hoffman, and the editorial staff at Eerdmans for their excellent help every step of the way.

I am most grateful to my wife Elizabeth and to my children, from whom I have learned the most about relationality and anthropology. This book is dedicated to them.

F. LeRon Shults

Introduction

John Calvin organized the first chapter of his 1559 *Institutes of the Christian Religion* around three claims. First, he insisted that "without knowledge of self there is no knowledge of God." Second, "without knowledge of God there is no knowledge of self." Third, this mutuality between knowing God and knowing ourselves occurs in the experience of facing "God's majesty."[1] Here Calvin rightly notes the inherent reciprocity between our awareness of God and our self-awareness. By emphasizing the existential "dread and wonder" *(horreur et stupeur)* out of which this knowing emerges, Calvin also models the appropriate starting place for theological inquiry. If the fear of the Lord is the beginning of wisdom and knowledge (Prov. 1:7; 9:10), then my attempt to understand my self in relation to God must start with acknowledging and embracing this delightful terror. I fear that which I cannot control, and this existential anxiety is most intense when I reflect on my ambiguous relation to the mysterious presence of God, which I am unable to manipulate, and on my futile attempts to secure a place for my "self" in the world. Theological anthropology articulates the gospel of grace manifested in the history of Jesus Christ, by whose Spirit I am set free from the binding pain of my attempts to control my own destiny and in whose Spirit I rest peacefully in the dynamic presence of divine love. But it is not simply about me and God.

What Calvin does not emphasize is the role that our relations to other persons play in mediating our knowledge of self and of God. The

1. John Calvin, *Institutes of the Christian Religion*, ed. John T. McNeill, trans. Ford Lewis Battles, LCC (Philadelphia: Westminster, 1960), pp. 35-39.

1

search for self-understanding in relation to the divine "Other" cannot be divorced from a trembling fascination with the human "other." My sense of self is called into being and formed through interaction with other persons within my particular set of overlapping communities. This mutual confrontation evokes an ambiguous transactional drama in which the boundaries of self and other are explored, negotiated, transgressed, or reified. Anxiety about my identity is intensified as I am repulsed and seduced by a multiplicity of encountered others — my ability to repress these fears and desires collapses when I fall asleep and dreams overtake me. Late modern theological anthropology must take into account not only our psychological and social relations to other persons, but also the physical and cultural relations that compose the matrices within which our lives are dynamically embedded. I find my self struggling to become wise, good, and free in my communal relations. When I seek to understand the origin, condition, and goal of this becoming, I am engaging in theological anthropology.

The Christian tradition has not always carefully attended to the social, cultural, and physical dimensions of humanity in its formulations of anthropological doctrine. The focus has often been on the abstract nature of the individual and the intellectual and volitional powers of one's soul. Today in our late modern culture we find a growing dissatisfaction with the denigration of human embodiment and sociality that characterized so much ancient and early modern anthropology. These concerns have arisen in connection with what I call the philosophical "turn to relationality." Chapter one traces the historical development of this shift by identifying some of the key turning points from Aristotle to Levinas. This brief overview outlines the context within which we must now engage in *reforming* theological anthropology. Although these developments challenge some ancient and early modern historical formulations, they also provide a new opportunity for theology to retrieve some of the inherently relational thought-forms of the biblical tradition. Christian theological anthropology has much to contribute to the contemporary dialogue on the intrinsically relational mediation of personal knowing, acting, and being.

The goal of reforming theological anthropology is reformative — not only to understand but also to facilitate the dynamics of spiritual transformation as we reach out in relation to ourselves, to others, and to God.[2] This means that our explorations of the conceptual space[3] of theological anthropology aim to serve the reformation of the existential space in which we together respond to the presence of divine grace. In part I, "Anthropology, Theology, and the Reader," this existential space is in the foreground. These chapters are not just preambles to the theological task, however, because the self-awareness that Calvin spoke of is essential for reforming theological anthropology. Reflecting on one's own relation to relationality is a crucial step for understanding the role and value of the concept of relationality. Encouraging this reflection is the purpose of chapter two, which engages in interdisciplinary dialogue with developmental psychology. How an individual holds on to a concept (such as "relationality") is shaped by one's order of consciousness, or what I call the "fiduciary structures" that underlie interdisciplinary method. This is important because the way the reader thinks about relating theology to other disciplines (such as philosophy and anthropology) will register its effect as one engages the historical and systematic work of chapters five-ten. As we will see already in chapter two, the "reader" does not stand alone in any of the developmental stages but is always socially situated.

Chapters three and four enter into dialogue with two other human sciences that also thematize these relations: educational psychology and cultural anthropology. Both chapters draw on the insights of practical theologian James Loder, whose passion for linking the resources of Reformed theology to the transformation of persons and society is evident in all his works. Loder demonstrates the mutual enhancement that can occur when theologians engage in interdisciplinary dialogue and transgress the boundaries of fields such as physics and anthropology. He believes that we should retrieve the ultimate relationality at the center of Christian faith, manifested in the doctrine of the Incarnation, and show how it illuminates proximate forms of relationality in other forms of human inquiry.

The focus of the third chapter is the repression of various fears

2. Cf. Henri J. M. Nouwen, *Reaching Out: The Three Movements of the Spiritual Life* (New York: Image, 1975). His "three movements" are correlated to the self, the other, and God.

3. It might be equally appropriate to speak of exploring "conceptual time" or "conceptual space-time." Conceptualizing occurs in time, with a specific history and trajectory. Speaking of conceptual space-time might help us emphasize the dynamic or kinetic characteristics of our thinking processes.

among seminarians that inhibit transformational learning. Of course, these anxieties are not unique to seminarians (or professors), but this is my own vocational context and so provides illustrative material that may be transposed to other contexts. A psychological perspective clarifies these repressive dynamics, but when the object of fear is theological, the problem is no longer too much but rather not enough fear — as the biblical authors knew. Defining fear as a response to our perceived inability to control an existentially relevant object helps us to understand how the dialectic between fear and love shapes the task of theological education, which is essentially reformative. Chapter four turns to an interdisciplinary dialogue with cultural anthropology, emphasizing some of the contributions of Claude Lévi-Strauss. This exercise in philosophical theology aims to show the illuminative power of the Christian belief that our personal identity is transformed through spiritual union with God in Christ. In both of these chapters, we will observe the impact of the philosophical turn to relationality on the anthropological sciences, which will help to set the stage for the material discussions of later chapters.

My proposal for reforming and reformative theological anthropology emerges out of my own embeddedness in the Reformed tradition, as becomes more evident in the chapters of part II. Reformed theology is characterized by a commitment to a hermeneutical openness to reforming the received tradition; not only the church but also theology is *reformata et semper reformanda*.[4] This reformation aims for the transformation of the whole church and the whole world under the authority of God's Word through the power of the Spirit. In the Reformed tradition, the life of the mind has been embraced as a legitimate and important way of serving God, and rigorous engagement with culture, including the arts and sciences, has been encouraged and valued as crucial to the success of the mission of the community of God.[5]

The task of reforming theological anthropology did not stop with

4. Cf. Jürgen Moltmann, "Theologia Reformata et Semper Reformanda," in *Toward the Future of Reformed Theology: Tasks, Topics, Traditions*, ed. David Willis and Michael Welker (Grand Rapids: Eerdmans, 1999), 120-35.

5. See the introduction to *Reformed Reader: A Sourcebook in Christian Theology*, ed. William Stacy Johnson and John H. Leith, vol. 1 (Louisville: Westminster John Knox, 1993); and chaps. 3 and 7 in John Leith, *Introduction to the Reformed Tradition* (Atlanta: John Knox, 1981).

John Calvin, Jonathan Edwards, Charles Hodge, or Karl Barth. It passes to each generation as we attempt to present the illuminative power of the gospel through engagement with contemporary philosophical and scientific interpretations of the world from within the living, dynamic biblical tradition. In the following chapters, the work of many Reformed thinkers will be mined for both inspiration and material help. Reforming theological anthropology is an ecumenical task, however, and our explorations will often lead us to be critical of some earlier Reformed models and to appropriate resources in theologians from other Protestant traditions, as well as from Roman Catholicism and Eastern Orthodoxy. As I argue throughout the book, the turn to relationality offers theology a new opportunity for presenting a Christian understanding of humanity in a way that upholds some key biblical intuitions that have sometimes been obscured or lost.

The concerns of philosophical, systematic, and historical theology intersect in each of the three chapters of part II, "Theology, Anthropology, and Relationality." These chapters share a basic theme, the hermeneutical function of anthropological relationality, but they focus on this function in methodology, the doctrine of Trinity, and Christology, respectively. Chapter five argues that the material "reciprocal relationality" evident in Schleiermacher's anthropology in his *Christian Faith* (1831) has a regulative function throughout his theological method. Many scholars have missed this connection and so have perceived a contradiction at the heart of his system. My suggestion is that attention to this relationality illustrates the coherence of his overall dogmatic proposal.

Chapter six demonstrates the inherent connection between constitutive relationality in the doctrines of the image of God and the Trinity in the work of Karl Barth and Wolfhart Pannenberg. By comparing and contrasting these theologians, one can illustrate the importance of relationality not only materially in particular doctrines but also formally in the actual performance of the theological task. Chapter seven examines the relation between anthropology and Christology by attending to the historical development of the *anhypostasis-enhypostasis* formula from Leontius of Byzantium in the sixth century to Karl Barth in the twentieth. The way in which theologians have imagined the relation between the substances of the soul and the body also structures the way in which they answered the question about the relation between the divine and human natures in the one person of Jesus Christ. Although the influence of Aristotelian and Platonic philosophical and anthropological presuppositions will figure more heavily in part III, we will often have the opportunity to observe their impact in several of these historical examples.

Building on the insights of these historical forays and maintaining my concern for practical reformation, I turn in part III to the explicit task of "Reforming Theological Anthropology." These final three chapters explore the importance of the concept of relationality for the three traditional loci of theological anthropology: human nature, sin, and the image of God. Each chapter has two major sections. First, I explore those traditional formulations in the doctrine that have been particularly problematic and show how a lack of emphasis on relationality may have contributed to some of the impasses in current debates. My focus here is on Western theology and the specific assumptions that have most influenced contemporary discussion. The second section of each chapter outlines the challenges and opportunities that the turn to relationality has raised in connection with these issues. Challenges to the traditional formulations come from research in biblical scholarship, from discoveries in science, and from philosophical reflection on human existence, all of which are linked to the shift toward relational categories in late modernity.

As I turn to this reformative task in the last three chapters, I do not leave behind the existential "dread and wonder" that Calvin argued ought to permeate all our theological inquiry. Human existence is characterized by a trembling fascination, a passionate longing for a secure relation with the other. Theological anthropology must account for this existential reality. In chapter eight I examine *epistemic* anxiety, the human longing for truth. The dominance of body/soul substance dualism and the faculty psychology that accompanied it have deeply shaped the Western way of thinking about human knowing, which in turn canalized formulations in the doctrine of human nature. Chapter nine treats the issue of *ethical* anxiety, our ambiguous longing for goodness. One of the most prevalent models in the West for explaining why humans find themselves unable to will the good is Augustine's theory of inherited sin. The diminishing plausibility of this hypothesis calls for a response. Finally, chapter ten explores what I call *ontological* anxiety — the human longing for beauty, which in its broadest sense involves a desire for belonging in a pattern of peaceful reality. Many classical interpretations of the doctrine of the image of God attempted to describe this longing as a result of our having lost our place in a primordial garden. In each case we will see that these formulations presupposed anthropological conceptions that have been radically challenged by the turn to relationality, which manifests itself not only in philosophy and science but also in the growing exegetical consensus surrounding the issues of biblical anthropology.

Reforming theological anthropology requires a response to the challenges raised in late modern culture after the turn to relationality in philosophy and science, which I trace in the first chapter. The nature of these challenges will come into focus as we proceed. However, it is important to begin by thematizing the way we respond to challenges generally. We can formally identify three broad types of responses to postmodernity. On the one side, we find a *de*constructive response — here the emphasis is primarily on engaging contemporary culture, with less interest in upholding or conserving the tradition. The other extreme is what we might call a *paleo*-constructive response, which would ignore or dismiss the challenges by appealing to an earlier premodern (or early modern) era in which truth and knowledge about God and humanity were allegedly unproblematic. This response is intent on maintaining a particular traditional formulation, with less interest in accommodating contemporary cultural concerns. While we might be able to find a few examples of fundamentalist repristinations or ultraliberal projects, neither pure fundamentalism (immunizing an old tradition from any contemporary influence) nor pure liberalism (completely freeing oneself from the influence of a tradition) is really possible. We find ourselves pushed and pulled between distanciation from and participation in the biblical tradition,[6] and most theological proposals operate within this tensive field between the extremes.

The *re*constructive response to the challenges of late modernity describes the wide middle ground, which is at once more interesting and more difficult to navigate. Naming this middle ground "reconstruc-

---

6. For discussion see J. Wentzel van Huyssteen, *The Shaping of Rationality: Toward Interdisciplinarity in Theology and Science* (Grand Rapids: Eerdmans, 1999); and Delwin Brown, *The Boundaries of Our Habitations: Tradition and Theological Construction* (Albany: State University of New York Press, 1994).

tive" does not determine a priori any material response to a particular issue, but it may raise our awareness of the forces pulling us toward either side. Behind these types of responses is a debate over the nature of human rationality. Foundationalist epistemology appeals to those tempted by the paleo-constructive response, while the threat of deconstruction often hangs over those who embrace antifoundationalism. In *The Postfoundationalist Task of Theology* I set out my own proposal for overcoming this double bind that structures the debate.[7] Building on the works of several philosophical theologians who aim to find a middle way between the extremes of absolutism and relativism, I challenge the common assumption that foundationalism and antifoundationalism are the only options. Joining the call for a postfoundationalist linking of epistemology and hermeneutics, I critically appropriate and refigure Wolfhart Pannenberg's methodology for this task. Although Pannenberg's way of conceptualizing the reciprocity between philosophical and systematic theology is helpful, I argue that we must take more seriously the challenges and opportunities that have arisen in postmodernity. The current book is an attempt to engage in this ongoing postfoundationalist task in relation to the doctrines of theological anthropology.

The reformation of theological anthropology operates at the intersection of the historical development of the lived biblical tradition and contemporary philosophical and scientific interpretations of reality. Theology is indeed to be reformed and it is always being reformed, but this reformation is *of* the biblical tradition. We must strive to understand those who carried it forward in the context of their cultures as we attempt to carry it forward in our own culture with the same courage and humility. It may be that the best way to conserve the intuitions of the biblical tradition is to liberate them for authentic dialogue with contemporary culture as we respond to the existential anxiety of those with whom we are called to enter into fellowship as we share together in the new relation to God made possible by the Spirit of Christ. This process will engender fear in many readers, for we are often most terrified of being forced to give up long-held beliefs. May we begin (and continue) the search for knowledge and wisdom by fearing God alone.

---

7. Shults, *The Postfoundationalist Task of Theology: Wolfhart Pannenberg and the New Theological Rationality* (Grand Rapids: Eerdmans, 1999).

My hope is that this book will help to clarify the crucial distinction between the reality of our existential creaturely relations and various doctrinal formulations about those relations. Our resistance to reforming theological anthropology may be due not simply to our desire to protect a particular biblical interpretation of the human creature in relation to God, but to a deeper fear of letting go of hidden philosophical and scientific presuppositions that constrain those readings of Scripture. The first step is to understand the major philosophical shifts that have led to a new appreciation of relationality in late modern culture.

1

The Philosophical Turn
to Relationality

Relationality is not a new concept for Christian theology. The doctrine of the Incarnation and the doctrine of the Trinity, which are defining characteristics of Christian faith, are inherently relational. Throughout the historical development of theological anthropology as well, whether the issue was the nature of humanity, sin, or the image of God, relations have been essential to Christian self-understanding. However, agreement on the nature and importance of relationality per se in these doctrines has not been uniform. This is due in part to the reciprocity between theological conceptions and the philosophical and scientific conceptions of any given culture and time. As several of the chapters in this book will show, the history of theology provides ample evidence of this mutual influence, and today this hermeneutical reciprocity continues in "postmodernity." This is one of the reasons it is important for us to understand the *philosophical* turn to relationality and its impact on our late modern scientific culture. The purpose of this chapter is to outline the historical development of the category of "relation" in some major philosophers from ancient Greece to the present in order to set the stage for the reconstructive work of the following chapters.

Before this turn to relationality, in which Kant and Hegel played a crucial role in philosophy, most Western formulations in theological anthropology privileged substance over relation. As we will see in part III, this is one of the primary reasons for the challenges to traditional theological anthropology in late modernity. This first chapter offers an overview of the philosophical currents that led to a new appreciation of relationality as an explanatory category. I believe that understanding these developments may allay some of the anxiety that often overshadows the reconstructive task of theology. My use of the word "turn" is not intended to suggest a completely new development in philosophy. Concern about relationality commonly played an important role in ethical and epistemological discourse in the West. The novelty is a new emphasis on the insertion of the category of relation into the heart of metaphysical discourse. After the turn to relationality, the concepts of being real and being in relation are thought together in a fresh way. I am using "turn" here in a fashion analogous to its function in the well-known phrases "linguistic turn" and "anthropological turn" — philosophers had not ignored language or humanity before these shifts, but their hermeneutical and metaphysical significance were not always recognized.

The major sections of this chapter review the philosophical turn to relationality in two stages: Aristotle to Kant, and Hegel to Levinas. I defend my decision for including particular thinkers and movements as I go along. Any attempt to treat such a broad and complex issue in a single chapter must inevitably be cursory; my goal is a modest one: to identify and explain the importance of some of the key turning points in this history. In a concluding section, I provide a brief reminder of the responsibility of theology vis-à-vis this shift. As we will see in the following chapters, the shaping influence has not been unidirectional — theological assumptions have often led to the formulation of philosophical and scientific categories. Today theology operates in a cultural context that has been radically altered by late modern philosophical reflection, and the task of reforming theological anthropology requires that we face these challenges and opportunities. At the conclusion of this chapter, I will explore the sense in which theology is responsible both for and to the turn to relationality.

Relationality from Aristotle to Kant

Most of the pre-Socratic Greek philosophers focused less on the relation of things to each other and more on the question of the essence of things. What "substance" stays the same beneath all the changes that we see in the world? They offered a diversity of answers, including water (Thales), air (Anaximenes), and fire (Heraclitus). This debate about being and becoming was in the background when Plato (428-347 B.C.E.)

proposed a metaphysical dualism between an immaterial realm of unchanging Forms or Ideas and a material realm of temporal change. In several of Plato's dialogues (e.g., *Theaetetus* and *Philebus*) the difference between the unchanging substance of a thing and its changing accidental qualities is presupposed, but it was his student Aristotle (384-322 B.C.E.) who developed a full theory of predication that carefully distinguished substance from accidents. Here we find the root of the Western philosophical privileging of substance over relationality.

In an early work called the *Categories,* Aristotle was interested in understanding how we *say* what a thing is *(to estin)*. Sometimes we simply speak of a thing itself (e.g., "the man" or "running"). At other times, as when we make a statement, we speak of a thing in combination with some other thing (e.g., "the man is running"). In other words, we say "things" about things and things are said about "things." This is hardly shocking. Aristotle wants to go further and determine what types of "things" we say about things, and to clarify the nature of the "things" about which other things are said. He argues that things that are said (simply, not in combination with other things) fall into ten categories: "each signifies either substance or quantity or qualification or a relative or where or when or being-in-a-position or having or doing or being-affected" (1^b25).[1] The term "substance" is not only first on his list, but also takes ontological priority because a substance must be included in any predication. That is, to make an affirmation (or negation) requires combining a substance, such as "the man," with a predicate that fits into one of the other categories, such as "running" (doing).

This is where Aristotle introduces his influential distinction between "primary" and "secondary" substances. Primary substances are particular things like an individual person. Secondary substances are the species and genera to which the particular thing belongs, which in the case of an individual person would be "rational" and "animal." The more concrete, the more substantial, argues Aristotle, for "of the secondary substances the species is more a substance than the genus, since it is nearer to the primary substance" (2^b7). All of the other categories are said of primary or secondary substances. Aristotle clearly

1. Quotations and references are from *The Complete Works of Aristotle,* ed. Jonathan Barnes, 2 vols. (Princeton: Princeton University Press, 1984).

13

gives the category of substance *(ousia)* priority over the fourth category, which is the category of relation, that is, the "toward something" *(pros ti)* of a thing. What we might call a thing's "towardness" does not really get at its "whatness" for Aristotle.

As illustrations of the category of relation, Aristotle offers the terms "half," "double," and "greater." He suggests that "we call *relatives* all such things as are said to be just what they are, of or than other things, or in some other way in relation to something else" (6^a37). Already in this early work we sense that he views the category of relatives as somehow farther from substantiality than the other categories. Yet Aristotle expresses a nagging feeling that he is missing something.

> Now if the definition of relatives given above was adequate, it is either exceedingly difficult or impossible to reach the solution that no substance is spoken of as a relative. But if it was not adequate, and if those things are relatives from which *being is the same as being somehow related to something,* then perhaps some answer may be found. . . . It is perhaps hard to make firm statements on such questions without having examined them many times. (8^a29-34, 8^b22-24)

In his later writings, Aristotle overcomes this hesitation; he is less reserved and argues explicitly that relatives are accidental and less real. In the *Metaphysics,* he explains that "the great and the small, and the like, must be relative to something; but the relative is least of all things a real thing or substance, and is posterior to quality and quantity; and the relatives are accidents of quantity" (1088^a21-25).[2]

Notice that each of his examples for "relatives" in the *Categories* implied a quantitative ratio and presupposed susceptibility of mathematical measurement. Here in the *Metaphysics,* "relation" is now explicitly an accident of "quantity." Although relatives are singled out, he seems to think of all of the other categories (except substance) as relative in a broad sense, and so accidental. The substance of a thing, as the "substratum" that underlies it, is "that which is not predicated of a subject, but of which all else is predicated" (1029^a28). Only substances can exist independently; relatives, like the other categories, cannot. While debate continues among Aristotle interpreters over his precise intentions here,

2. Cf. *Posterior Analytics* 83^a15-24.

the important point for my purposes is not controversial: his model led to a hard distinction between "substances" and "accidents" (including relations) in which the latter are not essential to what a thing is, and so less real. It came to be orthodoxy in Western philosophy that the relations of a thing to other things are not essential to defining or knowing what that thing is.

During the centuries that followed, Aristotle's list of ten categories was not universally adopted.[3] The Stoics typically have a shorter list of four "generic" concepts: substratum (or subject), quality (or essential attribute), state (or accidental condition), and relation. Much more influential, however, is the emergence of Neoplatonism, and especially the contribution of Plotinus (205-270 C.E.). He rejects both the Stoic and the Aristotelian lists, and takes the five "kinds" in Plato's *Sophist* as the ultimate categories: Being, Motion, Stability, Difference, and Identity (*Enneads* 6.1-2). Plotinus begins with "Being," which he takes to be obviously a primary genus, but then argues that the other four are not merely modifications of Substance (Real Being), nor are they distinct from substance; they are "constituents" of Substance. Immediately following his exposition of these five primary genera, Plotinus goes out of his way to stress that the term "Relation" is "remote from Being." He asks: "As for Relation, manifestly an offshoot, how can it be included among primaries? Relation is of thing ranged against thing; it is not self-pivoted, but looks outward."[4]

In the early Middle Ages we find a mixture of Neoplatonic and Aristotelian influences in the theological appropriation of the categories of substance and accidents.[5] Plotinus had insisted that one cannot apply the same categories in the same way to both the intelligible and sensible worlds, and he explored the way in which these "kinds" existed. Porphyry, who was a pupil of Plotinus, accepted the ten Aristotelian

---

3. This was exacerbated by the fact that he is internally inconsistent, offering different lists in various writings. The ten of the *Categories*, however, are usually considered the "Aristotelian" list. For a treatment of this background and a general historical overview, see H.-G. Steiner, "Relation," *Historisches Wörterbuch der Philosophie*, ed. Joachim Ritter and Karlfried Gründer (Basel: Schwabe, 1992), 8:578-611.

4. *Ennead* 6.2.16. In *Plotinus: The Enneads*, trans. Stephen MacKenna, new ed. (Burdett, N.Y.: Larson, 1992), 553.

5. For analysis of an example of a theological anthropology that adapts elements from both streams, see my treatment of Leontius of Byzantium in chapter seven below.

categories in his *Isagogue,* but asked very Plotinian questions about them. Do genera and species exist only in the understanding or also outside of it? If the latter, are these categories corporeal or incorporeal? Are they separable from, or do they only reside in, sensible things? When Boethius translated the *Isagogue* into Latin in the sixth century, he also offered his own answers to these questions. This set the stage for the debate over "universals" that dominated the High Middle Ages. Whether the answer is the moderate realism of Thomas Aquinas[6] or the nominalism of William of Ockham, the question is the same; Christian theologians for the most part accept the validity of Porphyry's way of formulating the issue, which presupposes a particular way of distinguishing between substance and (accidental) relations.

As early modern science arises out of the Renaissance, we see a slow but revolutionary shift in the understanding and use of categories. For Aristotle, the generic *qualities* of a thing (like its being "red" or "bovine") are very real; in fact, they are more real than the *quantitative* predicates that we apply to it like "large" or "half" (which are merely "relations"). As the mathematical models of Copernicus, Galileo, and others came to explain more and more of the world, philosophers began to think that quantitative analysis may get us closer to the "whatness" (or substantiality) of a thing than does a description of its qualities. The latter, after all,

---

6. Thomas's reliance on Aristotelian distinctions, including the categories of substance and accident, is well known. Because he accepted the idea that relations are not essential to a thing, he had difficulty thinking about the trinitarian relations as essential to the divine nature. It is interesting, however, that Thomas resisted giving up on the importance of relationality, which he believed is built into the nature of theology: "Now all things are dealt with in holy teaching in terms of God [*sub ratione Dei*], either because they are God himself or because they are relative to him as their origin and end. . . . All these indeed are dwelt on by this science, yet as held in their relationship to God [*ordinem ad Deum*]. . . . All other things that are settled in Holy Scripture are embraced in God, not that they are parts of him — such as essential components or accidents — but because they are somehow related to him" (*Summa Theologiae,* Blackfriars edition [New York: McGraw-Hill, 1964], 1:27 [I, Q. 1, Art. 7; cf. I, Q. 8, Art. 1]). Despite his difficulty in fitting them into the categories of his Aristotelian substance/accident metaphysic, Thomas could not give up on the central Christian intuitions about relationality in God (Trinity) and the relation of God to creatures. This tension was also evident earlier in Augustine. Despite his reliance on "substance" metaphysics, which I will illustrate in chapters eight and nine, Augustine's reflection on his own relation to the trinitarian God led him to recognize that when "things" are "said" about God "according to relation," these relations are not accidental (*De Trinitate* 5.5.6).

appears more subjective than the former. Perhaps the only "real" description of nature is provided by objective mathematical measurement. This bias was further strengthened by the increasing popularity of nominalism, which used Ockham's razor to cut off what appeared to be the unnecessary hypothesis of universal generic qualities. This severing encouraged the growing scientific interest in dissecting and naming particular phenomena. By the seventeenth century we find a rigorous debate on the nature of and distinction between "primary" and "secondary" qualities. In his *Meditations on First Philosophy* (1641) Descartes argues for a radical dualism between two types of substance: "extended thing" *(res extensa)* and "thinking thing" *(res cogitans)*. In this way he could protect the reality of secondary qualities like color and sound, but the price for this was segregating them into the subjective realm of *res cogitans.* Spinoza exemplifies the other extreme; he proposes a monism in which all that exists is Absolute Substance *(Deus sive Natura)*. In his *Ethics,* which was published soon after his death in 1677, he tries to maintain an infinite plurality of attributes of the one substance, although each attribute also expresses the essence of the one substance. The tension between these two philosophical extremes is still with us today.

During this era the sciences that we now call "physics" and "astronomy" were encompassed by the term "natural philosophy." The title of Newton's influential *Philosophiae Naturalis Principia Mathematica* (1687) underscores the important relation between science and philosophy. It also illustrates the growing faith in the explanatory power of mathematics. Here we have a picture of the universe in which bodies (material substances) move around absolute (static) space and bump into one another. Mathematics measures quantities and ratios that operate in accordance with the laws of inertial force. As the world of "subjective" qualities that the human mind perceives was made secondary to the "objective" qualities of nature, human subjects began to feel like aliens, unrelated to the cosmos.[7] Since that time, scientists have come to emphasize relationality much more radically. Einstein himself was aware of the philosophical underpinnings of mechanistic science, and even in

---

7. Partially for religious reasons, Robert Boyle tried to remind his scientific contemporaries of the de facto existence of human subjects, and insisted on the equal reality of "secondary" qualities. For a history of this development, see E. A. Burtt, *The Metaphysical Foundations of Modern Science* (Atlantic Highlands, N.J.: Humanities Press, 1932).

his explanation of the theory of "relativity," he felt it was important to point to developments such as nineteenth-century field theories of Michael Faraday and James Clerk Maxwell that led to understandings of reality not as "particles" of matter in the traditional sense, but as fields of energy.[8] Discoveries and developments in quantum theory led to a further outworking of relational thinking; particle physics is not really about particles anymore but about relationships — interpenetrating and mutually binding energy fields.[9] After the emergence of chaos theory in the late twentieth century, most physicists agree that units and relations are distinct but interdependent: "for an interaction to be real, the 'nature' of the related things must derive from these relations, while at the same time the relations must derive from the 'nature' of the things."[10]

Back in the early modern period, however, substance metaphysics was thriving, albeit in new dualist and empiricist forms. Its survival would require philosophical clarification on the issue of the distinct types of qualities. The distinction found its classical formulation in John Locke's *Essay Concerning Human Understanding* (1689). He explains that the primary qualities of "Body" that produce simple ideas in us are Solidity, Extension, Figure, Motion or Rest, and Number. Among secondary qualities, which "in truth are nothing in the Objects themselves, but Powers to produce various Sensations in us," he includes colors, sounds, and tastes (II.7.9-10). For our purposes, the important point is Locke's argument that the ideas of substance and accidents are not of much use in philosophy, because we do not know what substance is, except that which supports accidents. We have no idea of what it is, only an obscure and confused idea of what it does (II.13.19). Further, when he does treat of "Relation," he notes that "though it be not contained in the real existence of Things . . . yet the *Ideas* which rel-

---

8. See appendix V in Albert Einstein, *Relativity: The Special and General Theory* (New York: Crown, 1961). Cf. idem, "The Mechanics of Newton," reprinted in *Ideas and Opinions* (New York: Bonanza, 1954).

9. For introductions to these developments in physics and their theological implications, see Ian Barbour, *Religion in an Age of Science* (San Francisco: HarperCollins, 1990), 95-124; and Arthur Peacocke, *Theology for a Scientific Age: Being and Becoming — Natural, Divine and Human* (Minneapolis: Fortress, 1993), 29-43.

10. Ilya Prigogine and Isabelle Stengers, *Order out of Chaos: Man's New Dialogue with Nature* (New York: Bantam, 1984), 95.

ative Words stand for, are often clearer, and more distinct, than those Substances to which they belong" (II.25.8). So secondary qualities like smell and sound, which we might subjectively call beautiful or good, are merely powers in an extended thing that produce a particular *sensum* with which the mind forms an idea. The primary qualities, however, describe the "objective" world.

In the eighteenth century, David Hume tried to follow out the logic of Locke's position, which he believed led to skepticism. If Locke's "substance" (or substratum) is merely a "something we know not what," then we cannot predicate anything of it or know anything about it. In his *Enquiry Concerning Human Understanding* (1748), Hume argues that anything we do say about substances is merely habit or convention, because we cannot know or say what the thing *is*. This skepticism applies not only to substances but also to the connections (relations) we habitually associate between substances, relations such as cause and effect. Hume was clearly aiming at Christian theology here. In 1710 Leibniz had published his famous *Theodicy* in which he argued that we live in the best of all possible worlds, a world caused by a God who is perfectly good.[11] Hume was not impressed by this defense, as he makes clear in the *Dialogues Concerning Natural Religion* (not published until after his death in 1776). For our purposes, however, the important point is his devastating critique of the very idea of a "substance" that can be separated from all of its "accidents." By the time of Hume, many theologians had hitched their theological carts to the philosophical horse of substance metaphysics. Unlike the early Reformers, for whom relationality was a key concept for articulating (for example) a doctrine of the whole person as the image of God, the followers of Luther and Calvin were surprisingly quick to revert to Aristotelian categories, which they borrowed from the medieval scholastic discussion.[12] Not surprisingly, the doc-

---

11. Like Spinoza, Leibniz had made the concept of substance fundamental to his system, but rather than a single substance he proposed a multiplicity of "monads." These are simple immaterial substances that exhibit a preestablished harmony created by God.

12. For Luther, the justification relation is the key category through which all human understanding is judged. For Calvin, it is that the whole person who is called into a relational union with Christ by the Spirit. As we will see in chapter ten, both Strigel on the Lutheran side and Bucanus on the Reformed side differentiated between the substance of the "image" of God and the accident of "likeness" to God.

trine of the Trinity became less central during this period, and theologians turned their attention to proving the existence of God as an Immaterial Substance that was the First Cause of the world.[13]

Immanuel Kant credited Hume for waking him from his "dogmatic slumbers." Like most of us, he was resting peacefully in his assumption that he could know and speak of a thing as it really is. Kant's "critical" philosophy is a call to question such assumptions. He argues that we can speak of things as they appear to us (phenomena) but not of things in themselves (noumena). This is the main point of his critique of pure (theoretical) reason: showing its limits to "make room for faith." Kant believed that the time was ripe for revisiting the Aristotelian categories and the relative importance of the concepts of substance and relation. In Book I of the Transcendental Analytic in his influential *Critique of Pure Reason* (1787), Kant provides his own Table of Categories. The importance of this shift justifies my portrayal in Table 1 of these "predicables," which he calls the concepts of pure understanding.[14]

The most obvious discontinuity between the Western tradition up to this point and Kant's proposal is the latter's "Copernican revolution" in which he reverses the importance of human "subjectivity" and the "objective" world. Instead of beginning with the claim that an external (or noumenal) objective reality contains structures that are grasped by the mind, he proposes that the human subject itself provides the structural categories by which "objects" that appear (as phenomena) in human consciousness are "thought." The transcendental structures of human reason yield intuitions by means of sensibility and give rise to concepts through the understanding — these have purchase only in the realm of phenomena, or in the "appearance" of things in the mind. So he treats the categories not as realities or distinctions of "things in themselves" but as a priori categories of the understanding. This means that the categories "Of Relation" are forms through which the human subject understands a "thoroughgoing reciprocity" in the field of phenomena.

13. As Michael Buckley, S.J., has shown, atheism itself arose as a negation of modern "theism," which itself emerged when theologians turned away from the particularity of the Christian belief in Incarnation and Trinity and toward abstract philosophical categories as the basis of their attempts to defend the existence of God (*At the Origins of Modern Atheism* [New Haven: Yale University Press, 1987]).

14. Kant, *Critique of Pure Reason,* trans. Norman Kemp Smith (New York: St. Martin's Press, 1965), 113 (B106).

Table 1. Kant's Table of Categories

I
Of Quantity
Unity
Plurality
Totality

II	III
Of Quality	Of Relation
Reality	Of Inherence and Subsistence
Negation	*(substantia et accidens)*
Limitation	Of Causality and Dependence
	(cause and effect)
	Of Community (reciprocity
	between agent and patient)

IV
Of Modality
Possibility — Impossibility
Existence — Nonexistence
Necessity — Contingency

Two key points about Kant's table are relevant for my historical survey of the philosophical turn to relationality. First, notice that Kant explicitly makes "substance and accident" a subcategory of Category III, "Of Relation." This is a major adjustment and sets the stage for the radical developments I trace below in the second section of this chapter. In addition to his significant elevation of the category of relation, Kant's second major contribution is his unleashing of relationality from Category I, "Of Quantity," to which it had been tied by Aristotle. Later in the *Critique* Kant defines a system of "principles" of pure understanding that are correlated to the four "categories." These principles are applied *mathematically* for Categories I and II, but are applied *dynamically* for Categories III and IV.[15] The "analogies of experience,"

15. Cf. *Critique*, 196ff. This separation plays a key role in his proposed solution to the antinomies of pure reason later in the book (462ff. [A529]).

which are the principles derived from Category III (Of Relation), provide a way of salvaging the "qualities" central to human ethical and aesthetic life from the quantitative analysis of mathematics, while maintaining their importance for phenomenological analysis.

Despite his otherwise radical revisions, Kant still views substance in terms of permanence, and alteration as occurring only through the changing of accidents, described with the categories of cause and effect. Community (the third subcategory "Of Relation") is, Kant argues, simply the combination of the second subcategory with the first, that is, "the causality of substances reciprocally determining one another."[16] This important point of continuity with the Aristotelian substance tradition would be challenged by many who came after Kant, as we will see below. However, Kant's explicit critique of Aristotle's treatment of relationality provided the impulse for a series of philosophical developments that would open conceptual space for the rapid advancement of dynamic relational hypotheses in physics, psychology, and the other sciences that shape our contemporary culture.

Relationality from Hegel to Levinas

G. W. F. Hegel (1770-1831) contributed to the history of the concept of relationality in many ways, but three aspects of his work have been particularly influential: (1) challenging the basic separation of the category of accident from the category of substance; (2) insisting that the phenomena of relationality and process are essential not only to the reflective movement of knowing but also to being itself, which is self-related; and (3) emphasizing that the ultimate or absolute relation cannot adequately be defined by speaking of the Infinite over against the finite, because the "true" Infinite must somehow embrace the finite while transcending it. Hegel was by no means the first to make all of these claims, but he did articulate them in a way that has set the tone for much of the philosophical discussion over the last two centuries. For this reason, it makes sense to use Hegel as a kind of historical marker for an important pivot in the turn to relationality. After briefly outlining these three Hegelian emphases, I will point to some of the key

16. *Critique,* 116 (B111).

22

thinkers since Hegel who have shaped attitudes about relationality in the Western academy.

First, Hegel challenged the basic separation between the categories of substance and accident, a separation which most of the thinkers in the first section above, including Aristotle and Kant, had taken for granted.[17] We can find the core of Hegel's argument expressed in two closely related sections of his *Science of Logic:* "The Absolute Relation," which is the final chapter of volume 1 (*Objective Logic,* 1812), and "The Doctrine of the Notion," which is the first chapter of volume 2 (*Subjective Logic,* 1819).[18] Like Kant, Hegel brings substance and accidents under the category of "relation," but in a more radical way. For Hegel, both substantiality and accidentality refer to determinations of the totality or the whole; this "whole" is neither "being" nor "essence," however, but their dialectical unity in the reflective movement of the "absolute relation," which is the highest category in the objective logic. "Substance, as this identity of the reflective movement, is the totality of the whole and embraces accidentality within it, and accidentality is the whole substance itself." Hegel speaks of an "immediate identity" and a "unity" of substance and accidents; here again these are manifestations of the movement of the absolute relation. The extremes of accidentality and substantiality have no subsistence on their own. Accidentality is *"in itself* indeed substance," but as the "actuosity" of substance coming forth of itself, and substantiality is not substance "as substance," for it "has only accidentality for its shape or positedness."[19] This dialectical unity of substantiality and accidentality flows from Hegel's rejection of the hard distinction between form and content. For Kant, as for Aristotle, the logical categories were "forms" of reasoning and could be abstracted from "content." For Hegel form and content are inseparable in the dialectical process of logic, and method cannot be so easily separated from being: "The method is the pure Notion that relates itself only to itself; it is therefore the *simple self-relation* that is *being.*"[20]

This allusion to a self-relating "Notion" *(Begriff)* brings us to the

17. The substance-accident distinction was not as central to the Platonic tradition, as we saw in Plotinus, although "Relation" was still separated from substance.

18. Published together in *Hegel's Science of Logic,* trans. A. V. Miller, ed. H. D. Lewis (Amherst, N.Y.: Humanity Books, 1999).

19. All of these quotations are from *Hegel's Science of Logic,* 555-56.

20. Ibid., 842.

23

second of Hegel's themes that bear on the turn to relationality: his insistence that *process* is essential not only to reflection but also to being. Here substance is linked not only to relation but also to movement: "Substance as this unity of being and reflection is essentially the *reflective movement* and *positedness* of itself. This reflective movement is the reflective movement that is *self-related*, and it is thus that it *is*."[21] In his earlier *Phenomenology of Spirit* (1807), Hegel had argued that the cognition of the individual is participation in the Absolute Knowing of the Spirit, by which the Spirit becomes what it is in self-consciousness; substance is objectified and becomes Self in this process.[22] In the *Subjective Logic*, Hegel explicitly critiques Spinoza for stopping with the notion of Absolute Substance. This halt had left Spinoza with the problems of necessity that flowed naturally from his monism (pantheism). Hegel argues we should recognize the moment of truth in Spinoza but go further. It is not Substance but "Subject" that is Absolute; as the self-comprehending pure Notion, the Spirit (as Subject) consummates Spinoza's concept of substance by sublating its necessity into the freedom of the Notion.[23] Subjectivity replaces substance as the highest category, and "becoming" is radically incorporated into "being" (or vice versa). Hegel's "phenomenology," which held together the forms of thought and the content of being, was therefore an attempt to overcome the Kantian dualism between noumena (things in themselves) and phenomena (things as they appear).

The third Hegelian contribution was his rigorous reflection on the ultimate relationality, the relation between the Infinite and the finite. One might even argue that it was this reflection that led him to emphasize relationality and process in his understanding of phenomena. Finite things are finite because they are defined over against that which they are not. This limitation constitutes their finitude. The idea of the "Infinite" suggests that which is "not finite." Hegel points out that if the Infinite and the finite are thought together in a way that they are merely opposed to each other, then the Infinite is determined by the fi-

21. Ibid., 555.
22. Hegel, *Phenomenology of Spirit*, trans. A. V. Miller (Oxford: Oxford University Press, 1977), 479-93.
23. *Science of Logic*, 580-82. The term "sublating" refers to Hegel's well-known use of the German word *aufheben* to describe the negation as well as elevation of one idea or process into another.

nite. The Infinite is limited by the finite if it is defined simply as that which is not finite. If we speak of Infinity in this way, which Hegel calls the "spurious" or "bad" infinite, then in fact we have *two* determinate-nesses, two mutually limited worlds. In the relation between them, "the infinite is only the *limit* of the finite and is thus only a determinate infinite, an *infinite which is itself finite.*"[24] The "true" Infinite embraces both itself and finitude; it is a process that raises its difference from itself into the affirmation of itself, and through this mediation is becoming itself. Here it is important to distinguish between two clusters of ideas about the infinite in the history of philosophy. What we might call the "mathematical" cluster thinks of infinity in terms of endlessness, immeasurability, or unlimitedness, while the "metaphysical" cluster of ideas has emphasized the Infinite as wholeness, absoluteness, or perfection. Kant had separated "Of Relation" from "Of Quantity," but Hegel went further not only by making Relation an even higher category, but by explicitly tying it to Quality, which he then privileged over Quantity.[25] The mathematical (quantitative) infinite had dominated early modern consciousness; Hegel vigorously argued for a vision of the metaphysical Infinite as a self-related Absolute that could include finitude without being limited by it.

Like most Christian thinkers since that time, Søren Kierkegaard did not find Hegel's way of trying to solve the question of true Infinity compelling. On the one hand, it seems to vitiate the transcendence of God; and, on the other, it threatens the particularity of individual finite creatures who seem to be absorbed into an all-encompassing Subject. Kierkegaard's insistence on the "infinite qualitative distinction" between God and creatures was a response to both concerns. His whole authorship was driven by the question of the relation of the individual to the Infinite (or Eternal, or Unknown). Kierkegaard's pseudonymous writings can be understood as attempts to lead the reader through a process of intensification; the *Stages on Life's Way* (1845) are existence-spheres, or ways of relating to the self, the world, and God, through which readers are (indirectly) called to move. Despite his resistance to Hegel on so many other fronts, for Kierkegaard too "relationality" was a key concept. We may point, for example, to Kierkegaard's definition

24. Ibid., 140.
25. Ibid., 79. Hegel explicitly criticizes Kant in this context.

of the self in his *Sickness unto Death* (1849) as "a relation that relates itself to itself or . . . the relation's relating itself to itself in the relation; the self is not the relation but is the relation's relating itself to itself."[26] Many of the influential scholars associated with "postmodernity" were shaped by and contributed to the twentieth-century revival of Kierkegaard scholarship.[27]

Later in the nineteenth century the American philosopher Charles Sanders Peirce took up the question of "relations" and developed his own "New List" of categories in 1867. At this early stage he had five categories, with a major division between substance and being, the latter having the subcategories of Quality, Relation, and Representation.[28] Later these subcategories would become dominant, and he would give them names only a philosopher could love: Firstness, Secondness, and Thirdness.[29] Formally he called these the three "classes of relations" (monadic, dyadic, triadic). Materially, Firstness was linked to the *Quality* of Feeling, the "suchness" of immediate phenomenal experience; Secondness to the *Reaction* to some First, the "thisness" (haecceity) element of the phenomenon experienced in its "upagainstness"; and Thirdness to the *Representation* in thought that mediates the relation or "betweenness" of a Second to its First. These categories also led him to

26. Kierkegaard, *The Sickness unto Death*, trans. Howard V. and Edna H. Hong (Princeton: Princeton University Press, 1980), 13. In *Kierkegaard as Humanist: Discovering My Self* and *Kierkegaard as Theologian: Recovering My Self*, Arnold Come argues that the brief section in which this quote appears is the key to interpreting the whole Kierkegaardian corpus (London: McGill-Queen's University Press, 1995, 1997).

27. This is particularly evident in the work of Jacques Derrida, whose well-known emphasis on the category of *différance* has been so influential. For an example of his treatment of Kierkegaard, see *The Gift of Death*, trans. David Wills (Chicago: University of Chicago Press, 1995). For Kierkegaard's influence on other postmodern scholars, see the essays in *Kierkegaard in Post/Modernity*, ed. Martin J. Matuštík and Merold Westphal (Bloomington: Indiana University Press, 1995).

28. Peirce, "On a New List of Categories," in *The Essential Peirce*, edited by Nathan Houser and Christian Kloesel, vol. 1 (Bloomington: Indiana University Press, 1992), 6. At this early stage, he called the last three intermediate categories "accidents," but this terminology faded from importance in his mature work.

29. For an introduction to these categories, see Peirce's Harvard Lectures on Pragmatism, reprinted in *The Essential Peirce*, vol. 2, ed. Peirce Edition Project (Bloomington: Indiana University Press, 1998). Broadly speaking, these categories were related to pure possibility, actual existence, and real generality, respectively. His emphasis on Thirdness was an attempt to overcome the nominalism that had dominated science.

divide philosophy into three departments: "Phenomenology," which treats the qualities of phenomena in their Firstness; "Normative Science," which treats the laws and relations of phenomena in their Secondness; and "Metaphysics," which treats phenomena in terms of their Thirdness. Peirce's fascination with relationality is also evident in his suggestion that we may overcome idealism, dualism, and materialism with "synechism," the doctrine that everything is continuous.

The concept of "relation" was significantly affected by the divergence of two philosophical streams in the late nineteenth and early twentieth centuries. The first stream, which is commonly called the "analytic" tradition, has focused on relations in logic and language. Since Aristotle, logic had been limited to one-place categories (e.g., the man) and two-place predication (e.g., the man runs). Throughout the Middle Ages this had led to logical difficulties when dealing with relations between more than two categories; for example, the man runs at the cow, or the man bears the "is running toward" relation to the cow. This weakness in Aristotle's approach to logic was overcome by Georg Cantor's work in set theory[30] and Gottlob Frege's development of what is now called quantification theory. These tools allow logicians to signify and discuss the relations between multiple categories and sets of categories. In the analytic tradition, one of the most important debates has been over the issue of "internal" and "external" relations. Some relations seem to be essential (or internal) to a thing's being what it is, for example, my being "younger" than my grandfather. Other relations appear to be external to the essence of a thing, for example, my living east of the Mississippi River. Many philosophers have challenged the validity of this hard distinction for two reasons: first, ideas about which relations are "internal" or essential are gradational rather than absolute; second, judgments about which relations are internal (essential) are relativized by the interests of the one making the distinction.[31] Nevertheless, such distinctions are helpful for the purposes of logical or linguistic analyses, which operate within the defining mechanisms of predication.

30. As he developed set theory, which is still the basis of most contemporary theoretical mathematics, Cantor was led to postulate the idea of an "Absolute Infinite," which suggests theological reflection.

31. See the influential article by Timothy Sprigge, "Internal and External Properties," *Mind* 71 (1962): 197-212.

The second stream emerged out of a quite different understanding of language and of the task of philosophy. Although commonly called the "continental" tradition or "speculative" philosophy, for my purposes here I might risk the ambiguous appellation "phenomenology" for this stream of thought. Hegel's use of the term "phenomenology" was taken up and modified by a variety of nineteenth-century philosophers; one thinks immediately of Marx, who argued that the dialectical process of historical phenomena was material rather than spiritual; and of Dilthey, whose reflection on the relation between parts and whole in human understanding shaped the rise of historicist hermeneutics. In the twentieth century, however, "phenomenology" has been associated especially with the methodology of Edmund Husserl and those influenced by him.[32] In this school the focus is on *categorial intentionality*, the establishing of a categorial object by human consciousness. We may distinguish three aspects of this process. First, we have the passive perception of a thing, such as a barnyard scene. Second, a particular element of the whole comes to the foreground; for example, a kerosene lamp knocked into the hay by the cow. Finally, we have the registering of the relation between the whole and part, the simultaneous articulation of a state of affairs: the man is running toward the cow to put out the fire. This achievement of a categorial intuition comes all at once, but we may still distinguish the parts, the whole, and the relation between them in the phenomena. Notice that the interest here is not so much on listing types of categories, but on understanding the types of relations or distinctions that appear in consciousness.

Two of the most important philosophers of the twentieth century, Martin Heidegger and Jean-Paul Sartre, struggled with the relations inherent in being, although they interpreted it differently in that they focused on the phenomena of time and nothingness, respectively. Heidegger's thematic analysis of *Dasein* (being-there) led him to emphasize a whole host of relational distinctions including being-with, being-in, and his famous being-towards-death.[33] Sartre argued that the

---

32. For a more detailed treatment of the following issues, see Robert Sokolowski, *Introduction to Phenomenology* (Cambridge: Cambridge University Press, 2000).

33. Martin Heidegger, *Being and Time*, trans. J. Macquarrie and E. Robinson (San Francisco: Harper, 1962).

reciprocal relation of "being-seen-by-another" and "seeing-the-other" is an irreducible and fundamental relation that appears in consciousness; this relation of being-with and being-for-other *is* the self's being, or is the self as the apprehension of being. He was best known for his emphasis on the existential anxiety that emerges from the inability to control the inherent negation of these relations.[34]

The most important twentieth-century American philosopher who contributed to the growing dissatisfaction with the tradition of Aristotelian substance metaphysics, and its denigration of the category of relation, is Alfred North Whitehead. In *Modes of Thought*, he criticizes Aristotle's attempt to draw clear lines of division among genera and species. Nature is not so neatly divided. Tracing developments in the sciences, especially physics and biology, Whitehead argued that the fundamental concepts by which we understand the world are activity and process.[35] In *Process and Reality*, he set out his own eight "categories of existence"— these are Actual Entities (actual occasions), Prehensions, Nexus, Subjective Forms, Eternal Objects, Propositions, Multiplicities, and Contrasts. For my purposes, the key point is Whitehead's prioritization: "Among the eight categories of existence, actual entities and eternal objects stand out with a certain extreme finality" while the others have an "intermediate character."[36] He explicitly rejects the Aristotelian idea of "individual substances, each with its private world of qualities and sensations,"[37] and criticizes what he calls the "substance-quality" doctrine of actuality. In its place, Whitehead proposes a doctrine of "actual occasions" or "societies" in which reality is described in essentially dynamic and relational terms. Unlike Descartes (and others) for whom a physical body has the *attribute* of extension, for Whitehead physical "occasions" have the primary *relationship* of extensive connection to all things. To be an actual occasion (or entity) in the nexus of the physical world is to be a *relatum* in this fundamentally organic extensive scheme.[38]

---

34. Jean-Paul Sartre, *Being and Nothingness*, trans. Hazel E. Barnes (New York: Philosophical Library, 1956). See especially the section on "The Look" (252-302) and the Conclusion (617-28).

35. *Modes of Thought* (New York: Capricorn Books, 1938), 191.

36. *Process and Reality*, ed. David Ray Griffin and Donald W. Sherburne, corrected ed. (New York: Free Press, 1978), 22.

37. Ibid., 160.

38. Ibid., 288.

Process thought has had a tremendous impact on the way in which both philosophers and theologians think about the category of relation. The process concept of God and the God-world relation is unacceptable to most Christian theologians because it tends to subsume God and the world under a larger whole or totality, a tendency already evident in Hegel. Nevertheless, the emphasis on relationality as essential to reality has contributed to a renewed interest in the doctrine of the Trinity,[39] as well as to new attempts to overcome the problems in the early modern understanding of the God-world relation.[40] Debate continues among process thinkers over the way in which relations to past occasions are constitutive of present occasions, an idea that David Ray Griffin calls one of the "core doctrines" of process theology.[41] Lewis S. Ford believes that the future too must be conceptualized as a source of creativity in relation to present occasions, and not merely the past or present, as most process thinkers have argued.[42] One of the most important (sympathetic) critics of process philosophy is Robert Neville, who has underscored the necessity of the integrity of relata as well as the reality of relations themselves in cosmology.[43] In his response to Whitehead's idea that God must be the highest exemplification of our metaphysical categories, Neville also represents the classical insistence in Christian theology that created categories are not capable of completely explaining divine creativity.[44]

39. See, e.g., Joseph A. Bracken, S.J., and Marjorie Hewitt Suchocki, eds., *Trinity in Process: A Relational Theology of God* (New York: Continuum, 1997).

40. See, e.g., Philip Clayton, *The Problem of God in Modern Thought* (Grand Rapids: Eerdmans, 2000).

41. Griffin, "Process Theology and the Christian Good News," in *Searching for an Adequate God,* ed. John B. Cobb Jr. and Clark H. Pinnock (Grand Rapids: Eerdmans, 2000), 5.

42. Ford, *Transforming Process Theism* (Albany: SUNY Press, 2000).

43. "If things have no essential features over against their conditional features, they are reduced to their various relations with other things. But then it is the relations that are real, and the things are merely perspectives on the relations" (Robert Neville, *Eternity and Time's Flow* [Albany: SUNY Press, 1993], 73). He concludes that "things are harmonies of both conditional and essential features, conditional ones in order to be determinately related to other things with respect to which they are determinate, and essential ones in order to be determinately different from those other things" (75).

44. Neville, *Creativity and God: A Challenge to Process Theology* (Albany: SUNY Press, 1995), 140.

The philosophical turn to relationality has shaped not only the way we think about knowing and being, but also our understanding of human acting. In the early modern period human (free) agency had been dualistically separated from (mechanistically determined) nature, and this split registered its effect on anthropological theories. In contemporary psychology, and in the anthropological sciences generally, humans and communities are more often described in ways that recognize that their *relations* are constitutive. A person is no longer defined as an "individual substance of a rational nature" (Boethius) or as a "punctual self" (Locke). Instead of autonomous subjects that stand over against the natural world and other subjects, today human self-consciousness is understood as always and already embedded in relations between self, other, and world. Twentieth-century philosophical anthropology played a crucial role in this development; one thinks, for example, of the "personalism" of philosophers like Martin Buber, for whom the "between" of I and Thou is constitutive for personhood.[45]

In psychology proper, the turn is most obvious in "object relations" theory,[46] where the agential relation of a person to objects is essential to his or her developmental identity. These relations are not accidental or irrelevant but in some sense constitutive of the person. In part I, I explore in more detail the implications of these theories for understanding the interdisciplinary dynamics of theological inquiry. In the psychoanalytic tradition as well, one finds scholars who have recognized the centrality of the concept of relationality for understanding and helping persons.[47] Similar insights have arisen out of research in evolutionary biology in general and the neurosciences in particular, thus illustrating the blurring of boundaries between the "natural" and the "human" sciences. Today human acting is rarely described in terms of a substantial soul with abstract faculties (or powers) to influence the material world,

45. For some contemporary proposals in theological anthropology that have tried to account for these phenomena, see Stanley J. Grenz, *The Social God and the Relational Self* (Louisville: Westminster John Knox, 2001); and Alistair I. McFadyen, *The Call to Personhood: A Christian Theory of the Individual in Social Relationships* (Cambridge: Cambridge University Press, 1990).

46. See, e.g., Robert Kegan, *The Evolving Self* (Cambridge: Harvard University Press, 1982).

47. See, e.g., Stephen A. Mitchell, *Relationality: From Attachment to Intersubjectivity* (Hillsdale, N.J.: Analytic Press, 2000).

31

but more often in terms of a dynamic self-in-community. The material ramifications of these developments (and others) in the anthropological sciences is explored in part III when I turn explicitly to the task of reforming theological anthropology in late modernity.

Emmanuel Levinas seems an appropriate place to end this brief survey, not only because he so well illustrates the postmodern fascination with infinity, but also because he provides us with a clear example of the impact of the renewed philosophical privileging of ethics. First, Levinas is aware of Hegel's criterion of true Infinity, and although he rejects the idealist solution, he accepts the need to move beyond "bad" infinity. For Levinas the "in" of Infinity signifies both "non-" and "within." The Infinite's "very in-finity, its difference from the finite, is already its nonindifference to the finite."[48] For Levinas the Infinite produces the "primordial" relation between the I and the Other, which as an ethical (rather than ontological or epistemological) relationship precedes and subtends discourse and being. In face-to-face relations, we find ourselves called by and obligated to the other; in and through these relations we are also confronted with the presence of the absolutely Other, the Infinite. The Infinite is essentially beyond the grasp of the I, who cannot comprehend it, but its transcendent presence is mediated through the ethical relation to the other — precisely as that which is beyond essence.[49] This primordial relation, then, has become an overarching or underlying category. Rather, as Levinas would probably say, it is not a category at all, but beyond categorization — this is an even more radical prioritization of relationality. We have come a long way since Aristotle.[50]

---

48. "God and Philosophy," in *Emmanuel Levinas: Basic Philosophical Writings*, ed. A. T. Peperzak, et al. (Bloomington: Indiana University Press, 1996), 138.

49. For elaboration of these themes, see Levinas, *Totality and Infinity: An Essay on Exteriority*, trans. Alphonso Lingis (Pittsburgh: Duquesne University Press, 1969); idem, *Otherwise than Being or Beyond Essence*, trans. Alphonso Lingis (Pittsburgh: Duquesne University Press, 1981).

50. Many contemporary Aristotle scholars agree that today his view of substance must be expanded to incorporate the importance of a thing's relations. Aristotle was right that we say things about things, but we should also say that the relations of things are essential to their being thingy. For defenses and reconstructions of Aristotle, see the essays in M. L. O'Hara, ed., *Substances and Things: Aristotle's Doctrine of Physical Substance in Recent Essays* (Washington, D.C.: University Press of America, 1982); and D. M. MacKinnon, "Aristotle's Conception of Substance," in *New Essays on Plato and Aristotle*, ed. Renford Bambrough (New York: Humanities Press, 1965), 97-119.

The Responsibility of Theology

My focus in this first chapter has been on the philosophical dimensions of the turn to relationality, but one could not help observing that most of these philosophers were also concerned with explicitly theological questions. As I suggested in the introduction and as the following chapters will show, theology is in many ways responsible for this shift toward relational categories. It was through Hegel's struggle with Christian ideas about Incarnation, Trinity, and Spirit that he was led to link relationality and essence, and we should not let the fact that his constructive proposals are problematic cloud our recognition of this philosophical contribution. Hegel's worry about "bad" infinity was anticipated already in early church theologians like Gregory of Nyssa,[51] and in medieval theologians like Nicholas of Cusa.[52] Such thinkers fought against the Greek view of *apeiron* as negative infinity, and insisted that divine Infinity suggests something positive — an absolute perfection beyond the grasp of the human mind. Only because God is perfectly Infinite, as unlimited superabundance, are creatures able to exist in relation to God.

Our task is to retrieve and refigure the relational thought-forms of the biblical tradition that can help us respond to late modern anthropological self-understanding. Relationality has long been a staple of Christian theology; the early church debates focused most of their attention on the relations between God and humanity revealed in the person of Jesus Christ and on the relations between the Father, Son, and Spirit that constitute the essence of the divine being. Even the theme of "process" as essential to reality and even to God is not as for-

---

51. "The divine by its very nature is infinite, enclosed by no boundary. If the divine be perceived as though bounded by something, one must by all means along with that boundary consider what is beyond it. . . . In the same way, God, if he be conceived as bounded, would necessarily be surrounded by something different in nature" (*Life of Moses* 2.236; trans. and quoted in Everett Ferguson, "God's Infinity and Man's Mutability: Perpetual Progress according to Gregory of Nyssa," *GOTR* 18, no. 2 [1973]: 65).

52. For example, when Cusanus speaks of God as "Not-other" in his *De Li Non Aliud*, he insists this does not mean simply that God is "other" than creatures, but is the basis of the shining forth of all others. See Jasper Hopkins, *Nicholas of Cusa on God as Not-other: A Translation and an Appraisal of De Li Non Aliud* (Minneapolis: University of Minnesota Press, 1979).

eign to theology as we might think. Early theologians found it necessary to speak of "processions" as essential to trinitarian divine relations
and of the dynamic movement of the Logos in relation to the history of
Jesus of Nazareth. This emphasis emerged out of the trinitarian experience of the process of salvation that occurs through Christ by the
Spirit. Dependence on Greek substance metaphysics in the articulation
of the doctrines of the simplicity and impassibility of God made it difficult to render these doctrines consistent with the dynamic experience
of salvation as a "real" reconciliation with God and as a participation
in the divine nature (2 Pet. 1:4). The struggle to articulate a doctrine of
God that accounts for the insights of the (re)turn to relationality without collapsing into the problems that plague many forms of process
thought is an ongoing task, to which this book hopes to contribute, at
least indirectly.

Above I pointed to Kant as a pivotal thinker in the philosophical
turn to relationality; yet even his efforts were preceded by the work of
the Reformed theologian Jonathan Edwards, who, like Kant, was
deeply interested in responding to the new discoveries of early modern
science. Edwards explicitly modified Aristotelian substance categories
and developed an ontology of creation as inherently relational and dynamic. Sang Lee summarizes Edwards's relational metaphysics in
three statements: what an entity is, is inseparable from its relations;
relations determine the existence of an entity; the extent of the mutual relations of all entities is absolutely comprehensive. In Edwards's
view, "entities are related not only with *some* other entities in the system of being but indeed with *all* other entities — that is, with the
whole."[53] We can also point to Schleiermacher, who was thinking
theologically in the wake of Kant and alongside Hegel. As we will see
in chapter five, relationality was the key category for Schleiermacher's
interpretation of the pious self-consciousness, wherein a person is related to the divine not as an object of reason but in the realm of feeling, in the immediate self-consciousness. It has often been noted that
the relational Christian intuitions of nineteenth-century scientists
like Maxwell and Faraday surely contributed to their new ways of conceptualizing physical reality primarily in terms of fields rather than

53. Sang Hyun Lee, *The Philosophical Theology of Jonathan Edwards* (Princeton: Princeton University Press, 1988), 80.

substances. The most important Reformed theologian in the twentieth century was Karl Barth, who played a crucial role in the theological return to relationality. This is evident not only in his emphasis on
analogia relationis, but also in his insistence that the doctrine of the
Trinity be brought back to the beginning of the presentation of
church dogmatics. I return to these and other theological resources
often in the following chapters.

Theology is responsible in another sense — not only *for* but also *to*
the philosophical turn to relationality in contemporary culture. I believe that "reforming" theological anthropology is an important part
of this responsibility. The philosophical turn to relationality per se is
not hostile to Christian theology, though it may call us to a more critical evaluation of some traditional formulations that were overly
shaped by substance metaphysics. In this evaluation we may be aided
by the voices of those whose theological and anthropological categories have not been dominated by debate over substances. For many
non-Western Christians, the claim that relationality is central for theological anthropology is nothing new.[54] The chapters of part III (8–10)
summarize some of the most promising opportunities for reconstruction in light of the challenges that face theological anthropology today.
Because my goal is to thematize the reciprocity between conceptions of
relationality and doctrinal formulations, that exploration is preceded
in part II by analysis of some historical examples of this reciprocity vis-
à-vis theological method, Trinity, and Christology (chaps. 5–7). Illustrating the operation of these relational dynamics in the theological
performance of some major theologians in church history may also
help us overcome our fear of facing these dynamics in our own cultural
context. I have asserted and will attempt to argue for the claim that the
demise of the substance metaphysics of ancient Greece and early modern science is a happy occasion for theology and for Christian praxis.
For many readers, however, engaging the challenges of late modern cul-

---

54. In the African culture of Ewe-Mina, "being" is interpreted not in terms of essence and substance, but in terms of communal relations. As Christian theologian Efoé
Julien Pénoukou explains, this society perceives the Supreme Being as simultaneously
proposing and disposing "the becoming of the human being within a network of constitutive relations." The ontological dependence of humanity is "defined first and fore-
most in terms of fundamental relationships." "Christology in the Village," in *Faces of Jesus in Africa,* ed. Robert J. Schreiter (Maryknoll, N.Y.: Orbis, 1998), 24-51 at 33.

ture will be (at least initially) an occasion for fear rather than joy. Rather than suppress this anxiety, let us face head-on the psychological, social, and cultural dynamics that any truly reformative theological anthropology must engage.

ANTHROPOLOGY, THEOLOGY, AND THE READER

2   Relationality and
        Developmental Psychology

This book is about the relations in and between theology and anthropology. Our general task is to explore opportunities for reforming theological anthropology in late modernity after the turn to relationality in philosophy and science, which I have just traced in the first chapter. Later chapters deal with specific implications for particular doctrines in light of the material challenges that have arisen from other anthropological sciences.

In this chapter, however, I invite the reader to engage in a propaedeutic self-exploration of the formal structures that inevitably shape all of one's exploring. This is a difficult and often unwelcome task — criticizing our criticality, reflecting on the structures of our reflection, thematizing the nature of our thematization. Here we engage the discipline of developmental psychology not merely for abstract understanding but with the goal of more intentional self-understanding. I began in the introduction by noting Calvin's claim that knowledge of self and knowledge of God are linked. If this is so, then we may hope that our efforts in extending our self-awareness may also lead us to a deeper awareness and knowledge of God (and of our neighbors).

Many proposals for a methodological relating of developmental psychology and theology focus on the content of the disciplines or the communities that work in them. In this chapter I argue that such approaches leave out a crucial first step: taking account of the individual interdisciplinarian and the way his or her structure of consciousness upholds or subtends the relation between the disciplines. From the perspective of both developmental psychology and theological anthropology, it seems a glaring omission to try to build an interdisciplinary method without including the irreducible influence of the developing person as he or she constructs and utilizes any such method. The model proposed here classifies three ways of holding on to the theology-psychology relationship, focusing on how the underlying "fiduciary structure" of the individual shapes interdisciplinary method.

We must recognize that we are dealing here with a hidden curriculum. Developmental psychologist Robert Kegan suggests that an unseen "assignment" lies beneath the mental demands of modern life. The complexities of our society and shared life together have resulted in a cultural design that requires of us a qualitative transformation of mind that goes as deep as the change "from magical thinking to concrete thinking required of the school-age child or the transformation from concrete to abstract thinking required of the adolescent."[1] Kegan goes further and argues that even if we are able to make this transformation and fulfill the demands of modern life, a whole new set of postmodern mental "assignments" awaits that will require an even more complex order of consciousness.

As Christian interdisciplinarians, we find ourselves caught in a double bind. On the one hand, we are pressured to acknowledge the postmodern critiques that have demonstrated the provisional, subjective and contextual nature of our disciplinary knowledge and theorizing. On the other hand, we desire some way of talking about "objectivity" so we can judge the truth claims in and between theology and psychology within the broader pluralist conversation.[2] How can we develop an interdisciplinary method in this intellectual and social milieu without either embracing relativism at the expense of Christian faith, or retreating from the pluralistic conversation into a solipsistic fideism? What is hidden in the "postmodern curriculum" is that it is unfair (or at least unkind) to demand that individuals develop or adopt a complex interdisciplinary method without recognizing their need, first of all, to develop an underlying structure of consciousness that can adequately uphold such a relationality.

This current epistemological exigency requires a developmentally

1. Robert Kegan, *In Over Our Heads: The Mental Demands of Modern Life* (Cambridge: Harvard University Press, 1994), 11.

2. For a discussion of the issues of truth and knowledge in dialogue with postmodernity, see chap. 2 of my *Postfoundationalist Task of Theology* (Grand Rapids: Eerdmans, 1999).

more complex way of constructing the relation of the self to its knowledge. "Relational" language is quite common in the current dialogue between psychology and theology, but one may wonder whether particular interdisciplinarians are relating to the relationship between the fields in a way that is up to the task of subtending inherently relational concepts. That is to say, have the relational structures of our frame of reference developed sufficiently to support the explanatory concepts that are referents in the frame? Focusing on the way we as individual scholars/practitioners construct our interdisciplinary methods may help us learn how to maintain the relation between our disciplines and theories without falling into either extreme: the Scylla of relativism or the Charybdis of absolutism. Our chances of success in this endeavor can be improved as we develop qualitatively more complex ways of holding on to our knowledge and our disciplinary identity. For us to work through the curricular demands of postmodernism, new interdisciplinary methods may need to be upheld by a new kind of "methodological faith."

Methodological Faith

Early in the twentieth century this phrase would have seemed oxymoronic. At that time the dominant positivist view was that scientific thought was free of all reliance on any kind of "faith" or commitment. In our postpositivist milieu, it is well known that all scientific theories are underdetermined by the data. Today most readers will not be surprised to hear that scientists (including psychologists) bring beliefs and assumptions to experimentation, data gathering, and theory building. The rest of this chapter explores the way we are bound to our methodological assumptions and how this shapes our interdisciplinary constructs in theology and anthropology.

The root of the Greek word *pistis*, which is usually translated as "faith" in the New Testament, means "to bind." This meaning can be seen in derivative English terms such as "faithfulness," and is also evident in Latin words related to *fides* (fidelity, fiduciary) that refer to being bound in a relationship or to a contract. Faith has to do with relationships. I am using the expression "methodological faith" in this context to refer to the way a person is related to knowledge, that is, the

41

way one "holds" the relation of the self as knower to the objects studied by each discipline. The metaphor of "holding on" is not meant to imply a conscious grasping or an attitude toward knowledge, but refers instead to a prior epistemic "relating" out of which one constructs knowledge. I use the expression "fiduciary structure" in order to emphasize this deeper sense of one's *hold* on the theology-psychology relation. Unlike the commitment one necessarily has to one's worldview (which one must have in order to ask whether anything is true),[3] the "faith" I am concerned with here is at the deeper level of the "holding structure" that subtends the self and its relation to its worldview.

Before moving on to lay the groundwork for understanding the relation between fiduciary structures and interdisciplinary method, it is essential to emphasize that methodological faith is found in socially situated individuals. The classical model of rationality, which sought certain and self-evident foundations for knowledge, and clear rules to follow based on those foundations, has collapsed under the pressure of the clamoring throng of the postmodern crowd. Harold Brown has shown that we always need a reason for why we select the foundations we do (or why we know they are self-evident). The classic model of rule-following, foundationalist rationality results in an infinite regress: searching for foundations for foundations. Brown proposes a new model that features "judgment" within a community. The details of his proposal are less important for my purposes than the fact that he takes the notion of a rational agent "as fundamental, and such notions as 'rational belief' as derivative in the sense that a rational belief will be one that is arrived at by a rational agent."[4] The positioning of "interdisciplinary method" not primarily in a set of propositions or in a community, but in culturally embedded individual agents, is crucial for understanding the purpose of this chapter. In making this transfer, one must recognize that the capacity of the knower to hold on to the theology-psychology relationship finds its boundaries within one's underlying fiduciary structure.

3. Cf. Mary Midgley, *Science as Salvation: A Modern Myth and Its Meaning* (New York: Routledge, 1992), 57.

4. Harold Brown, *Rationality* (New York: Routledge, 1990), 185. Cf. A. A. Van Niekerk, "To Follow a Rule or to Rule What Should Follow? Rationality and Judgement in the Human Sciences," in *Knowledge and Method in the Human Sciences,* ed. J. Mouton and D. Joubert (Pretoria: HSRC, 1990), 179-94.

Orders of Consciousness

My goal in this section is to show how Robert Kegan's "subject-object" theory outlined in his book *In Over Our Heads* provides a developmental scheme that can help us explain the relation between fiduciary structures and interdisciplinary method. In an earlier work, *The Evolving Self*, Kegan described the evolution of the self as developing through a set of stages called "evolutionary truces." These are temporary solutions "to the lifelong tension between the yearnings for inclusion and distinctness."[5]

In his later book, he expands his theory to clarify the central importance of the underlying structure of the subject-object relation within each stage. Kegan speaks of five "orders of consciousness," each evolving to take as object what was previously lived or experienced as subject (thus the name "subject-object" theory). This theory grew out of his desire to elucidate the core structural commonalties underlying the cognitive and interpersonal characteristics of the developmental stages. For my purposes, the critical orders of consciousness are the third, fourth, and fifth, which Kegan refers to as "traditionalism," "modernism," and "postmodernism," respectively. (When I propose and explicate the parallel concept of *fiduciary structure* in the next section, I borrow these three descriptive terms as Kegan broadly defines them.) Let us review each briefly, with reference to table 2. The first thing to notice about the table is that the contents of the "subject" box are moved into the "object" box with each new order of consciousness. For example, in the second order one constructs knowledge *out of* one's point of view (childhood), while a person in the third order "backs up," so to say, and objectifies his or her own point of view as one among others (typical of adolescence). The qualitative nature of this transformation obtains for each new emergent order.

Kegan illustrates the difference between the third and fourth orders of consciousness by describing a couple who are struggling with the issue of interpersonal intimacy in their marriage. He notes that if each spouse constructs the self at a different order of consciousness, each will have a different idea of what it means to be intimate, or to be

5. Robert Kegan, *The Evolving Self: Problem and Process in Human Development* (Cambridge: Harvard University Press, 1982), 108.

Table 2. Summary of Kegan's Five "Orders of Consciousness"

	Subject	Object	Underlying Structure
1	Perceptions Impulses	Movement Sensation	**"Single Point/Immediate/ Atomistic"**
2	Concrete Point of View Enduring Dispositions	Perceptions Impulses	**"Durable Category"**
3	**Traditionalism** Abstractions Interpersonalism Inner States	Concrete Point of View Enduring Dispositions	**"Cross-Categorical, Trans-Categorical"** Stepping outside one's "point of view," to see it as *object* among other possible "points of view"
4	**Modernism** Abstract Systems Ideology Self-Formation	Abstractions Interpersonalism Inner States	**"System/Complex"** A mental structure that "subtends, subordinates, acts upon, directs, and actually generates the meaning of relationships"
5	**Postmodernism** Trans-Ideological Inter-Institutional Self-Transformation	Abstract Systems Ideology Self-Formation	**"Trans-System, Trans-Complex"** Systemic knowing itself is relativized, made *object* instead of *subject*. Relationship is seen as prior to the elements in relation.

(Adapted from Kegan, *In Over Our Heads,* 314)

near another "self." In the fourth order, the self becomes subject to its third-order constructions "so that it no longer *is* its third order constructions but *has* them . . . [now] the sharing of values and ideals and beliefs will not by itself be experienced as the ultimate intimacy of the sharing of selves, of who we *are.*"[6]

6. Kegan, *In Over Our Heads,* 114.

The move to the fourth order requires a qualitatively different way of structuring knowledge; it involves more than just the inclusion of more complex content within the mental constructions. The third order, with its underlying cross-categorical structures, is transformed from whole to part, that is, from subject to object. This move is not something that can be taught like a new skill. It involves growth, transformation, evolution, and takes time to develop. Introducing new complex ideas constructed by a fourth order of consciousness to a person who still constructs the subject-object relation in the third order will not by itself accomplish a transformation. Rather, the person will simply fit the new concept into the old order and "make the best use it can of the new ideas *on behalf of the old consciousness!*"[7] For this reason, spouses with different orders of consciousness may find communication difficult. As we will see below, a similar phenomenon occurs when we introduce the requirements of postmodernist interdisciplinary method to someone who constructs the subject-object relation from a "traditionalist" or "modernist" fiduciary structure.

Although Kegan focuses most of his case material on helping us to understand the movement to the fourth order (which his research indicates most adults have not reached), he points out that our culture is quickly developing levels of complexity that call for the fifth order. This is his interpretation of the emergence of postmodernism in various disciplines and cultural spheres. These new demands in so many arenas of life "all require an order of consciousness that is able to subordinate or relativize *systemic knowing* (the fourth order); they all require that we move systemic knowing from *subject* to *object.*"[8]

To understand the fifth order more clearly, it is helpful to examine two of Kegan's examples. First, he applies his model to "conflict" between two disputants or views, such as in marriage counseling or international peace talks. The fourth order approaches conflict by beginning with the two positions as separate, and goes from there. The relationship is an "after-the-fact" inconvenience, with which each side must contend. The approach of the fifth order of consciousness, on the other hand, suggests that the conflict is probably the result of one or both parties "making prior, true, distinct, and whole our partial po-

7. Ibid., 97.
8. Ibid., 316.

sition. . . . We may have this conflict because we need it to recover our truer complexity."[9] Even more strongly, Kegan suggests that while the fourth order disputants have the perception "of the logical priority of their distinct existences," the fifth order (or postmodern) interlocutors start with the belief that "the conflictual relationship creates the parties; the parties do not create the relationship."[10]

A second example that is particularly relevant to our topic is Kegan's discussion of "knowledge creation" from a fifth order of consciousness, and its relation to postmodernism. The move out of the fourth order means a relativizing of the "system" from its throne as subject, recognizing that all of its constructions are grounded in subjectivity. This involves a process of "differentiating" the self from the fourth order of knowing. But then, asks Kegan, is *post*modernism (being "beyond" the fourth order) also about a new kind of "integration" after the "differentiation," or is the creation of knowledge hopelessly ungrounded? Here he distinguishes between two kinds of postmodernism: deconstructive and reconstructive. Both point to the limits of knowledge, to the "unacknowledged ideological partiality" of every discipline and theory. For the deconstructivist this can be taken to imply the unacceptability of any position and lead to the the devaluation of all commitments. The reconstructive approach, on the other hand, makes into "objects" the limits of our disciplines and theories "for the purpose of nourishing the very process of reconstructing the disciplines and theories. . . . When we teach the disciplines or their theories in this fashion, they become more than procedures for authorizing and validating knowledge. They become procedures about the reconstruction of their procedures. The disciplines become generative. They become truer to life."[11] As a theory about theory making and a stand-taking about the way we take stands, a reconstructive response to postmodernism makes judgments concerning theories and stands that are not aware of the relativized mental structures that uphold them. The more complex order of consciousness is "privileged" only because it is "closer to a position that in fact protects us from dominating, ideological absolutes."[12]

9. Ibid., 319.
10. Ibid., 320.
11. Ibid., 330.
12. Ibid., 333.

In essence, the move to the fifth order of consciousness requires that one take the relationship itself as prior to its parts: "Do we take as prior the *elements of* a relationship (which then enter into relationship) or *the relationship itself* (which creates its elements)?"[13] This primacy of relationality is central to the postmodernist fiduciary structure that I explore below. To describe this fifth order, Kegan uses terms like "dialectical," "interpenetration of selves," and "trans-system." As we examine the shaping of interdisciplinary method by our underlying fiduciary structures, it is important to remember that these relational terms refer to the underlying structure of the subject-object relation within self-consciousness, not to the objects of our construction.

Ways of Holding on to Interdisciplinary Method

One of the benefits of interdisciplinary studies is discovering new insights in the relationality between fields, disclosing aspects of reality that would have remained concealed if we had hidden behind disciplinary walls (or remained in a second order of consciousness). We cannot speak of a disciplinary community or of a methodology moving to a higher order of consciousness, but if we focus on the need for individuals as interdisciplinarians to develop more complex fiduciary structures, we may indirectly contribute to progress on material and methodological discussions as well. It is critical that we attempt such a move because we are today in a situation worse than that described several decades ago by C. P. Snow in his concern over the "two cultures" of the arts and sciences that can no longer communicate. Today we have dozens of "cultures" (disciplines) that cannot communicate, with the threat of further fragmentation (deconstruction) from those who would argue that each one of us wholly constructs our own culture. The interdisciplinary dialogue between psychology and theology has contributed greatly toward the healing of this cultural split.[14] However, most discussions of interdisciplinary method have focused on the content of the disciplines or the communities that inhabit them.

13. Ibid., 313.
14. Cf. Stanley L. Jones, "A Constructive Relationship for Religion with the Science and Profession of Psychology," *American Psychologist* 49, no. 3 (1994): 184-99.

47

I am attempting here to draw attention to the *individual's* fiduciary structure, or underlying way of *holding on* to relationality (which subtends the content of the disciplines), as a crucial factor in interdisciplinary dialogue. I use the term "fiduciary structure" (instead of Kegan's "order of consciousness") to emphasize the influence of the knower's faith in (or "boundness to") knowledge. The model I propose here suggests that a transformation of one's fiduciary structure analogous to a move from the fourth to the fifth of Kegan's "orders" is necessary to uphold the kind of interdisciplinary method required by the demands of postmodernism. Children or adolescents with first and second orders of consciousness are at a developmental stage incapable of holding on to an understanding of relations between disciplines. In the first-order (atomistic) individual, there would be no consciousness of relationality, no sense of a distinct discipline. For an individual at the second order (durable category), the concept of a discipline emerges as a "category," but experience can be constructed or understood only from within the category. A fiduciary structure (or methodological faith) sufficiently complex for interdisciplinary discourse is possible only after movement to the third order of consciousness.

For each fiduciary structure (see table 3), I have described the general way of approaching the relationality between disciplines, that is, the shaping of interdisciplinary method. I have also indicated the tendency an individual at each fiduciary structure will exhibit in responding to the postmodern epistemic double bind; viz., how can we make rational judgments about absolutes or "objective" reality with our relative and "subjective" knowledge? It is important to recognize that while there is a shaping influence between fiduciary structures and the way an individual holds on to the theology-psychology relation, this is not a rigidly deterministic influence. The classification of three fiduciary structures is an attempt to describe the way the self tends to its theories, not the inherent value of the theories themselves. The point is that individuals with traditionalist or modernist fiduciary structures may talk about relational concepts but put them to use in the service of constructing a less complex methodological faith, which makes them prone to misunderstanding. The concepts in the mind of an interdisciplinarian are not like eggs in a basket that can be taken out and replaced; there is a reciprocal relation between content and fiduciary structure that cannot be ignored. I will de-

Table 3. Fiduciary Structures and the Shaping of Interdisciplinary Method

Fiduciary Structure	*Shaping of Interdisciplinary Method*
Traditionalist Fiduciary Structure (parallel to Kegan's third order of consciousness)	**Interdisciplinary Method:** *ex parte* **relationality** Relation between disciplines is viewed "from one side only." Tendency of the interdisciplinarian to collapse the double bind by leaning toward the absolute or objective pole.
Modernist Fiduciary Structure (parallel to Kegan's fourth order of consciousness)	**Interdisciplinary Method:** *ab extra* **relationality** The relationality (between disciplines) itself becomes the object of reflection, but one starts with the disciplines as separate, and then analyzes the relation "from the outside." Tendency of the interdisciplinarian to collapse the double bind by leaning toward the relative or subjective pole.
Postmodernist Fiduciary Structure (parallel to Kegan's fifth order of consciousness)	**Interdisciplinary Method:** *ab intra* **relationality** The relation of the disciplines is *held on to* "from within" the relationality itself. One starts by indwelling the tensional unity that constitutes the interdisciplinary relation. Tendency of the interdisciplinarian to allow the prior relationality of subject-object in knowledge to shape the resolution of the double bind.

scribe each structure briefly, and then turn to some material case studies.

With a traditionalist fiduciary structure, the possibility for interdisciplinary discourse first emerges because the individual's own point of view becomes an object and not only the subject of one's constructions. A transcategorical consciousness is generated by the recognition that others have a different point of view (or discipline) that guides the questions they ask. This person is more likely to exhibit what I call *"ex parte* relationality" in his or her interdisciplinary method, constructing judgments on the relation between psychology and theology "from one side only." One tends to lean toward the absolutism side of the postmodern double bind and continues to search for certain foundations for knowledge (typically rooted in one's own discipline). The point here is not the content, but the way the new interdisciplinarian *holds on* to the relationship.

"Ab extra relationality" refers to the way a person with an underlying modernist fiduciary structure typically approaches the relation between theology and psychology. Here the relationality between various foundations, sets of rules, and communities of discourse, rather than one discipline (pole) or another, becomes the object. But the relation to the relation between disciplines is still based on the poles, and starts "from outside" the relationality itself. One begins by abstracting the fields of study as though they were not in relation, and then asks how to relate them. More so than a traditionalist, a person with a modernist fiduciary structure may be tempted by the relativism side of the double bind. It makes sense to think that most theologians and psychologists, especially those who are struggling with the issues of epistemology and interdisciplinary method, have reached at least this level of methodological faith. One can see, for example, in Ian Barbour's description of "dialogue" models for relating science and religion that these methods begin with the disciplines as separate, and then try to work out the relation between them.[15]

A postmodernist fiduciary structure, on the other hand, operates out of a prior awareness of the tensive bipolar relational unity of the disciplines that hermeneutically precedes the description of the disciplines as separate poles. Here we find an intuitive recognition that disciplinary identities are dialectically related and so mediated (even if negatively) by their embeddedness in a broader relationality. *"Ab intra* relationality" is my way of describing the way a person with this underlying fiduciary structure (parallel to Kegan's fifth order of consciousness) tends to the relation of psychology and theology. An interdisciplinarian with this type of methodological faith can recognize the contextual, provisional nature of the subject pole, but simultaneously

15. Ian Barbour, *Religion in an Age of Science* (San Francisco: HarperCollins, 1990).

affirm the real, objective existence of the object pole, because knowledge is constructed from within the relationality itself. In the theology-psychology relation, figure and ground are reversed; interdisciplinary method is turned inside out.

In this way of thinking, the interdisciplinary relationality helps us to understand the disciplines, which can be fully explained only by accounting for their being-in-relation. This emphasis on the "field" that constitutes the tensionality of the "fields" can ultimately result in a mutually enhanced understanding of both disciplines. This is not an attempt to end discussion by sliding into a solipsism of subjective knowing (as the traditionalist might think), or surreptitiously smuggling a new kind of absolutism into knowledge (as the modernist might think). The fact that interdisciplinary method is shaped by this underlying structure does not mean all our theories will fall into the same mold. Indeed, I argue that Kegan's functional definitions (while extremely useful and illuminative) do not take us far enough; we still need to think theologically about holding on to relationality.

Developing Fiduciary Structures

It is important to acknowledge that we do not have access to some neutral standpoint from which we can know the relation between the inner structures of another person's consciousness and the content of his or her conceptions. Indeed, it is difficult enough to ascertain our own way of holding on to knowledge as we struggle to understand our relation to ourselves, to others, and to God. As we engage in this search for intelligibility, however, we may find resources to help us develop more complex orders of consciousness. In what follows, I have selected some particular proposals that use language and imagery that may facilitate this development. Let me emphasize that my intention is not to place these authors in a particular box or order. My task is the identification of developmental resources for the perilous and promising journey toward knowing as we are known. We examine these formulations of interdisciplinary relationality in order to ask: How might this way of talking about the relation between theology and psychology help lead a person toward a more complex fiduciary structure? The taxonomy is not intended to judge the adequacy of interdisciplinary constructs or to measure intelligence. The point of exploring underlying fiduciary structures is not the content of a method, but the way it is held on to by an interdisciplinarian. With these caveats, I invite readers to join me in self-reflection as we think about ways of thinking about interdisciplinary relationality.

The Traditionalist Fiduciary Structure

I will spend the least time on this type of methodological faith because it is generally the starting point for most individuals interested in the theology-psychology relationship. Here one finds oneself in a discipline and then reflects on its relation to another discipline. If the other discipline is perceived primarily as a threat to one's own discipline, then one can easily be tempted to remain in the comfort of a traditionalist fiduciary structure. Although the constructs of theories that are materialistically behaviorist or spiritually reductionist are radically diverse,[16] individuals (from either side) who feel comfortable with these formal antagonistic ways of constructing the relation between disciplines may be operating with the same third order of consciousness.

J. Wentzel van Huyssteen has pointed out that a similar foundationalist epistemology appears to drive individuals from both sides. Treating the general relation between theology and science, he notes that foundationalist interlocutors often share the following characteristics: "Both believe that there are serious conflicts between contemporary science and religious beliefs; both seek knowledge with a secure and incontrovertible foundation, and find this in either logic and sense data (science), or in an infallible scripture or self-authenticating revelation (theology); both claim that science and theology make rival claims about the same domain and one has to choose between them."[17]

In the terminology I have been developing, we could say that materialistic behaviorism and spiritual reductionism may fit more comfortably within an underlying traditionalist fiduciary structure. Both com-

16. B. F. Skinner, *Beyond Freedom and Dignity* (New York: Knopf, 1971), may be an example of the former; "nouthetic counseling," of the latter.
17. J. Wentzel van Huyssteen, *Essays in Postfoundationalist Theology* (Grand Rapids: Eerdmans, 1997), 240. For a full treatment of these issues, see his *Shaping of Rationality* (Grand Rapids: Eerdmans, 1999).

52

mitments can lead to an interdisciplinary approach limited to *ex parte* pronouncements, chipping away at the foundational pillars that support the opponent's epistemic temple. Clearly this kind of methodological faith is not up to the task of resolving the postmodern double bind; it tends to exempt itself from the provisionality, contextuality, and fallibility that characterize all human inquiry.

Developing a Modernist Fiduciary Structure

The methodological faith of a modernist fiduciary structure may uphold and shape interdisciplinary method in a qualitatively different way. The cross-categorical structures of the third order of consciousness (traditionalism) become object instead of subject. This fiduciary structure can more adequately grasp the complexities of relating psychological and theological theories. Kegan's research suggests that this is the structure out of which most graduate-level educated persons operate. Indeed, one of the most important goals of college and graduate school is to help develop higher levels of critical thinking. This makes all the more relevant the task of clarifying how these structures can shape the way we hold on to the relation between theology and psychology (and other disciplines). In this section we look at three examples of proposals that use relational imagery that may lead us and help us lead others toward developing a modernist fiduciary structure for subtending the disciplines.

In his proposal for a "psychology of Christian living," which would involve the creation of a new subguild of specialized practitioners, A. A. Sappington enters into dialogue with some popular models in industrial/organizational psychology that are interested in understanding and influencing a "class of behaviors." In a similar way, Sappington suggests that Christian practioners might focus on increasing "behavior that conforms to the Golden Rule."[18] To describe the relation between Christian faith and psychology, he offers the image of a person praying to God for help in crossing a river, while a rowboat sits nearby.

18. A. A. Sappington, "Psychology for the Practice of the Presence of God: Putting Psychology at the Service of the Church," *Journal of Psychology and Christianity* 13, no. 1 (1994): 6.

While admitting God could miraculously provide transport, Sappington suggests that the rowboat (psychology) may be the answer to the prayer.[19] This parable opens us up to the possibility of imagining a more complex relation between theology and psychology in which the two are intimately related and not simply two separate options for facilitating behavioral change. Notice that his subtitle ("putting psychology at the service of the church") explicitly leads us to thematize the interdisciplinary relation per se.

Another example of interdisciplinary discourse that encourages us to focus on the integral relation between theology and psychology is the work of European practical theologian Johannes van der Ven. A leader in the growing empirical theology movement, his own approach is characterized by "the use of empirical methods and techniques of conceptualization, operationalization, and statistical analysis by theologians themselves in order to explore and to treat specific problems in practical theology."[20] Bringing psychological modes of inquiry and assessment directly into theological method is clearly a model that recognizes the mutual relation between the disciplines. Van der Ven argues that questions like which processes of change in the church are cleansing or purifying *(reinigen),* and which social conditions must obtain for the church to influence these changes, "demand an answer, but without the direct use of social science instruments, it is not possible to answer them."[21] The essential relation between the disciplines, and especially the implicit impact of psychological thinking on theological thinking, is brought into focus. Of course, it is also important to acknowledge the way in which theological thinking (e.g., reflection on ultimate values) may shape the direction of psychological research. Nevertheless, van der Ven's integration helps us thematize the relationality itself, and so lures us toward a more complex fiduciary structure.

Everett Worthington speaks of three phases of interdisciplinary in-

19. Ibid., 13.

20. Johannes van der Ven, "Practical Theology as Critical-Empirical Theology," in *Les Etudes Pastorales à l'Université,* ed. Adrian Visscher (Paris: Presses de l'Université d'Ottawa, 1990), 239. Cf. his *Practical Theology: An Empirical Approach* (Kampen: Kok Pharos, 1993).

21. J. van der Ven, "Unterwegs zu einer empirischen Theologie," in *Theologie und Handeln: Beiträge zur Fundierung der praktischen Theologie als Handlungstheorie,* ed. O. Fuchs (Düsseldorf: Patmos, 1984), 112.

tegration, and suggests that we are now in the third phase, which involves *intra*disciplinary integration: the task of integrating "Christian values, beliefs, and assumptions and various theories of therapy."[22] His proposal for a "blueprint" to assist in this task is extremely helpful because it points to the role of the individual in relating psychology and theology. Worthington's discussion leads us to examine the conceptual relation between "Christian values" and "theories of therapy." The individual practitioner must integrate these concepts, and the image of a "blueprint" helps us imagine the relationality itself as the object of reflection: interdisciplinary method is something the Christian therapist "writes" and "rewrites."[23] Worthington's proposal makes the relation between theology and therapy the focus of interdisciplinary discourse, thereby offering language and imagery that can lead us toward upholding the disciplines in a way that can better account for the complexities of their reciprocity. Further, he draws attention explicitly to the importance of the individual interdisciplinarian's own way of holding on to the relation between psychology and theology.

Developing a Postmodernist Fiduciary Structure

All of these proposals help us thematize relationality itself as we move forward in the interdisciplinary task of reforming theological anthropology. In light of the radical turn to relationality in late modern culture, however, we should continue to explore other ways to develop more complex fiduciary structures for holding on to the relational constructs that have led to challenges to traditional formulations of doctrine in Christian anthropology. The remainder of this book is just such an exploration, and so I limit myself here to pointing out the resources available in the work of practical theologian James Loder, to whom we will often have occasion to return.

The theme of "relationality" pervades Loder's writings, as well as his pedagogical and therapeutic practice. His passion was to lead others into a deeper understanding of the illuminative and transformative

22. Everett L. Worthington, "A Blueprint for Intradisciplinary Integration," *Journal of Psychology and Theology* 22, no. 2 (1994): 79.
23. Ibid., 85.

power of the ultimate relationality between God and humanity revealed in Jesus Christ. Loder's goal was not merely to engender an abstract understanding about christological relationality, but to facilitate the passionate self-involvement of the reader or listener so that he or she might participate more intensely in this relation to God made possible by the Spirit of Christ. In one of his last articles, he argues that practical theology should be guided by an explicit theological position, namely "the Chalcedonian formulation of the relationality between the Divine and the human natures in the one person of Jesus Christ. This relationality is characterized in Barthian terms as 'indissoluble differentiation,' 'inseparable unity' and 'indestructible (asymmetrical) order.' More succinctly, this constellation of factors is designated as asymmetrical, bipolar, relational unity which is self-involving through faith."[24] In other words, the relational logic of Incarnation and redemption should be at the heart of practical theology, both methodologically and materially.

Loder's writings are filled with language that challenges us to start with *(ab intra)* the relationality of the disciplines and to recognize the irreducible influence of the knower in the act of constructing an interdisciplinary method. He would often speak of a figure-ground reversal between relationality and its polarities, so that relationality was viewed as fundamental. In a work coauthored with physicist W. Jim Neidhardt, he explains that "the central orientation of this book is not science on the one hand versus theology on the other; rather it is upon a fundamental epistemology."[25] This epistemology is explicitly related to Christology for Loder. He argues that the Chalcedonian fathers started with the relational unity of Jesus Christ as truly God and truly human.[26] They included their own roles as knowers and worshipers in their description of the knowledge of the One who can be known completely and truly only through participating in his inner life with the Father by the Spirit. This was not an attempt to force two opposites together, but the struggle of "participating" knowers to carry out the most rigorous effort reason could make. For Loder, the logic of Chalce-

24. James Loder, "The Place of Science in Practical Theology: The Human Factor," *International Journal of Practical Theology* 4 (2000): 23.

25. James Loder and W. Jim Neidhardt, *The Knight's Move: The Relational Logic of the Spirit in Theology and Science* (Colorado Springs: Helmers and Howard, 1992), 89.

26. James Loder, "Practical Theology and Interdisciplinary Method," paper presented at the International Academy of Practical Theology, Bern, Switzerland, 1995, 18.

don provides us with the relationality needed to relate God's self-revelation to God's creation, especially in the sphere of human action: "the hypostatic union . . . constitutes the ontological ground for claiming that relationship is definitive for reality."[27]

As professor of the philosophy of Christian education at Princeton Theological Seminary, Loder often dealt with the epistemological, ethical, and metaphysical issues that underlie various models of the dynamics of redemptive transformation. Although he did not publish extensively on the philosophical concept of relationality, he did deal with it indirectly and implicitly in his various treatments of Kierkegaard, Bohr, Piaget, Polanyi, and others.[28] Loder refused to immunize his view of theological relationality from critique, but engaged in rigorous interdisciplinary dialogue, identifying proximate patterns of relationality in other fields of study such as physics and psychology, patterns that he believed pointed toward the ultimate relationality revealed in Jesus Christ. In physics Loder was particularly interested in the relationality depicted in the Copenhagen interpretation of the quantum reality of light, commonly called "complementarity."[29] In psychology he focused on the dynamics of relationality that characterize the process of human development, building on the work of Piaget and others as he outlined an ontology of relationships that could account for our experience of spiritual transformation.[30] Loder showed us the valuable mutual enhancement that can occur when we transgress the boundaries of the traditional disciplines of theology, physics, and psychology.

As is evident from the quotation above, Loder's own way of conceiving relationality was deeply influenced by Karl Barth, and by Reformed theology in general. Barth's own theology focuses on the revelation of the Word of God in Jesus Christ, and his understanding of

27. *Knight's Move,* 200.

28. Loder spells out his understanding of relationality in greatest detail in *The Knight's Move,* but an implicit treatment of philosophical relationality is already present in the book based on his dissertation, *Religious Pathology and Christian Faith* (Philadelphia: Westminster, 1966).

29. See especially *Knight's Move* and his later "Barth, Bohr and Dialectic," in *Religion & Science: History, Method, Dialogue,* ed. W. Mark Richardson and Wesley J. Wildman (New York: Routledge, 1996), 271-89.

30. See especially *The Logic of the Spirit: Human Development in Theological Perspective* (San Francisco: Jossey-Bass, 1998).

that revelation is inherently relational, both materially (as is evident, e.g., in his doctrine of the Trinity) and formally (as is evident in his commitment to *analogia relationis*). The philosophical theologian who most influenced Loder's view of relationality was Søren Kierkegaard; this influence is implicit in the reference above to self-involvement through faith,[31] but is made explicit in several of his works — from his dissertation on Kierkegaard and Freud to *The Knight's Move*. Loder's resolution to what I have called the postmodern double bind of relativism-absolutism builds on Kierkegaardian themes: "only through deeply indwelt particularity is universality able to be known and appropriated."[32] Like Kierkegaard, Loder believed that the relationality disclosed in the God-man is a basic hermeneutical category and that each individual is called to appropriate this relationality existentially through inward passion. The Christian experiences this as spiritual transformation in relation to Jesus Christ.

Relationality Transformed by the Spirit of Christ

In all of these discussions of relationality, we encounter the amazing fit between human intelligence and creation's intelligibility. The knower is irreducibly caught up in the act of knowing and composes the world in a relational way that mirrors the relational unity of the self. This relationality built into human experience might be expressed in Polanyian terms as "tacit and focal awareness"; in cultural anthropology as "binary kinship structures"; in depth psychology as *coniunctionis oppositorum;* in the psychoanalytic tradition as the subconscious and the conscious; in Kierkegaardian terms as the tension of the "infinite qualitative distinction" between temporal existence and eternity. These diverse examples suggest that human *knowing* can do the work of constructing only because human *being* is so constructed; that is, knowledge emerges out of relationality inherent in reality.

It appears that we are "made" for relational knowing and that the world is "made" for being known relationally. When relationality becomes a "positive third term" it takes on a life of its own, mutually

31. "Place of Science," 23.
32. *Knight's Move*, 104.

transforming the poles-in-relation. For this reason, we must develop a theological understanding of relationality that goes beyond Kegan's functionally defined "orders of consciousness." Relationship, left to itself, can distort the poles; it can lead to codependency or oppression. The quality of the relationship, which gets at the *why* and not only the *how* of our therapeutic and pedagogical efforts, must be defined in theological and spiritual terms. Think of the fortune-telling slave girl of Acts 16. She spoke the truth: "These men are slaves of the Most High God" (v. 17). The content of her proclamation is accurate. But it is the distortedness of the way she was holding on to the knowledge, the "demonic" way she was related to the truth, that led Paul, "very much annoyed," to command the spirit to leave her (v. 18). Having the right content in our interdisciplinary method is not enough.

Indeed, even having a postmodernist fiduciary structure is neither a necessary nor a sufficient condition for knowing or being related to God. This model does not imply that salvation is dependent on developing a more complex fiduciary structure. Such a conclusion would involve a functional reduction of faith into ego capacity. One cannot posit a direct correlation between complex cognitive capacities and advanced levels of religious development. I would argue that spiritual transformation may occur at any developmental stage. On the other hand, a person may compose the world out of a more complex fiduciary structure, but have no positive relationship to God. As I understand faith development, God's gracious presence that calls us to become sharers in the trinitarian divine relationality (cf. 2 Pet. 1:4) does not depend on our fiduciary structures. When the relationality in question is God's relation to the self, the human way of holding on to relationality becomes the object, so to say, and God is the Subject. In the experience of transformational faith, the believer is upheld by God as she or he is caught up into the Son's knowledge of the Father by the Spirit, providing a new center for the relationality that composes the self. God's holding on to us transforms human relationality as we are united with Christ through the communion-creating presence of the Spirit.

When we turn to the specific task of understanding and describing the relationality that obtains between our disciplines and theories, however, a postmodernist fiduciary structure (in the reconstructive sense described above) is indeed to be valued as more proficient. This mode of relational imagination may be more capable of constructing complex ways of conceptualizing God's relation to the world, resulting in a heightened self-understanding of one's own relational existence. Therefore, movement to more complex fiduciary structures should be encouraged and facilitated, but not relied upon as a substitute for spiritual formation nor as a panacea in pastoral care. Kegan's subject-object theory suggests that we cannot force a person to think in a higher order of consciousness. If one proposes new relational models and interdisciplinary ways of thinking that require a postmodernist fiduciary structure, then those with less complex structures will often place the new ideas at the service of their current order of consciousness. Like a good therapist in a session with a client or like a sensitive professor with a new student, one should meet the interdisciplinarian where he or she is. It is well worth the effort to take the time necessary to help people develop a new way of holding on to the relation between theology and other sciences. This is why all of the chapters of part I encourage the reader to thematize her or his own relation to theology and anthropology before we thematize their material reciprocity in part II and explore the impact of the turn to relationality on material doctrinal themes in part III.

In the context of the general flow of this book the current chapter is intended to set before us early a reminder that *we* are doing theological anthropology. Our efforts to respond to the challenges of late modernity may be undergirded by a deeper examination of the methodological faith or underlying fiduciary structures out of which we hold on to the relation between our disciplines and to specific doctrinal formulations. A focus on this relational dimension of knowledge may disclose new therapeutic, pedagogical, and theological insights, transforming interdisciplinary method into a very personal way of helping to repair the cultural bifurcation between faith and reason. The deeper causes of the mental pain of being in over our heads will not be healed by our ignoring them and hoping that postmodernism will go away. Instead, we may be able to take an active role in transforming culture through a theological engagement with late modern philosophy and science. Many readers may still fear this engagement and will ask for an explicitly theological rationale for such an enterprise. The next chapter attempts to set out such a rationale by exploring the fear of God as the beginning of knowledge and wisdom, focusing on the specific dynamics of transformational learning in theological seminary education as a case study.

3
Relationality and Pedagogical Practice

In his celebrated book *Pedagogy of the Oppressed,* Paulo Freire helped raise our consciousness of the influence of social oppression on a student's capacity to learn. On the basis of his experience working with illiterate peasants in South America, Freire called for transformed models of education that engage the whole praxis of the individual learner as an agent in a socioeconomic context.[1] In North American institutions of higher education, Freire's work has contributed to an awareness of the extent to which our cultural systems oppress minorities and women, as well as the poor. Freire's emphasis on problem-centered education and linking praxis to critical reflection has strengthened our understanding of and ability to fulfill the task of preparing students for (and in) Christian ministry.[2]

In spite of many similarities, however, the barriers to transformational learning that hinder most North American seminarians (and

1. Paulo Freire, *Pedagogy of the Oppressed* (New York: Continuum, 1985). See also the articles collected in Freire, *The Politics of Education: Culture, Power, and Liberation,* trans. Donaldo Macedo (South Hadley, Mass.: Bergin & Garvey, 1985).

2. North American theological educators who have appropriated aspects of Freire's thought are too numerous to mention here. Some important examples include Robert K. Martin, "Congregational Studies and Critical Pedagogy in Theological Perspective," *Theological Education* 33, no. 2 (1997): 121-46; Michael Welton, "Seeing the Light: Christian Conversion and Conscientization," in *Adult Education and Theological Interpretations,* ed. P. Jarvis and N. Walters (Malabar, Fla.: Krieger, 1993), 105-23; Russell A. Butkus, "Linking Social Analysis with Curriculum Development: Insights from Paulo Freire," *Religious Education* 84 (Fall 1989): 568-83; Elisabeth Schüssler Fiorenza, "Theological Education: Biblical Studies," in *The Education of the Practical Theologian,* ed. Don Browning, et al. (Atlanta: Scholars Press, 1989), 1-19.

61

laypersons) are quite different from those faced by Freire. In addition to sociological oppression, what keeps many of our theological students from learning is psychological *repression*. Of course, these intercalated factors (along with others) cooperate to inhibit learning, and both are present in all learning environments; yet repression often appears more dominant in our context. Or better: the particular forms of repression characteristic of North American learners present a unique challenge to seminary educators. While many students surely feel the weight of oppression, they also suffer from the pain of repressed fears. Without downplaying the former, I propose in this chapter to focus on the latter — what we might call the "pedagogy of the repressed."

My method is explicitly interdisciplinary, examining the complementary perspectives of psychology and theology on the role of fear in seminary education. Of course similar dynamics are operative in the local church, and the principles outlined in this chapter could also be applied to other ecclesial contexts. I begin by offering a definition of terms and setting out the conceptual framework (borrowed from James Loder) that will structure my proposal. I then treat the problem of fear from a psychological perspective, providing a brief summary of some of this discipline's salient contributions. The main purpose of this chapter, however, is to propose a deeper theological understanding of fear in relation to education; this is carried out in the final major section. While we have done well at appropriating the research of educational psychology and other fields that help students adapt to their setting, perhaps we have not always done so well at remembering that we are engaged in *theological* education. When the object and context of one's inquiry is *theos*, the Holy One who is the transcendent source of all things, learning to adapt to one's culture and its patterns of learning (albeit necessary) may not be sufficient. Far from denigrating the contribution of educational psychology and other anthropological disciplines, I suggest (to paraphrase Einstein) that the anthropological sciences without theology are blind, but theology wholly divorced from the anthropological sciences is lame.

Repression, Pedagogy, and Transformation

By adopting the term "repressed," I do not intend to weigh in on the intramural debate among psychologists (e.g., Freudians, Jungians, object-

62

relation theorists) about precisely what qualifies as repression and how it is caused. Rather, my goal is simply to refer to the broadly accepted description of ego dynamics wherein a person's capacity to function is hindered by psychological defenses that one has constructed to deal with one's fears. Repression seems to involve both external and internal factors — we see a reciprocal influence between the inner fears of an individual and societal pressures and expectations. The general concern of this chapter, then, is our pretheoretic intuitions about individuals (seminarians) whose ability to learn has been blocked (or at least hindered) by their self-enclosure as a result of fear.

The key point for our purpose here is that repression in all its various forms is based on experiences of fear. But what do all experiences of fear have in common? Whatever the object of fear (whether related to class load, to ridicule by peers, to the future demands of ministry, or to being compelled to give up cherished beliefs), there is a sense that one cannot control that object. I cannot control my peers, so I fear they may reject me. I cannot control time, so I fear being overwhelmed and failing a class. I cannot control my parishioners, so I repress my true feelings of anger or anxiety. I cannot control all truth with my finite mind, so I fear any new idea or set of categories that may challenge my comfortable ways of structuring the meaning of reality. In order to capture this generic aspect of fear, then, I offer the following definition: fear is *a response to the perceived inability to control an existentially relevant object*.[3] From a theological perspective, this generic definition allows us to ask how education is affected when God is the object of fear.

Although it is used to refer to educational practice generally, "pedagogy" literally means leading or facilitating change in children; the term is derived from the Greek words *paid-* (child) and *agōgos* (leader). Malcolm Knowles, a key figure in the emergence of the field of adult education, introduced the term "andragogy" in order to emphasize that facilitating learning in adults differs from facilitating learning in children. While the term itself has virtually dropped out of circulation (probably because "andragogy" is too androcentric), the stress on the difference between childhood and adult learning remains a major

---

3. The modifier "existentially relevant" is added to exclude things like quasars in distant galaxies, which although we may not be able to control them do not affect our response to the world.

theme in the field.[4] Christine Blair offers a helpful summary of some characteristics of adult learners: they learn best when the learning environment feels safe and supportive, when their minds are engaged, when their learning is grounded in their experience, when they are self-directed, and when education speaks to mind, heart, and soul.[5] Despite its etymology, I will conform to disciplinary parlance and speak of the "pedagogy" of seminarians, with special attention to their unique needs qua adult learners.

The term "transformation" is quite popular in the field of adult education, for it serves to emphasize that the goal in adult learning is not merely *form*ation (a dominant motif with children), but *trans*formation; i.e., not simply the socialization into a particular culture's way of formulating meaning, but the facilitation of new critical reformulations.[6] While we should avoid a forced dichotomy (for working with children involves transformation, and adults are also in formation), this is a valid distinction that points to the qualitatively different mental structures that emerge through the various stages of life. Ideally modes of learning continue to change throughout life's stages, moving toward complexification of meaning schemes that render intelligible the self-world nexus. The relevant literature on developmental psychology has been summarized elsewhere.[7] In thematizing the pedagogy of adults, the goal of seminary educators is to appropriate findings from psychology as an aid to facilitating the transformation of seminarians' sense of identity, so that they may function in the ministry contexts to which they are called as whole (psychologically integrated) and holy (theologically integrated) persons.

4. See, e.g., Stephen Brookfield, *Understanding and Facilitating Adult Learning* (San Francisco: Jossey-Bass, 1988); and Sharan B. Merriam and Rosemary S. Caffarella, *Learning in Adulthood* (San Francisco: Jossey-Bass, 1991).

5. Christine Blair, "Understanding Adult Learners: Challenges for Theological Education," *Theological Education* 34, no. 1 (1997): 11-24.

6. See, e.g., Jack Mezirow, *Transformative Dimensions of Adult Learning* (San Francisco: Jossey-Bass, 1991), 3.

7. I limit myself to recommending James E. Loder, *The Logic of the Spirit: Human Development in Theological Perspective* (San Francisco: Jossey-Bass, 1998); and Robert Kegan, *In Over Our Heads: The Mental Demands of Modern Life* (Cambridge: Harvard University Press, 1994).

The Four Dimensions of Human Existence

In order to highlight the differences between psychological and theological perspectives as we approach the topic of fear in seminary education, I borrow a conceptual framework developed by James Loder. In *The Transforming Moment,* Loder explores the human longing for and drive toward transformation of the self, a dynamic process that operates within what he calls the four "dimensions" of human existence: the lived world, the self, the void, and the Holy. "Being human entails environment, selfhood, the possibility of not being, and the possibility of new being. All four dimensions are essential, and none of them can be ignored without decisive loss to our understanding of what is essentially human."[8]

Loder uses the rubric of the *lived world* to stress the constructive, compositional character of the environment in which humans have their existence. Humans are conditioned by their composed situation, their cultural and historical embeddedness; they cannot completely rise above this situatedness and escape from the finite social world in which they live. In what follows, I adopt Loder's usage of the term "world" to refer to a particular, lived embodiment in a composed environment. The seminarian's "world" is the whole complex of systemic relations (physical, psychological, sociological, etc.) that constitute his or her existence.

The second dimension Loder describes is the *self* that transcends the embodiment of being human in order repeatedly to recompose its "world":

> this is the knower; the self is embodied in the lived "world" and at the same time stands outside it. By virtue of this duality of the self, it is evident that human being both *is* its environment and *has* its environment. . . . Ontogenetically the lived world is engrossing and very largely determinative of the ontic, or particular shape of the self; in this sense, the environment composes the self. Ontologically the self is primary in that (1) self-transcendence or openness to one's own being is universal and independent of the environment and (2) the lived world must finally be the self's own composition of the environment as given with birth.[9]

8. James E. Loder, *The Transforming Moment* (Colorado Springs: Helmers and Howard, 1989), 69.

9. Ibid., 69-70.

These first two dimensions, the self in its relation to the lived world, are properly the subject matter of psychology (and the other anthropological disciplines).

These two dimensions of human being are weak, however, when confronted with the third: "the possibility of annihilation, the potential and eventually inevitable absence of one's being." Loder uses the term "void" for this dimension, which is the end result of each human being, implicit in existence from birth and explicit in death. The void is understood as the ultimate telos toward which all experiences of nothingness point — these experiences (such as loneliness and despair) are the "faces of the void." In periods of anxiety, we glimpse the void, but the ultimate experience of the void is death. Death is something all humans face, an essential aspect or dimension of our existence.

Loder describes experiences of the fourth dimension, the *Holy*, as occurring when "being" is present not only implicitly in beings but explicitly manifest as "being-itself." This *mysterium tremendum et fascinans* is not a privileged awareness, but a constitutive dimension of personal human experience. The various religions are responses to "being-itself" as it is mediated through language, culture, and community. It is essential to being a human, argues Loder, that one worships what is holy. When the sense of "the Holy" is projected onto the profane, "worship" (and this essential aspect of being human along with it) collapses into the embodied environment as idolatry and thence into nothingness. Loder suggests, however, that "at the center of transformational knowing in science, esthetics, or therapy the imaginative, constructive insight or vision is an undoing of nothingness; it is a proximate form of the ultimate manifestation of 'the Holy' in revelation. . . . Faith sees that being-itself may be interpreted as 'God' and that the ultimate manifestation of being-itself is Jesus Christ."[10] Theology is primarily concerned with these last two dimensions of human existence, although it is concerned with them in order to understand how they bring transformation to the first two dimensions.

Psychological adaptation is the attempt to control things and ourselves in reaction to objects we cannot control, to "get a grip" on the world and the self, to overcome our fears. But what about the fear of God? The Holy is not something *we* grip, but that which *grips us* at the

10. Ibid., 70-71.

deepest level of existence. Just as all of our predicates are radically qual-
ified when applied to God, so too when the object of fear is the Holy
One who absolutely cannot be controlled. As we will see below, both
the Hebrew Bible and the New Testament clearly call us to fear God;
moreover, transformational learning ("the beginning of wisdom") is
linked to this command.

I suggest that the ultimate remedy to the repression that keeps
seminarians from transformational learning is to fear the only One
worth fearing, so that they can overcome the fears of this world. For
truly transformational learning to occur in seminarians, it is crucial for
us to provide an integrative environment in which they see their intellectual task (theological exploration) as inherently connected to their
relation to God (spiritual and personal formation) and to their ministry with the people of God (transformational leadership). This chapter,
then, follows the dialectic between the ultimate (theological) experience of fear and the proximate (psychological) experiences of fear and
their repression, in order to identify that which inhibits transformational learning in seminarians.

Transformational Learning in Psychological Perspective

What keeps seminarians from transformational learning? The psychological answer is *too much fear*. The focus here is on the subjective pole
of the fear experience, that is, how the individual student handles experiences of fear. Whether it is of failure, of exposure, or of rejection, the
psychological perspective illuminates the ego dynamics of the subject
that allow the fear to prevent transformational growth.

Psychology and the Fearful Subject

The relation between lived world and self (Loder's first two dimensions) is the conceptual arena in which most psychological analyses
and prescriptions occur. These dimensions figure prominently in
Freire's work. He differentiates between a "banking" model and a
"problem-posing" model of education. In the banking approach, students are viewed as containers, ready to be filled with knowledge de-

posited by the teacher. The student then masters the task of making withdrawals from the stored knowledge in response to the appropriate questions. This confirms in the student's mind that he or she has little or nothing to contribute in the "transaction." In problem-posing education, on the other hand, the learners and the teachers together explore and interact with conceptual reality (Loder's "lived world"). For Freire, pedagogy of the oppressed must begin with a raising of the learners' consciousness of their oppression, so that (after naming it) they can move toward changing it. In a similar way, we must raise seminarians' awareness of the debilitating effects that their fears (and their repression) have on them, so that they too can move toward transformation.

Several scholars have examined the psychological effects of oppressive ideology within the lived world of the *ekklēsia*. For example, R. K. Martin builds on the work of Freire and others, calling for the inclusion of "emancipative rationality" in the analysis of congregational dynamics. He argues for a radical inclusion of trinitarian thinking within a "theological rationality" that views the ground of ecclesial and all Christian praxis "ontologically beyond themselves in the Triune God revealed through Jesus Christ."[11] British religious educator John Hull warns churches of the dangers of maintaining the puerilization of their members (keeping them childish in their thinking). While many adults continue to develop critical-thinking skills in other areas of life, some religious institutions retard this development in matters of faith, again out of fear that their members will think for themselves and become "uncontrollable." This can lead to boredom with the church, or to an intentional avoidance of doctrine (as can be seen, e.g., in the compartmentalization of beliefs about creation and evolution in so many parishioners). Hull claims that "the principal problem in the growth of consciousness is the overcoming of fear,"[12] a fear that we find (I suggest) on both sides of the pulpit or professorial lectern.

---

11. Martin, "Congregational Studies," 143.

12. John M. Hull, *What Prevents Christian Adults from Learning?* (Philadelphia: Trinity Press International, 1991), 165.

Educational Anesthesia

One unfortunate way of dealing with this fear is what I call "educational anesthesia." Of course, few professors actually desire to put their students to sleep, and few students prefer an extremely passive (banking) model of education. However, fear on both sides can lead to a state of affairs in which boredom and irrelevance reign. Moreover, many students come to seminary apathetic, numbed by doctrinal wars, seeing theological education as something to be endured, like an operation (which makes the imagery of anesthesia even more poignant). The "anesthetic" metaphor has two functions here. First, it refers to the deadening or numbing of the learner prior to the cognitive surgical operation of the teacher. Most of us have experienced teachers who seem to prefer that students be anesthetized, discouraging questions and resisting alternative, experientially oriented methods of learning.

Second, the metaphor points to the removal of the aesthetic (anaesthetic) from the learning environment. "Anesthesia" derives from *anaisthētos* (having no feeling). The aesthetic dimension in theological learning includes the pleasure and pain of the learner's life story, one's systemic and sensible relations to community, one's emotive and optative investment in the whole history of humanity, and of course one's experience of God. So "aesthetic" here is used in a general sense to refer not merely to the arts, music, and literature but to the innate human longing for transcendence signified by these activities. Of all modes of human inquiry, theology in particular should deeply integrate the drive inherent in these spiritual aspirations into its pedagogical practice.

A psychological perspective illuminates the factors in the dimensions of the self and lived world that hinder transformational learning, and provides resources and tools for helping to conquer the fears that inhibit the seminarian's adaptation to the challenges of Christian ministry. Factors that contribute to overcoming repression include models of learning that enhance self-direction, problem-oriented strategies, and an environment that facilitates the student's sense of belonging to a safe educational community. It is important to note that fear is not wholly negative; it can be a stimulus for growth in an educational setting. Even its positive function, however, is negatively mediated — fear is something to conquer.

From a theological perspective, however, even this delight in conquering repressed fears does not answer our deepest longings for transformation. Theologically, we must speak also of the need to remain conquered by fear of God. This recognizes other dimensions in the pedagogical task: our goal should be to overcome educational anesthesia without inadvertently anesthetizing students to the dimensions of the void and the Holy as these inevitably break into the learning environment. Conversely, we must be careful that a theological perspective does not ignore or crush the essential psychological integrity that is crucial for thriving in the first two dimensions.

Transformational Learning in Theological Perspective

What keeps seminarians from transformational learning? The psychological answer, as we have seen, is too much fear. The theological answer is *not enough fear*. Both answers are correct, but in our theological analysis we turn our focus most decisively to the *object* of fear. The question here is what impact fear of the Holy, which alone can ultimately conquer and transform the void, has on learning. Several scriptural maxims make the connection for us: the fear of the Lord is the beginning of wisdom (Prov. 9:10) and knowledge (Prov. 1:7); in fact it *is* wisdom (Job 28:28). It seems that fear per se (and not merely overcoming it) is necessary for transformational learning! Ellen Charry has reminded us that theology is supposed to be good for you,[13] and I suggest this is clearly the case when dealing with the concept of fearing God. I want to emphasize again that the theological answer does not ignore the psychological answer, but buttresses and clarifies it. We see this too in Scripture, for it is precisely the (theological) fear of God that overcomes worldly (psychological) fears (e.g., Exod. 20:20; Ps. 27:1; Isa. 8:12-13; Tob. 4:21). Before exploring some of the implications for overcoming the stultification of transformational learning in seminarians, let us carefully examine the biblical emphasis on the "fear of the Lord."

13. Ellen Charry, *By the Renewing of Your Minds: The Pastoral Function of Christian Doctrine* (Oxford: Oxford University Press, 1998).

Fearing God Is Good for You?

We must first clarify the kind of fear under discussion: What is the fear appropriate to this existentially relevant object, the Holy One of Israel? Seminary professors might be tempted to mumble something about it being synonymous with "reverence" or "awe" and move quickly to the next doctrinal or biblical issue. Often we find the pendulum has swung too far in one of two directions. On the one side the need for fearing God is diminished or denied — God is conceptualized as a user-friendly deity who helps us accomplish our lived-world objectives. On the other side are those who so overemphasize the fear of God that we are led to imagine an angry deity who can hardly wait to punish us. While the former approach focuses only on predicating love (of a certain sort) of God, the latter seems to forget that God *is* love. Perhaps a review of the biblical data is the best first step toward finding a more balanced view. What did the ancients know about fearing God that we seem to have missed?

In the Hebrew Bible, the concept of "fear" *(yare')* functions as a comprehensive and summary description of the proper relation to God. "So now, O Israel, what does the Lord your God require of you? Only to fear the Lord your God, to walk in all his ways, to love him, to serve the Lord your God. . . . You shall fear the Lord your God; him alone you shall worship" (Deut. 10:12, 20). The fulfillment of the law is tied to this fear; "The whole of wisdom is fear of the Lord, and in all wisdom there is the fulfillment of the law" (Sir. 19:20; cf. Sir. 21:11; Ps. 2:11; 1 Sam. 12:24; 2 Chron. 19:9). It is significant that one of the names of YHWH, parallel to "the God of Abraham," is "the *Fear* of Isaac" (Gen. 31:42), illustrating the importance of this concept in relation to God.

One way to fill out the material content of "fear of the Lord" is to note its linkage to various ideas in Hebrew poetry. We see, for example, that this fear is the source of life: "The fear of the Lord is a fountain of life, so that one may avoid the snares of death" (Prov. 14:27); "The fear of the Lord is life indeed" (19:23). A second parallel concept is righteousness or (put negatively) overcoming sin and evil: "by the fear of the Lord one avoids evil" (16:6) and "fear the Lord, and turn away from evil" (3:7; cf. 8:13; Ps. 19:9; 2 Esd. 16:67). The ancient Israelite poets also connected the fear of the Lord to other concepts, such as love, light, and true judgment: "The fear of the Lord is the beginning of love for him" (Sir. 25:12), "the fear of the Lord is their path" (50:29), and "those who fear the Lord will form true judgments, and they will kindle righteous deeds like a light" (32:16; cf. 23:19; Wis. 17:12).

Observing the relationship of God to God-fearers is quite enlightening, and tells us more about the kind of "fear" that is proper when the Holy One is its object. "The friendship of the Lord is for those who fear him" (Ps. 25:14). In relation to those with this fear, God "has compassion" like a father (103:13), fulfills their desire and saves them (145:19), and takes pleasure in them (147:11). Finally, the psalmist insists: "*Happy* are those who fear the Lord" (112:1; cf. Isa. 33:6). For the Israelite, the fear of the Lord was a desirable thing, in fact the most desirable thing of all. Nothing compares to it in fulfilling the longing for transformation that all humans experience. This attitude is expressed eloquently in the apocryphal book of Sirach:

> Nothing is better than the fear of the Lord, and nothing sweeter than to heed the commandments of the Lord. (23:27)
>
> Fear of the Lord surpasses everything; to whom can we compare the one who has it? (25:11)
>
> Riches and strength build up confidence, but the fear of the Lord is better than either. There is no want in the fear of the Lord, and with it there is no need to seek for help. The fear of the Lord is like a garden of blessing, and covers a person better than any glory. (40:26-27)
>
> The fear of the Lord is glory and exultation, and gladness and a crown of rejoicing . . . the fear of the Lord delights the heart, and gives gladness and joy and long life . . . the fear of the Lord is the crown of wisdom, making peace and perfect health to flourish. (1:11, 12, 18)

The fear of God continues to play an important role in the New Testament. Jesus urged his listeners not to fear those who can kill the body, but "rather fear him who can destroy both soul and body in hell" (Matt. 10:26; Luke 12:4-5; cf. 4 Macc. 13:14-17). The whole of Jesus' ministry reflects the anticipation expressed by Isaiah: "The spirit of the Lord shall rest on him, the spirit of wisdom and understanding, the spirit of counsel and might, the spirit of knowledge and the fear of the Lord. His delight shall be in the fear of the Lord" (11:2-3a). Paul summarizes the status of unbelievers: "there is no fear of God before their eyes"

(Rom. 3:18). In 2 Corinthians 5:11 he describes his relation to God: "knowing the fear of the Lord, we try to persuade others." Picking up the theme of its link to righteousness, Paul urges the Corinthians to make "holiness perfect in the fear of God" (2 Cor. 7:1). The secret to church growth also appears to be related to fear of the Lord: "Living in the fear of the Lord and in the comfort of the Holy Spirit, it [the church] increased in numbers" (Acts 9:31). First Peter puts it bluntly: "Fear God" (2:17), and readers are encouraged not to fear what the world fears (3:14, 18). The book of Revelation claims that the eschatological reward is for "all who fear your name" (Rev. 11:18; cf. 19:5). Clearly, the "fear of the Lord" is a central dynamic that must be inherently related to transformational learning among those who are called as ministers of the gospel.

Theology and the Object of Fear

In spite of all this, many may still feel uncomfortable with the idea that God is the proper object of fear. Perhaps a heuristic analogy will help. Let us reflect on the dialectic between fascination and fear among human lovers. Human love too is characterized by *mysterium tremendum et fascinans*, although the "other" as object of love is not "the Other," who *is* Love. In human love, the lover is unable to control the beloved (as other). However, a good lover does not desire to control the beloved; the lover rejoices in the freedom of the beloved to respond to love. The beloved is the beloved precisely as an uncontrollable, existentially relevant object (of a special kind); if controlled, the beloved ceases to be the object of *love*. Fear (as I have defined it) is an essential element of love. Part of the ecstasy of human intimacy is the delightful terror *(tremendum)* that derives from not being able to manipulate the beloved. True love does not eradicate the element of fear, but takes it up into itself, transforming it so that it becomes a trembling delight *(fascinans)*. This is indeed a "terrific" mystery.

When God is the object of fear (and so, in this sense, the Beloved), we must move beyond the human analogy. When God is the Beloved (and so, the feared), we are confronted with the constitutive presence of the truly infinite and eternal Creator, whose love is the basis of the existence of the self and its lived world, whose creative activity overcomes

73

the void. When the divine source of truth, goodness, and beauty is the object of fear, recognition of the unmanipulability of this object evokes faith and hope. Human love of God includes the element of fear, but it is transformed infinitely into the terrific delight of worship, not merely a worship that is ritualistically compartmentalized, but a doxological way of living in relation to the Holy that constitutes the whole of one's identity in the lived world (Rom. 12:1).

While this vision of life fascinates us, we are tempted to ignore or bypass the third dimension of our existence — the void. True transformation by the Holy is always mediated, however, through the overcoming and negation of the void. Superficial forms of psychotherapy and pedagogical practice may succeed in patching over the cracks in the lived world through which the void is seeping, but while this way of adapting the self to the world may temporarily camouflage loneliness and depression, it is only at the price of cutting off the self from the only One who ultimately conquers the void.

We cannot overcome the void through the repressive capacities of our ego structures; we can only conceal the widening fissures of nothingness with the wallpaper of our psychic busyness. Carl Jung claimed that after age 35 all psychological healing is inherently religious. Such healing is not simply religious in content but involves an existential confrontation of that which is beyond the first three dimensions. This is probably because by this age most people are beginning to face their inability to conquer the void — the youthful naiveté that hopes to stave off death indefinitely is quickly vanishing. Interestingly, the average age of seminarians is now approximately 35.

Abrogating the need to deal with the void and the Holy may remove (anesthetize) some of the pain of the lived world, but it hinders true transformation. Ironically, some approaches to overcoming educational anesthesia may result in theological anesthesia if they deaden the learner's sensitivity to the third and fourth dimensions. Loder notes that humans long for more than simple adaptation to the first two dimensions; existential transformation of the self "works to redeem the significance of the whole sequence, including the depression, as a passageway to centeredness in the Holy."[14] Only from the side of the Holy can we hope for the gracious act of redemption that provides

14. Loder, *Transforming Moment,* 89.

a share in eternal life unthreatened by the void. We long for unity with the infinite source of new being, yet we turn away from that source and attempt to establish on our own the conditions of our existence. It is this two-dimensional ego-controlled life that we must lose in order to gain true life; dying to the lived world, we are linked to Christ's death and resurrection, through which the void was conquered. We find ourselves radically and robustly embedded in the same lived world, but now everything has changed — now our lives are hid with Christ in God (Col. 3:3), which is the only peaceful place to be.

The theological search for wisdom as transformational learning takes up and includes within itself the psychological task of conquering fear of the world; it does so by orienting the whole self to God through a holistic act of worship that is a being conquered by the love of the Holy. This occurs within community, for as we fear God truly, and share in the trinitarian life of unity and peace, that peaceful unity shapes our life together (John 17:20-23). For the seminary classroom, this implies that professors and students may explore together all four dimensions of human existence as they bear on the conceptual and practical problems involved in redemptively transforming the lived worlds of family, *ekklēsia,* society, and the whole of human culture.

Perfect Fear Casts Out Love

First John 4:18 tells us that "there is no fear in love, but perfect love casts out fear." This appears to raise yet another objection to my panegyric on the fear of God and its salubrious effects on transformational learning. But about what kind of fear is the apostle writing? Not fear of God, but fear of worldly things. Perhaps we could say with equal truth that perfect fear casts out love, that is, the perfect fear of God casts out the love of the lived world, the self-love that hopelessly endeavors with its two-dimensional strength to control the void. Only as seminary students are spiritually transformed by true fear of God will they overcome the fears of the lived world that keep them from transformational learning. This wholehearted singularity of vision is captured in Thomas Merton's query: "Why should I fear anything that cannot rob me of God, and why should I desire anything that cannot give me possession of him?"[15] Kierkegaard argued that purity of heart is to will one thing — and only the Good may be willed purely as one thing. Similarly, I suggest that purity of heart is to *fear* one thing — and only the Holy may be feared purely as one thing. This willing and fearing (which is also a resting and a loving) set one free *from* repressed fear of the world, and set one free *for* works of love in the world. The pure in heart shall see God, and surely that is the goal of theological education. Not only the formal structures of our educational systems, however, but all our ways of searching together for knowledge should be explicitly con-nected to our deeper longing for a spiritual transformation in which we all come to experience the intimacy of knowing and being known by God.

15. Thomas Merton, *New Seeds of Contemplation* (New York: New Directions, 1961), 159.

Relationality and Spiritual Transformation

In 1 Corinthians 6:17 Paul states that "the person who is joined to the Lord becomes one spirit with him." This text draws us into a nexus of doctrinal issues in theological anthropology, Christology, pneumatology, and soteriology, and raises practical concerns about the outworking of Christian life. What are the implications of the apostle's claim about the relational unity that constitutes the Christian's identity with Christ? What does it mean for a finite, temporal human being to become "one spirit" *(hen pneuma)* with the infinite eternal Lord? Paul is clearly referring not merely to some remote future existence, but to the person here on earth who is currently linked to Christ. But how can I really be one with God without losing my own identity? In this chapter I outline a philosophical-anthropological model that may help us articulate the Christian vision of persons in community who are being transformed by the regenerative work of the Spirit of Christ.

The possibility of spiritual union with God strikes a deep chord within us — we desperately long for such an intimate "oneness." Yet at the same time the idea of getting so close to God may also be frightening. Will this new identification with God mean I am dissolved into God? Will I still be "me"? To the Galatians (2:20), Paul says that his relation to the Lord is one in which "it is no longer I who live, but Christ who lives in me."[1] We are bound to wonder: how can it be "I" living and

---

1. Other key passages that address the issue of the Christian's relational union with God include: John 17, where Jesus prays that we may become one in God just as Jesus and the Father are one; Gal. 4:19, which indicates that not only are we "in Christ" but

"Christ" living at the same time? How can I retain my identity, be my "self," while being so related to an infinite "Other" that we are "one spirit"? How can the divine *Spiritus Creator* and the human creaturely spirit become one? If the Spirit of God is the determinative force in my life (the source of my actions and identity), then what space does that leave for my little human spirit?

Interdisciplinary Strategy

This chapter is an exercise in philosophical theology, in thinking through the truth conditions of theological claims in dialogue with the relevant conceptual sciences.[2] It explores the relation between the structural dynamics of the intrinsic human longing for a secure identity (outlined by philosophy and cultural anthropology) and the Christian theological articulation of the experience of finding true identity outside oneself in Christ (outlined by theology). From the anthropological direction, I examine the claim that human cultures exhibit embedded patterns of meaning that reflect a longing for a transformation of identity — a radical transformation that reconstitutes the existential and social situation of the individual. From the theological direction, I argue that these patterns serve as a heuristic lens to clarify the patterns of transformation in the doctrine of regeneration by the Spirit of Jesus Christ, and (conversely) that the operation of this regeneration (or converting) of the individual identity in Christ is the ultimate fulfillment to which the various proximate cultural transformations point.[3]

Let me state the thesis even more strongly: the longing for unity with the divine that one finds in the various myths of world cultures,

---

Christ is being formed "in us"; and 1 Cor. 12, which describes us as being in the one Spirit and the one Spirit in us.

2. For a fuller analysis of the relation between philosophical and systematic theology, see my *Postfoundationalist Task of Theology* (Grand Rapids: Eerdmans, 1999), chap. 4.

3. The use of the terms *proximate* and *ultimate* in the interdisciplinary linking of the human sciences and theology is borrowed from Loder. See, e.g., his *Transforming Moment*, 2d ed. (Colorado Springs: Helmers and Howard, 1989), 172; idem and W. Jim Neidhardt, *The Knight's Move: The Relational Logic of the Spirit in Theology and Science* (Colorado Springs: Helmers and Howard, 1992), 13, 273.

in the structures of human self-consciousness, and in philosophical reflection on metaphysics, is fulfilled in and through the spiritual regeneration of those who become "one spirit" with the Lord. The anthropological analysis points toward a fulfillment in the theological domain, while the theological doctrine discloses the creaturely integrity of anthropological self-understanding. I will suggest a specific way of defending the scriptural language about the relation of Holy Spirit to human spirit as both coherent and experientially adequate. The goal is not to "prove" a Christian doctrine based on neutral foundations, along the lines of early modern natural theology, but simply to present the explanatory power of the Christian claims about Jesus Christ as the transformer of human identity. My strategy is to engage in an interdisciplinary dialogue with philosophy and cultural anthropology, which attempt within their own disciplinary guidelines to describe the nature and structure of the human grasping after union with the divine.

Claude Lévi-Strauss, one of the founders of cultural anthropology, has argued that there are "deep structures" underlying the myths or transformational stories in a variety of cultures. Before we move on to an analysis of his anthropological contributions, I need to make two points of clarification. First, I am well aware of the poststructuralist critiques of Lévi-Strauss and of the dangers of totalizing structuralist claims. My goal here is to appropriate the insights of his cultural analysis while resisting the absolutizing tendencies and positivistic assumptions that deconstructivists have rightly challenged. Second, the term "myth" is used here not as synonym for "untrue" but in the technical sense as the ultimate explanation a culture gives for social and cosmic order.

Lévi-Strauss makes the startling claim that, despite material differences, each myth (considered as an aggregate of all its variants) corresponds to the formula below.[4]

---

4. Lévi-Strauss proposed the formula first in a 1955 article, "The Structural Study of Myth," reprinted in *Structural Anthropology*, trans. C. Jacobson and B. G. Schoepf (San Francisco: Basic Books, 1963), 228. In his more recent *The Story of Lynx*, trans. C. Tihanyi (Chicago: University of Chicago Press, 1995), Lévi-Strauss reasserts the formula and points to a wide range of scholars who have appropriated its explanatory value (e.g., 104, 133). In *Transforming Moment* (186-87n1), Loder suggested that this Lévi-Straussian formula could be applied to the redemptive activity of the incarnate Christ. This chapter is an attempt to follow and expand this line of thought vis-à-vis the Christian experience of spiritual transformation.

$$f_x(a) : f_y(b) :: f_x(b) : f_{a^{-1}}(y)$$

Here he has adopted the language of mathematics and set-theoretic function theory in order to represent the logical relations that inhere within the dynamics of human transformation, as expressed in cultural myths and folklore. The terms in parentheses (a, b, y) are "agents" in the story; the subscripts (x, y, a^{-1}) represent events or forms of existence (domains) in which they are placed. Lévi-Strauss suggests that human beings in the cultures he studied appear to have a built-in openness and longing for a mediator (b), or an agent who is a savior, who can mediate the opposition of two existence-spheres (f_x and f_y). These spheres are different in every story; they may represent male and female, yin and yang, land and water, human and divine life, and so on. By engaging these structural dynamics of transformation identified by anthropological research, I hope to show how the Spirit of Christ illuminates and fulfills the longing for a mediator who can transform the human spirit and create a new "dialectical identity." Following Loder, this is the term I use for the scriptural concept of "I, yet not I, but Christ."

An important aspect of set-theoretic functions necessary for understanding why Lévi-Strauss used this apparatus, and how it can serve as a heuristic device for us as well, is that each *set* of symbols $f_{[\,]}(\,)$ (i.e., a function sign with a subscript and a term) mathematicians think of as "one" or a "unity"; this new unity refers to the object or situation that results when the agent term (a or b) enters into or is acted on by the "event-existence" associated with the subscript (indexed as x and y). The formula could be read like this: "function sub-x of a is to function sub-y of b as function sub-x of b is to function sub-a(inverse) of y." In the opposition of f_x and f_y, typically the former is "negative" in the story, while the latter is "positive."

It is critical to note that the mediator must operate in both spheres. $f_x(b)$ is called the "negative" function of the mediator, because it negates the negative dilemma of the protagonist. Following Loder again, I use the term "double negation" for this action.[5] The transformation ef-

---

5. See, e.g., *Transforming Moment*, 105; *Knight's Move*, 103. The need to include the role of "negation" in human transformation was already emphasized by Loder in his early work, e.g., *Religious Pathology and Christian Faith* (Philadelphia: Westminster, 1966); cf. "Negation and Transformation: A Study in Theology and Human Development," in *Toward Moral and Religious Maturity* (Morristown, N.J.: Silver Burdett, 1980).

fected by the mediator results in a new kind of identity $[f_{a^{-1}}(y)]$, in which the original agent (a) is "inverted" and becomes a function of the positive action (y) of the mediator. A permutation (change of place) is noted; what was a function (y) becomes an agent, what was an agent (a) becomes a function. A theoretical mathematician would say that the agent is "hypostatized in the domain" (a phrase that is at least suggestive for potential dialogue with Christology). Because we are talking about stories, these "domains" denote modes of agential existence. If we believe that God created the proportional structures of the universe and the patterns reflected in the intelligibility of human consciousness (embodied first in the mathematical intuitions of small children), then it should not come as a shock that the dynamics of regeneration produced by the Holy Spirit would fulfill the longing of our created spirits, which are embedded in the proportionality of spatiotemporal existence.

Harvard anthropologists Elli and Pierre Maranda expanded Lévi-Strauss's model by adding arrows to the formula:[6]

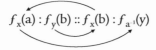

$$f_x(a) : f_y(b) :: f_x(b) : f_{a^{-1}}(y)$$

They wanted to move beyond a linear or purely synchronic analysis, arguing that the mathematical analogy (A is to B as C is to D) goes only so far. They emphasized the diachronic or dynamic dimensions of transformation by adding arrows. This illustrates the "twists" that we find in actual myths. With this new linguistic or syntactic dimension, so to speak, the formulaic design now provides a tool for mapping the "grammar" of transformation, which takes place in real historical time.

The crucial point here is that in a wide variety of cultures, past and present, we find a recognition that for a real transformation involving gain in the identity of an individual to occur, the transforming event must follow the formulaic pattern; the gain on the part of the original agent (a) involves the ongoing influence of the positive domain (y) of the mediator (b) after the negation of his or her negative existence in the original domain (x).

6. Elli and Pierre Maranda, *Structural Models in Folklore and Transformational Essays* (The Hague: Mouton, 1971), 28.

81

Spiritual Union with God?

Cultural stories often evince these structural dynamics when describing the transformation of an individual's identity from, for example, unmarried to married, or low class to high class. However, what would such a transformation of identity look like if f_x represented the broken finitude of the human spirit and f_y represented the infinitude of the life of the Spirit of God? The answer to this question is shaped by one's understanding of biblical language, which sometimes speaks of the Spirit as "indwelling" (or "infusing") the Christian, and other times as a "paraclete," one who is called alongside. I return to this hermeneutical question in a later section.

Let me back up for a moment and paint in broad strokes the background against which we can understand the scope and complexity of this issue: How can two qualitatively different beings, human spirit and divine Spirit, be united into one? This issue of "spiritual unity" is a conceptual problem with which great thinkers have struggled for millennia, and it is an existential problem that hits close to home as we find ourselves in a situation of painful separation from God. I will touch on three perspectives that bear on the issue and try to show their interconnection: psychological, philosophical, and theological.

First, we can view the problem from a psychological perspective. As we saw in chapter two, developmental psychologists study how the identity of an individual is related to the way one resolves the tension between "I" and "other." The way of connecting these two "poles" takes various forms as the ego emerges with increasingly complex ways of composing the relation between self and world. As the self matures, it handles the tension between self and other by trying to maintain an equilibrium between "independence" (or apartness) on the one side and "inclusion" (or assimilation) on the other. We long to be intimate with the other, to get back the sense of unity and wholeness that obtained when as infants our sense of identity and belonging was constituted by the face of the loving mother (or primary caregiver).

But as we grow, we are afraid of being absorbed by the other (or diffused into otherness), which would destroy our sense of self-differentiation, and so the two-year-old says "No-no-no" to everything, sharply distinguishing the self from that which is not-I.[7] At each stage through adolescence and beyond, we try to negotiate relations with others in which we can protect the integrity of our identity while simultaneously longing to be included wholly in the love of the other. We maintain ego defenses and develop role structures in order to keep the "self" in and the "other" out, but these temporary solutions, aimed at avoiding absorption or abandonment, do not fulfill our deepest needs for love and unity. This failure of the self in relation to other has become a central theme in postmodern analysis of the human condition.

We can also see how unity with the divine has been a perennial issue in philosophy. In Plato's *Symposium,* for example, Aristophanes gives a speech in which he tells a story to explain why humans have a longing to love and be loved. The primeval human was round like a ball, he explains, having one head with two faces, having four hands and four feet, and so on. Humans were becoming so powerful that Zeus wanted to destroy them, but they offered worship to the gods and he would miss that. The ingenious solution was to cut these spherical humans in half, which resulted in less powerful subjects, but twice as many worshipers. Then Apollo healed their wounds and composed their forms, as we now see them. Aristophanes explains, "Now, since their natural form had been cut in two, each one longed for its own other half, and so they would throw their arms about each other, weaving themselves together, wanting to grow together."[8] This story reminds us of the Genesis 2:24 reference to a man and woman becoming "one flesh" (the same analogy that Paul uses in 1 Cor. 6:16 for becoming "one spirit" with the Lord).

The larger point I am trying to make is that philosophers have long recognized the problem of spiritual unity and identity; many non-Christian religions recognize the importance of the human longing to be one, to be united to an ultimate other. This is easy to illustrate. The ancient Egyptians believed that the pharaoh was the divine representative of *Re;* thus the people's relation to the divine was mediated through his (or her, in the case of Hatshepsut) presence and will. On a

7. See Loder, *The Logic of the Spirit: Human Development in Theological Perspective* (San Francisco: Jossey-Bass, 1998), esp. chap. 4.

8. Plato, *Complete Works,* ed. John M. Cooper (Indianapolis: Hackett Pub. Co., 1997), 474.

cosmic scale, the Neoplatonic philosophers spoke of the longing of the soul to merge with God, or as Plotinus put it, to ascend to union with the One. Hegel's system was an attempt to explain how our individual identities could participate in the actualization of the Absolute Geist. The Bhagavad-Gita asserts that salvation or union with ultimate reality (Brahman) is achieved through asceticism and loving action. Because God and humans are on different "levels," religious systems have had to try to explain how they can be united.

This brings us to the Christian theological perspective, which answers the question with the doctrine of the incarnation of the Son, whose work is appropriated by humans through the regenerative activity of the Holy Spirit. How has the Christian tradition struggled with the idea and promise of being "at one" with God? How can we talk about divine being related to human being in a single identity? Of course, we think immediately of the Council of Chalcedon (451 C.E.) and its description of the two natures of Christ in his one person. Much scholarly effort has been put into the christological question of the hypostatic union, and I believe we may learn from these efforts in discussing the transformation of human spirit through union with Holy Spirit. Although we must be careful to protect the uniqueness of Jesus Christ and the incarnation, we may recognize in this ultimate divine self-revelation the relational pattern of God's dealings with humans in history. The events leading up to and following Chalcedon illustrate the importance of emphasizing what we should *not* say about the union of divine and human — that is, the need to set boundaries for orthodoxy. On the one hand, we should not push the *Logos-sarx* framework of Alexandria to the extreme as Eutyches did, affirming only one nature. On the other hand, we should not push the *Logos-anthrōpos* framework of Antioch to the extreme as Nestorianism did, affirming a separation of the two natures.[9] That is, we must avoid either a total confusion or a mere conjunction of the divine and human.

Similar boundaries might be proposed for the doctrine of regeneration; i.e., for imagining the dynamics of spiritual transformation. We should not say that "indwelling" means a fusion of Holy and human

9. The distinction between the *Logos-sarx* and *Logos-anthrōpos* Christologies of the patristic period is developed and described by Aloys Grillmeier, *Christ in Christian Tradition* (New York: Sheed and Ward, 1965).

spirit, nor should we say that "paraclete" means that the Holy Spirit is just a really close associate. The Eastern Orthodox concept of *theōsis* has often been understood as committing the former mistake, while much Protestant piety commits the latter. How can we claim that the creature is "one" with the Creator unless we have some robust sense of their unity? Setting aside some of the infelicitous ways of articulating unity with God, we may still agree with proponents of *theōsis* that we are called to be "one" with God. Promising work is being done in the new Finnish interpretation of Martin Luther that identifies "union with Christ" as the Reformer's key ontological motif for the doctrine of salvation.[10] This recognizes that we are dealing not just with static entities, but with agents in historical movement. In Reformed circles we find a similar growing interest in Calvin's significant use of the concept of "union with Christ" and its similarities to medieval mysticism.[11]

Interestingly, the success of the Chalcedonian Council in correlating the two frameworks of Alexandria and Antioch was due, in the view of many scholars, to the intervention of Leo's *Tome*, which was less focussed on "substances" and more interested in the structural dynamics of redemption: pre-existence, kenosis, and exaltation.[12] I suggest that in understanding the relation of Holy Spirit to human spirit, we need a similar thought pattern that incorporates the irreducibly kinetic dimension of such a relational unity. The Marandas' diachronic refiguring of Lévi-Strauss's model of the structural transformation in myth may contribute to the development of such thought patterns.

For those who may be nervous about my use of the word "myth," I believe C. S. Lewis's experience is insightful here. After his conversion, he wrote to a friend that before his conversion he was powerfully affected by pagan myths, that he was moved by the idea of a god who dies

10. Carl E. Braaten and Robert W. Jenson, eds., *Union with Christ: The New Finnish Interpretation of Luther* (Grand Rapids: Eerdmans, 1998). For more resources on similar kinds of dialogue, see Robert Rakestraw, "Becoming Like God: An Evangelical Doctrine of Theosis," *Journal of the Evangelical Theological Society* 40, no. 2 (1997): 257-70; and Paul R. Hinlicky, "Theological Anthropology: Toward Integrating *theosis* and Justification by Faith," *Journal of Ecumenical Studies* 34, no. 1 (1997): 38-73.

11. Cf. Dennis E. Tamburello, *Union with Christ: John Calvin and the Mysticism of St. Bernard* (Louisville: Westminster John Knox, 1994).

12. This is helpfully outlined by Jaroslav Pelikan in *The Emergence of the Catholic Tradition* (Chicago: University of Chicago Press, 1975), 263ff.

and lives again (Balder, Adonis, Bacchus), as long as it was anywhere except in the Gospels. After his conversion, Lewis now sees the story of Christ as the *true myth*, and argues that it works on us in a similar way, but with "the tremendous difference that *it really happened*."[13] This suggests that humans are created, or "high-wired," to use Loder's term,[14] to experience regeneration in a way that fulfills our sense of longing to be one with God, a longing that is reflected in non-Christian myths that illustrate the inherent human desire for a special kind of transforming event.

The Need for a Mediator in the Transformation of Identity

In his various books (which have titles like "the raw and the cooked") Lévi-Strauss offers dozens of examples of the kinds of opposites that are mediated in myths. His early work pointed to parallels between the American Ash-Boy story and the European Cinderella story, both of which mediate low class and high class. He analyzed a myth of the ordering of the world by a duck, who mediated between solidity and nonsolidity. In one of his last works,[15] he applies the formula to several Amerindian myths; for example, an indiscreet sister mediates adornments and wounds, the concept of "protuberance" mediates male and female, and several other examples that tend to shock our contemporary "Western" sensibilities. In all cases the structure of the myth points to an inherent openness and longing in human beings for a mediator that can resolve opposites through a double negation that results in an ongoing dialectical identity.

Now what if the situation that needs a mediator is the ultimate opposition: estrangement of human being from divine being — the distance between the finite and the Infinite, the temporal and the Eternal? In their various attempts to explain how the ultimate opposites of divine and human could be mediated, many myths seem to miss the double negation of the human existence-sphere and the resulting dia-

---

13. Quoted in R. L. Green and W. Hooper, *C. S. Lewis: A Biography* (New York: Harcourt Brace Jovanovich, 1974), 118.

14. *Knight's Move*, 285.

15. Lévi-Strauss, *Story of Lynx*.

lectical identity. I suggest that Christian doctrine fulfills these intuitions and explains these conditions in its teaching of the incarnation
of the Word and of the ongoing work of the Spirit. Christianity asserts
that humans are sinful and cannot achieve at-oneness with the Eternal
through their own efforts; the Eternal must graciously move toward us.
I suggest that this "moving toward" should not be simplistically imagined as a spatial coming from afar, but as the incursive presence of
God, who grants us existence and calls us toward fellowship in the divine trinitarian life. Of course, our source of this knowledge is not anthropological formulae but God's gracious self-revelation in Jesus
Christ by the power of the Spirit. In light of our experience of this revelation, however, we may be able to see things in the human condition
that were there all along.

Turning again to the inherent structural grammar that shapes the
human longing for transformation, let me suggest a way of recognizing
the dynamic pattern of the formula in the regenerative work of the
Holy Spirit.

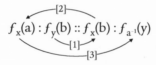

$$f_x(a) : f_y(b) :: f_x(b) : f_{a^{-1}}(y)$$

I have added enumeration to the arrows, signifying the following
labels: [1] represents what I am calling "mediation of opposites," [2]
"double negation," and [3] "dialectical identity." The mediator (b) is the
Spirit *of* Christ, who takes the initiative in regeneration. First (arrow 1)
it is the Spirit of Christ, who as the incarnate One is the union of God
and humanity in one person; therefore this Spirit is able to mediate the
opposites of human and divine. But the transformation also involves a
negation (arrow 2) so that the Holy Spirit, whose very being is the divine life (denoted by f_y), really does enter into the existence sphere of
the human spirit (f_x) and cancels out the negative action of the defensive ego, whose task is avoiding abandonment or absorption. Arrow 3
points to the final outcome [$f_{a^{-1}}(y)$] of these "positive" and "negative"
actions of the Holy Spirit in the regeneration of a new identity for the
human spirit. This new "dialectical" identity involves a permutation in
which there is something like a figure-ground reversal; the original

agent (a) is inverted and now exists as a domain in which the divine life of the Spirit (y) is "hypostatized." This outcome is an ongoing event-existence that constitutes the identity of the Christian, whose life is hid with Christ in God (Col. 3:3).

One more methodological note before I turn to putting the model to work theologically by offering some more material examples. We remember Karl Marx's famous claim that he had "turned Hegel on his head," switching the priority of matter and spirit. Less well known is Hegel's claim that his dialectical system was an attempt to "put Spinoza in motion." Let me try to put my proposal in a broader context by reaching further back in time than these two philosophers, and then bringing us up to date on the metaphysical dialogue. Plato conceived of the relation between divine and human as one in which love (Eros) aided the soul in ascending to contemplation of the Good. Plotinus put emanations in Plato. Spinoza collapsed Plotinus by fusing God and nature *(Deus sive Natura)*. Hegel put Spinoza in motion. Marx turned Hegel on his head. Durkheim buttressed Marx through social determinism of religious myth. Lévi-Strauss structuralized Durkheim. The Marandas put Lévi-Strauss in motion. And now I want to turn the Marandas on their head. But I want to turn them on their head in a specifically christomorphic way. That is, I want to say that it is not the formal grammar of permutation that has conceptual priority for understanding the human longing for transformation. Rather, the material history of the Incarnation of the Logos through, in, and for whom all things were made (and by whom all things will be transformed) discloses the ultimate relational unity of the divine and human to which our proximate longings only point.

Double Negation and Dialectical Identity

Now let us explore more deeply the structural grammar of transformation and see how it may illuminate the theological concept of spiritual unity. Psalm 63:8 says, "my soul clings to you; your right hand upholds me." Philippians 2:12-13 urges readers to work out their own salvation in fear and trembling, for it is God that is working in them. In Mark 13:11 Jesus tells his disciples: "do not be anxious beforehand about what you are to say; but say whatever is given you in that hour, for it is not you who speak, but the Holy Spirit."[16] Who is holding whom? Who is really "working" and "speaking" — the human spirit or the Spirit of God?

Conceptual models of the relation between Holy Spirit and human spirit often focus too exclusively on one or the other of these two "sides" (divine/human) of the dialectical identity. On the one hand, overemphasizing the "indwelling" imagery of Scripture may lead to the view that the Holy Spirit takes over my mind, and I become merely an instrument or vessel. This fails to uphold the integrity of the created human spirit. On the other hand, exclusive stress on the biblical "paraclete" imagery can lead to a view of the Holy Spirit as merely a confidant or copilot. This fails to account for the radical union through which the Spirit truly is the primary composer of Christian identity and action. Although they may fail for quite different reasons, both these extremes tend to affirm the positive action of the mediator but miss the need for double negation, that is, the "negative" action of the mediator. Yes, the Spirit gives new life — but first the Spirit kills. The Spirit negates the ego-controlled sinful nature of the "flesh" that is bound by sin. Only after dying to sin and to self is the Christian freed to new life. We must be united to Christ in death before we are united to him in resurrection (Rom. 6:3-11). To gain our lives, we must first lose our lives (Matt. 16:25). Models that do not account for this negation cannot adequately explain how regeneration resolves the deep human longing to be transformed, to live within the "dialectical identity" that is suggested in Paul's "I, not I, but Christ."[17]

Let me offer two examples of what becoming "one spirit with the

16. Other verses that suggest the tension of a dialectical identity include Col. 1:29 ("I toil and struggle with all the energy that he powerfully inspires within me") and Heb. 4:11 ("strive to enter that rest").

17. We are often eager to bypass "negation" because it sounds so depressing. However, the New Testament makes clear that we must "die" in order to live. It is interesting that most scholarly appropriations of Loder's work have passed by his treatment of negation, focusing instead on his (equally important) description of the five steps of "transformational logic" in human development; see, e.g., Michael Welton, "Seeing the Light: Christian Conversion and Conscientization," in *Adult Education and Theological Interpretations,* ed. Peter Jarvis and Nicholas Walters (Malabar, Fla.: Krieger, 1993), 105-23. Loder's analysis of the four "dimensions" of human existence (including the "void," or threat of nonbeing) has unfortunately not been sufficiently explored, perhaps due to our dislike or fear of negation. However, as I argued in chapter three, it is precisely through the void that the Holy transforms us and gives us new being.

89

Lord" might look like in the terms of the formula. First, let us look at the Johannine portrait of Peter. After three years of trying to hold things together and help Jesus usher in the kingdom, Peter finds himself undone on the night of the betrayal. When he was asked whether he was a disciple of this man, we see the profound implications of his response for his sense of identity; he says: "I am not." Three times he says "I am not." He is in the domain of human not-being: unable to "be" the person he longs to be. In John's Gospel Peter was present when Jesus pronounced his well-known "I AM" statements (e.g., John 8:58; 18:5), linking his presence with the God of Israel (I AM WHO I AM, Exod. 3:14). Entering into the domain of existence in which death and nonbeing reigned, and conquering them through the victory of the cross and resurrection, Jesus Christ manifests the mediated relational unity of God and human being. The second Petrine epistle (1:4) speaks of becoming "sharers of the divine nature," partakers in the divine BE-ing *(theias koinōnoi physeōs)*. Peter is remembered as one whose transformed and inverted life became the domain of the positive action of the One who IS.

Let us take the philosophical-anthropological concept of "exocentricity" as a second example. "Exocentric" refers to the idea that to be a self involves a being centered outside oneself through the mediation of knowing (and being known by) the other, while at the same time being centrally organized by the agency of the ego.[18] Part of the self-identity of the knowing subject is its awareness of what it is not, viz., the other, that which is not-I. The self holds together the meaning of the world, so to speak, through the ego, which is both centripetally figured and centrifugally oriented. My identity as a self is conditioned by my relation to others; the "ego" is the agency by which I try to compose a meaningful life, to make sense of my ultimate destiny. But in knowing and being known by Jesus Christ, where the not-I is the presence of the Spirit of God, my very identity as a self is transformed and inverted; my dialectical identity is newly composed by the Infinite and

18. For a historical review and assessment of the concept of exocentricity, see Wolfhart Pannenberg, *Anthropology in Theological Perspective*, trans. Matthew J. O'Connell (Philadelphia: Westminster, 1985), esp. chap. 2. I discuss the possibility of linking Loder's interdisciplinary model with Pannenberg's approach to systematic theology in *Postfoundationalist Task*, chap. 4.

Eternal not-I, who cancels my need to compose my own ultimate identity through the ego.

$[f_x(a)]$ represents the initial sinful condition of the individual, whose exocentric ego tries to posit conditions for its own existence as a defensive mechanism. $[f_y(b)]$ is the positive function of the Holy Spirit, who recenters the self in God, providing the only ultimate way of grounding the self. $[f_x(b)]$ is the "double negation," whereby the ego is negated as the central organizer of the self; this "negative" function of the Holy Spirit underlines the impossibility of transformation outside the grace of God's initiative. It is the hypostatizing of the mediator (b) into the domain of my ego-controlled existence, negating and inverting it, that makes me, for the first time, truly free to love.

$[f_{a^{-1}}(y)]$ is the ongoing outcome of a "dialectical identity," in which the inverted individual becomes a function of the positive action of the mediator. This new identity is radically *trans*formed. In the normal (i.e., sinful) process of identity formation, the ego strives to hold its world together around itself. But for the kind of relational unity in which we are "one spirit with the Lord," the ego (as a functional structure striving to posit the conditions for the existence of the self) must be inverted so that the self as human spirit can rest transparently in the Infinite Power that established it (to borrow Kierkegaard's phrase); it now accepts its identity and destiny as a gift of grace. This was intuited by Martin Luther when he insisted that believers exist *extra se in Christo* (outside themselves in Christ).

I have tried to illustrate the explanatory power of an anthropological formula that points toward a theological fulfillment. But this interdisciplinary effort shares one important limitation with all theological language. It does not exhaust the divine act or circumscribe it. It is not intended to explain God's action comprehensively, or reduce it to anthropological "depth descriptions." For when the opposites that are mediated are the ultimate opposites of Creator and creature, the model itself is inverted and transformed by the Spirit of Christ. The formula simply helps us formulate an explanation for our Christian experience of spiritual regeneration; it aids us in our search for ultimate intelligibility — a search that reaches consistently through all of creation from mathematical structures to structures of the mind to structures of the cosmos. Anthropological explanations cannot exhaust the religious dimension of human existence, but they can point toward the need for fuller theological explanations. The apologetic force of this argument is not based on incorrigible foundations that compel universal assent. Rather, it is an appeal to the explanatory power of the Christian claim that the Spirit of Christ fulfills the inherent longing of human beings. It is an attempt to witness to the promise of the Holy Spirit to transform lives — to say: this is what you really want! This is the answer to your deepest need for love and belonging — a way has been made for you to participate in God's eternal life of peace and love.

Fellowship in the Trinitarian Life

Systematic theology has a term for the kind of relational spiritual unity we have been discussing, a term that goes far beyond "permutational" and "dialectical." This is the Greek word *perichōrēsis,* which refers to a concept that emerged in the early church as a way of describing the mutual coinherence of the three persons of the Trinity. The Latin translation was *circumincessio,* implying a movement in, through, and with one another. The Greek etymology (*peri,* "around," and *choreō,* from which we get "choreography") suggests a dynamic ontological movement, an intercalation of identities. The point of the doctrine of perichoresis is that in the Trinity, personhood and relation-to-other are not separated as they are in us. The divine persons and the divine relations are mutually constitutive. The event-existence associated with the divine life (y) is one in which there is no tensive anxiety between being a person and being-in-relation.

This is the peaceful life of God, who is love, who is Spirit. We long to know and be known by God, to love and be loved by God. We strive to be united with God, to find peace in our troubled lives. We were created to throw ourselves on God's mercy and trust wholly in gracious divine love. All of creation is from God, through God, and to God (Rom. 11:36). However, this relation cannot be upheld from the side of the creature. As long as we attempt to establish our identity by our own efforts, the relation between us and the source of our identity (of our very life) is broken. We cannot hold our personhood and our relations to others (or to *the* Other) together. The defenses of our autonomous ego keep our self-identity separate from our self-alterity, our relation to other persons. But there is One whose personhood is constituted by self-relationality and infinite love, in whom there is no bifurcation be-tween being and relation, One who holds all things together.

We were created for fellowship with this trinitarian One, to be spir-itually united to God in Christ. We are called to a *koinōnia* with God, a union that is so deeply perichoretic that our anxiety about losing our personhood through relation with the other is dissolved as we rest in the One whose personhood is constituted by self-giving love. In the work of the Spirit of God called "regeneration," our defenses that keep us from real love are negated, and we are freed for a new integration, a new identity received by grace, in which our selfhood is recentered in the divine life of the Spirit. The event-existence of the perichoretic di-vine life transforms and upholds us so that we can live in, by, from, through, and to the Spirit of Christ, becoming "one spirit with the Lord."

The way in which we conceptualize the relationality between Holy Spirit and human spirit shapes and is shaped by our understanding of other theological uses of relationality. Elsewhere I have explored the mutuality of anthropological self-understanding and ideas of God in the Christian view of salvation and the doctrine of God.[19] The chapters of part II explore additional historical examples of this hermeneutical reciprocity, which is evident in methodology as well as in material doc-trines such as the Trinity and Christology. Acknowledging this mutual-ity of relational thought forms that transverse the webs of our theolog-ical discourse may open us up to new ways of knowing, acting, and being in relation to the biblical God. This in turn will facilitate the ref-ormation of theological anthropology as we seek to conserve the intu-itions of the tradition by liberating their illuminative power in dia-logue with scientific anthropology after the philosophical turn to relationality.

19. See part 2 of my "Sharing the Divine Nature: Transformation, *Koinōnia* and the Doctrine of God," in *On Being Christian . . . and Human,* ed. Todd Speidell (Eugene, Ore.: Wipf and Stock, 2002), and chapter 5 of my book (with Steven Sandage) *The Faces of For-giveness: Searching for Wholeness and Salvation* (Grand Rapids: Baker Academic, 2003).

THEOLOGY, ANTHROPOLOGY, AND RELATIONALITY

Anthropology and Theological Method: Regulative Relationality in Schleiermacher

The three chapters that follow operate at the intersection of historical, philosophical, and systematic theology. In each case I focus on the link between patterns of relationality in theological anthropology and similar relational thought forms that appear in other material areas such as Christology and the doctrine of God. In previous chapters I have already hinted at this isomorphism across doctrinal loci, especially between anthropology and Christology. Chapter 7 treats the latter explicitly by tracing a particular christological formula through fourteen centuries to show how it was influenced by changing anthropological presuppositions. Chapter 6 examines the connection between patterns of constitutive relationality in the doctrine of Trinity and the "image of God" by comparing and contrasting the formulations of Karl Barth and Wolfhart Pannenberg. In this chapter, I focus on one theologian who provides a particularly helpful case study because of his interest in and contributions to the need for reforming theological anthropology in the early nineteenth century.

The concept of the pious self-consciousness plays a central role for Schleiermacher's theology, and recognizing the exact nature of its role is crucial for understanding both his anthropology and his general theological method. My thesis in this chapter is that the concept of "reciprocal relationality" is central to his view of this self-consciousness and, further, that this principle serves as a heuristic lens (providing constructive insights) and a hermeneutical horizon (providing epistemic limits) for his whole dogmatics. In other words, the relational structure that is constitutive for Schleiermacher's theological anthropology is regulative for the rest of his theology. While this might initially appear surprising, such a conclusion would be consistent with his earlier lectures on *Dialektik*, where, as Terrence Tice has expressed it, "constitutive and regulative principles are seen by Schleiermacher to be one and the same."[1]

A failure to recognize the principle or rule of reciprocal relationality has led many scholars to argue that Schleiermacher was inconsistent in adhering to his methodological intentions stated in the introduction of the second edition (1830-31) of *Die christliche Glaube* ["The Christian Faith"], which is often called by its nickname — the *Glaubenslehre*.[2] As we will see below, Schleiermacher has been charged with methodological inconsistency in his psychology, in his doctrine of God, and in his Christology. I argue against these claims, and suggest that Schleiermacher's allegedly ambiguous epistemic, ontic, and soteric statements can be defended as wholly congruous with his method by interpreting them in light of "reciprocal relationality," a principle that is embedded in his theological anthropology.

For Schleiermacher reciprocal relationality is constitutive for the pious self-consciousness and regulative for theological anthropology. This is demonstrated in the first two sections. First I outline constitutive relationality through a careful exposition of the early paragraphs of the *Glaubenslehre*. Second, I demonstrate its regulative role in anthropology in the context of a response to some of Pannenberg's objections to Schleiermacher's psychology. In the third section I briefly pursue a final goal, providing the outline of an argument that suggests that reciprocal relationality has a regulative function beyond the domain of theological anthropology, indeed, that it ramifies throughout Schleiermacher's entire dogmatics. The next two chapters explore additional examples of the intercalation of relational thought forms in anthropology, Christology, the doctrine of God, and theological method.

To thematize this deeper rationality that shapes Schleiermacher's

---

1. Terrence Tice, "Editor's Postscript," in F. Schleiermacher, *Brief Outline of Theology as a Field of Study*, trans. T. Tice (Lewiston, N.Y.: Edwin Mellen, 1990), 198.

2. Two volumes, edited with an introduction by M. Redeker (Berlin: de Gruyter, 1960). For background on the early controversies surrounding his dogmatics, see Schleiermacher, *On the* Glaubenslehre: *Two Letters to Dr. Lücke*, trans. J. Duke and F. Fiorenza (Atlanta: Scholars Press, 1981). See also his early philosophical theological reflections in *On Religion: Speeches to Its Cultured Despisers*, trans. and ed. Richard Crouter (Cambridge: Cambridge University Press, 1996), which shaped his later theological proposals.

dogmatic propositions requires a figure-ground reversal of relationality and doctrine. That is, I intend to draw out into the foreground Schleiermacher's use of relationality qua relationality. Now, the importance of relationality in Schleiermacher's theology has been recognized by many authors; they speak of his use of "polar dialectical reciprocity,"[3] "co-inhering polarity,"[4] *"Relationalität,"*[5] "polar duality in knowledge as well as being,"[6] "dipolar dynamics,"[7] and "synoptic, mediated, polar relationship."[8] However, most treatments of Schleiermacher's relationality view it merely as one element of his system, as a *result* of his method, as something that appears *after* dealing with doctrinal issues. I hope to show that relationality is for Schleiermacher not just a conclusion but also the starting point of his dogmatic method, and that it functions as a fundamental regulative principle.

Reciprocal Relationality and the Pious Self-Consciousness

The most important sections for understanding the structure of the pious self-conscious are §§3-5 of the Introduction to the *Glaubenslehre,* where Schleiermacher offers a description of the reciprocal relationality that holds together the unity of self-consciousness. There he argues that the self-consciousness has a "double constitution" (p. 13).[9] It

3. R. Vance, "Sin and Consciousness of Sin in Schleiermacher," *Perspectives in Religious Studies* 13, no. 3 (1986): 241-62.

4. H. Richard Niebuhr, *Schleiermacher on Christ and Religion* (New York: Scribner, 1964).

5. C. Albrecht, "Schleiermachers Theorie der Frömmigkeit: Ihr wissenschaftlicher Ort und ihr systematischer Gehalt in den Reden, in der Glaubenslehre und in der Dialektik," in *Schleiermacher-Archiv,* ed. H. Fischer, et al., vol. 15 (Berlin: de Gruyter, 1994).

6. G. Spiegler, "Theological Tensions in Schleiermacher's *Dialektik,*" in *Schleiermacher as Contemporary,* ed. R. W. Funk (New York: Herder and Herder, 1970).

7. M. Nealeigh, "The Epistemology of Friedrich Schleiermacher from a Dipolar Perspective," in *Schleiermacher in Context,* ed. R. D. Richardson (Lewiston, N.Y.: Edwin Mellen, 1991), 174-202.

8. Karl Barth, *Protestant Thought: From Rousseau to Ritschl,* trans. B. Cozens (New York: Harper, 1959).

9. Page numbers in the text refer to the English translation of *Die christliche Glaube* as *The Christian Faith,* trans. H. R. Mackintosh and J. S. Stewart (1928; reprint Edinburgh: T&T Clark, 1989). Hereafter abbreviated as *CF.*

is a coexistence of the "highest" self-consciousness and the "sensible" self-consciousness in the same moment, "involving a *reciprocal relation* of the two" (p. 21). Life is "conceived as an alternation between an abiding-in-self *(Insichbleiben)* and a passing-beyond-self *(Aussichher-austreten)* on the part of the subject" (p. 8). Schleiermacher viewed self-consciousness as constituted by the relational unity of reciprocal elements or "poles." He expressed this in various ways, placing several other pairs of terms into this kind of relation.

> Thus in every self-consciousness there are two elements, which we might call respectively a self-caused element *(ein Sichselbstsetzen)* and a non-self-caused element *(ein Sichselbstnichtsogesetzthaben)*; or a Being and a Having-by-some-means-come-to-be *(ein Sein und ein Irgend-wiegenwordensein)*. . . . In self-consciousness there are only two elements: the one expresses the existence of the subject for itself, the other its co-existence with an Other. (p. 13)

These relations, and other pairs that are similarly related throughout the System of Doctrine, are represented graphically in table 4. I recognize that any attempt to develop a graphic representation or topology of the psyche can easily lead to oversimplification or reductionism. The table is intended only as a pedagogical tool, designed to illustrate the importance of the relationality in Schleiermacher's view of the self-consciousness. The point is to stress the fact that the two elements are "combined" *(verbindung,* p. 124) or "conjoined" *(Zugleichgesetztsein,* p. 21), but never "fused" *(verschmelzen,* p. 23). This table should not be taken as a "picture" of the self-consciousness, but only as a heuristic model for thinking about its structure. With these caveats, let me now attempt to put the model to work.

Think of the arrows in table 4 as the "figure," and the box itself (the whole self-consciousness) as the "ground"; our attention is on the figure, the relationality itself. The arrows represent the conjoining of the two potencies of higher self-consciousness and sensible self-consciousness, which are related to each other "in the unity of the moment." These elements are inseparable, but they are never "fused" (p. 23). The dotted line to the left of the reciprocity arrows demarcates the area in which antitheses may occur; this indicates that the relationality itself is included in what he later calls spheres of "more or

Table 4. "Reciprocal Relationality"

"Constant" element	↔	"Variable" element
Being	↔	Having-by-some-means-come-to-be
Abiding-in-self	↔	Passing-beyond-self
Self-positing element	↔	Non-self-posited element
Existence of subject for itself	↔	Coexistence of subject with an other
Pure receptivity	↔	Relative receptivity/Activity
Feeling	↔	(Knowing) Doing
Absolute dependence	↔	Relative dependence/Freedom
Highest self-consciousness: no antithesis; feeling of absolute dependence on God	↔	*Sensible* self-consciousness: antithesis of unpleasant and pleasant, e.g., sin and grace

less." In other words, the quantitative antitheses in experience also encompass the manner in which the elements are related (p. 23). The element to the left of the dotted line is untouched by any antithesis. There are several different German expressions that are translated by the English word "reciprocal" (the most common is *Wechselwirkung,* but one also finds *gegenseitigen Einwirkungen, Bezogensein, Verhältnisse zueinander*), but they all refer generally to the same idea of reciprocity, or mutual interaction between elements, without fusion.

For Schleiermacher, self-consciousness is the reciprocal relational unity of the two elements. The terms in the left column represent the "constant" element in self-consciousness, while the terms in the right column refer to the "variable" element. The "essence of the subject itself" is not a third thing, but the relational unity of the two elements (pp. 8, 21, 124). Though the "potency" of one element may be stronger than the other, the relationality between them cannot be eradicated. That relationality is "reciprocal," for "the total self-consciousness made up of both together is one of *Reciprocity* between subject and corresponding Other. ... That term 'reciprocity' is the right one for our self-consciousness in general, inasmuch as it expresses our connexion with everything which either appeals to our receptivity or is subjected to our activity" (p. 14).

One should note that the last pair in the table are terms that describe only the "pious" self-consciousness (which is a modification of the immediate self-consciousness). This pair is therefore described in the System of Doctrine proper, while the others are outlined in the early paragraphs of the Introduction. Prior to regeneration, the sensible self-consciousness dominates the feeling of absolute dependence. After Christ's redemptive assumption of the individual into the fellowship of grace, the feeling of absolute dependence dominates the sensible self-consciousness. The immediate self-consciousness is then modified or determined as "pious" self-consciousness. This modification does not negate the relationality between the two potencies; it simply removes the "constraint" from the already present God-consciousness so that it dominates the relational unity.

The main subheadings of the System of Doctrine in the *Glaubenslehre* are: (I) "The development of that pious self-consciousness which is always both presupposed by and contained in every Christian pious affection," and (II) "Development of the facts of the pious self-consciousness, as they are determined by the antithesis of sin and grace." This division makes clear that the pious self-consciousness is central to Schleiermacher's method. In fact, he explicitly affirms that "we shall exhaust the whole compass of Christian doctrine if we consider the facts of the pious self-consciousness" (p. 123). But this self-consciousness itself is constituted by the relationality between the "presupposed" element (the feeling of absolute dependence) and the "determined" element (antithesis of sin and grace). This means, I believe, that these two major parts of the System of Doctrine may themselves be in a reciprocal relational unity, the first describing the self-identical element, the second explicating the determined element.

Table 4 also illustrates why "feeling" is so important to Schleiermacher. Of course, he is not referring with this term merely to affect, mood, or sensation. Feeling is "the immediate presence of whole undivided being" (p. 7). As immediate self-consciousness, feeling is the "mediating link" in the transition between moments in which knowing and doing predominate (p. 8). This has led some process theologians to say that Schleiermacher has a dipolar view, with feeling in the center as a merging of doing and knowing.[10] But this misinterpretation is based on a failure to see that feeling is able to serve as a "mediating link" not because it is in the middle, but because it is the constant, self-identical element of self-consciousness (on the left side of table 4). While doing is wholly a "passing-beyond-self," and knowing is a form of consciousness but becomes real only by a "passing-beyond-self," feeling alone belongs "altogether to the realm of receptivity, it is entirely an abiding-in-self" (p. 8).

It is important to ask why Schleiermacher took the approach he did in developing a reciprocal relational understanding of self-consciousness as the basis of his theological anthropology. According to Thandeka, Schleiermacher's goal, especially in the 1822 lectures on *Dialektik,* was to "find" the self that Kant "lost." Arguing that Kant's division of pure and practical reason failed to ground transcendental consciousness (because it was still enclosed in "thinking"), Schleiermacher wanted to find the "common seed" of both types of reason.[11] Thandeka explains that Schleiermacher "believed that the self he discovered by means of his *Dialektik* can only be disclosed in an actual act of self-consciousness. This actual act is beyond the purview of thinking."[12] We have seen that Schleiermacher makes this clear also in the Introduction to the *Glaubenslehre,* where he argues that feeling (the self-identical element) is always the "mediating link" between moments in the sphere of "more or less" (the determined element) in which doing and knowing vacillate in predominance. He recognized that the gap left by Kant cannot be repaired or filled by "thought." It must be *felt* in the deeper relational unity that is the "essence of the subject itself" (*CF,* p. 8).

The evolution of Schleiermacher's view of self-consciousness has been helpfully traced by Maureen Junker-Kenny, who suggests that there is a noticeable shift between the first and second editions of the *Glaubenslehre,* with a distinct "transcendental turn" in the latter edition. She argues that the first edition described only a feeling of dependence (not absolute) and showed its relation to his view of God,

10. For example, Nealeigh, "Epistemology."

11. Thandeka, "Schleiermacher's Dialektik: The Discovery of the Self That Kant Lost," *Harvard Theological Review* 85 (1992): 439. Cf. W. Anz, "Schleiermacher und Kierkegaard: Übereinstimmung und Differenz," *Zeitschrift für Theologie und Kirche* 82, no. 4 (1985): 429.

12. Thandeka, "Schleiermacher's Dialektik," 443.

which he developed separately in *Dialektik*. In the second edition, however, the name "God" is posited as the "Whence" (*CF*, p. 16) of the feeling of absolute dependence, which Schleiermacher develops out of his transcendental analysis of the constitutive elements of human subjectivity. Junker-Kenny observes:

> In the original draft both the consciousness of ourselves as "always remaining the same" and the consciousness of ourselves as "variable" were considered "only elements of each determined self-consciousness, because each of them is the human person's immediate consciousness of herself as changed" (§9,1). In the corrected version the human person's consciousness of herself as "remaining the same" is not just counted as one element of determined self-consciousness, but as the condition of the possibility of identifying the changing conditions of consciousness as her own.[13]

In the final edition, then, it is precisely the double constitution of the self (and not only the determined element) that provides the basis for his view of self-consciousness. Although either element may "almost disappear," both are always present. This double constitution finds its form or structure in what I have been calling reciprocal relationality. This principle is regulative for all human knowing because the self cannot escape the limits of its relational constitution, which determines all experience as "reciprocal." Thereby it confines all scientific (i.e., positive) theological statements about apparent antitheses in the sphere of reciprocity to descriptions of "more or less." Only by rejecting any real qualitative polarity of opposites (in the highest self-consciousness) can we be faithful to what is presupposed in self-consciousness: that every part of the world (nature-system) exists in equivalently absolute dependence on God.

---

13. M. Junker-Kenny, "Schleiermacher's Transcendental Turn: Shifts in Argumentation between the First and Second Editions of the *Glaubenslehre*," *New Atheneum/Neues Atheneum* 3 (1992): 25.

The Regulative Function of Reciprocal Relationality in Theological Anthropology

In the first section I have attempted to demonstrate the way in which Schleiermacher's reciprocal relationality functions constitutively for pious self-consciousness. Now I hope to show that it also serves as a heuristic lens (providing constructive insights) and as a hermeneutical horizon (providing epistemic limits) for his theological anthropology. To reiterate, my goal is to effect a figure-ground reversal, drawing out the relationality qua relationality that is tacit in Schleiermacher's method in order to dispel the putative ambiguity of some of his dogmatic propositions. By interpreting these doctrines through the lenses of reciprocal relationality, I hope to respond to his critics' charges that he has inconsistently carried out his method.[14]

On this issue Pannenberg has been particularly critical, and I focus here on his concerns. I use Schleiermacher's view of the identity of the self as a point of entry, as we follow through the logic of his transcendental description of the reciprocal relationality that constitutes the self, to show that he works out the psychological implications of his anthropology in a way consistent with his method. Even if one follows Pannenberg's material critique of Schleiermacher in light of modern psychological and anthropological research, I believe that where Pannenberg sees internal inconsistencies, it is due to the fact that he has not perceived the reciprocal relationality that grounds Schleiermacher's view of the self. I examine three alleged inconsistencies.

The first two are related to the use of the term "immediate self-consciousness." In *Anthropology in Theological Perspective*, Pannenberg argues that Schleiermacher's interpretation of the feeling of absolute dependence is an "entry of finite relations into the book of 'immediate consciousness'; when the latter is also conceived as consciousness of God it can hardly be called 'immediate' any longer in view of the exten-

---

14. See, e.g., the criticisms of Thomas Pröpper, "Schleiermachers Bestimmung des Christentums und der Erlösung: Zur Problematik der transzendental-anthropologischen Hermeneutik des Glaubens," *Theologische Quartalschrift* 168, no. 3 (1988): 193-214; and Jan Rohls, "Frömmigkeit als Gefühl schlechthinniger Abhängigkeit: Zu Schleiermachers Religionstheorie in der Glaubenslehre," in *Internationaler Schleiermacher-Kongress Berlin 1984*, ed. K.-V. Selge, Schleiermacher-Archiv 1/1 (Berlin: de Gruyter, 1985), 221-52.

sive effort of reflection required for this."[15] What Pannenberg has missed here is that Schleiermacher is talking about a specific modification of immediate self-consciousness, namely, *pious* self-consciousness, in which a person recognizes that the feeling of absolute dependence *is* God-consciousness. In this "state of grace," the redeemed person now looks back and sees that he or she has been unaware that the self-identical element of self-consciousness, in which one has the feeling of absolute dependence, was in fact a relation to God all along (*CF,* p. 18). For Schleiermacher, however, that feeling is still "immediately" present in self-consciousness.

Pannenberg is also concerned with Schleiermacher's use of the term "self-consciousness" to describe feeling generally. He argues in *ATP* that "we should not follow Schleiermacher in giving the name 'self-consciousness' to this phenomenon, especially since even according to Schleiermacher it includes more than simply the ego or self as distinct from the world."[16] Pannenberg thinks that Schleiermacher's reliance on this key concept of transcendental idealism (i.e., the term "self-consciousness") has led him into an inconsistent description of feeling, which fails to recognize the priority of the distinction between the "I" and the object in the self. He makes a similar point in his *Systematic Theology.*

> In *Christian Faith,* §5.1, Schleiermacher shows interest in the fact that in feeling we do not stand opposed to others, but he relates this only to the element of dependence, which in his view is contained already in the immediate self-consciousness (§4), whereas in fact, as his own argument shows in §4.2 (interaction with others), the distinction of the self and the object is presupposed already in sensory awareness.[17]

Pannenberg sees this as a contradiction. However, my analysis of Schleiermacher's reciprocal relationality suggests that he can consistently say both that "in *feeling* we do not stand opposed to others" and that the distinction of the self and the object is "presupposed already in *sensory awareness.*" He can do this because "feeling" refers to the self-identical element (i.e., "abiding-in-self") and "sensory aware-

15. Pannenberg, *ATP,* 253.
16. Ibid., 250.
17. Pannenberg, *ST,* 2:192n58.

ness" refers to the determined element (i.e., "passing-beyond-self") in self-consciousness. The former represents the "highest" grade of self-consciousness and the latter represents the "sensible" grade. These two grades cannot be abstracted from their reciprocal relational unity in the self-consciousness. However, Schleiermacher is careful to emphasize that the two elements are never "fused" (*CF*, pp. 21, 23). Pannenberg's charge of inconsistency seems to assume a relationship of fusion.

A third alleged inconsistency has to do with the contrast between dependence and freedom. Pannenberg argues that Schleiermacher

> all too quickly interpreted the element of receptivity and stateness as dependence in contrast to freedom. . . . I say "all too quickly," because the concept of dependence has its proper place in the area of "reciprocity between the subject and the corresponding Other" (§4,2) and therefore in the relation of the person to the world. . . . The definition of freedom as spontaneous activity in contrast to receptivity, which lies behind the thesis that the denial of absolute freedom forms the meaning-content of immediate self-consciousness, must likewise be judged inadequate, because it does not do justice . . . to the concept of freedom as the expression of achieved identity with one's own being.[18]

Here too my disagreement with Pannenberg is based on an analysis of Schleiermacher's reciprocal relationality. He still seems to be assuming that Schleiermacher has a "fusion" model of self-consciousness. For Schleiermacher, however, both dependence and freedom can be found in the "reciprocity between the subject and corresponding Other," because they both occur on the right side of table 4, that is, both are determined by the "more or less" relationality that is a consequence of the relational tension between the sphere of the sensible self-consciousness and the highest self-consciousness. The feeling of absolute dependence is found only in the latter self-identical element of the relational unity.

I believe these examples show the importance of examining the role of constitutive relationality itself in Schleiermacher's theological anthropology. As a conjoining without confusion, it protects the feel-

18. *ATP*, 253.

ing of absolute dependence from any possible corruption. This function is critical, for without it, Schleiermacher says, the whole edifice "falls to the ground" (*CF,* p. 193). I argue in the third section that a correct understanding of reciprocal relationality in self-consciousness illustrates his methodological consistency in "all religious expressions" (to use Schleiermacher's phrase), even in his highly controversial treatment of the divine attributes and the doctrine of redemption, where he has been most vigorously attacked.

The Regulative Function of Reciprocal Relationality in All Religious Expressions

In describing the facts of the pious self-consciousness, Schleiermacher insists one must never contradict the feeling of absolute dependence, which is "presupposed." To avoid this contradiction, he must affirm that all apparent antitheses or "relative oppositions" are only expressions of a "more or less" *(mehr oder weniger)* within the sphere of the sensible self-consciousness. The importance of this "more or less" relationality for Schleiermacher cannot be overemphasized. It serves to "bracket" all antitheses so they do not corrupt the feeling of absolute dependence. In the crucial first section of the First Part of the System of Doctrine (§36), he deals with creation and preservation, which together are "the original expression" of the relation between the world and God expressed in the pious self-consciousness (p. 142). These doctrines describe the immediate feeling that the world exists only in absolute dependence on God. Each of his propositions, he explains, "puts forward a greatest and a least and, showing that the feeling of [absolute] dependence holds good in an equivalent way for both limiting cases, establishes this equivalence as the rule for all religious expression" (p. 193). So, for example, the antithesis of good and evil is based on "the greatest and the least in the harmony of universal reciprocal activity with the independent being of the individual."

The insistence that all propositions conform to this feeling (that all things in every sphere are equivalently absolutely dependent on God) is rooted in the twin doctrines of creation and preservation, but consistently maintained beyond them. In fact, this quantitative (more/less) relationality is found throughout the *Glaubenslehre*. For example, it is applied (using the phrase "more or less") to the relation of the sensible and higher self-consciousness in "redemption" (p. 55), to the receptivity of the Christian and the activity of Christ (p. 371), to Christ's "humiliation and exaltation" (p. 105), to the measured degree of the potencies in sanctification (p. 478), to the negative and positive qualities of race consciousness (p. 559), and to the multiplicity of forms of underlying disposition (p. 726). The "more or less" rule of equivalence implicitly informs his propositions elsewhere as, for example, in describing sin as a "vanishing quantity" in the regenerate (p. 508). My point in listing these examples is to illustrate that this relational thought form permeates his dogmatics. Further, this rule of "more or less" relationality cannot be understood by examining either one or both elements of the pious self-consiousness (or the parts of the System of Doctrine); rather it must be grasped intuitively out of the relationality itself that constitutes their unity.

At the beginning of the First Part of the System of Doctrine, he makes clear that "great discrimination" should be used in discussing attributes of God and the constitution of the world, even as they appear in pious self-consciousness. This is due to the danger that they may allow in some statement in excess of the "immediate content of that [pious] self-consciousness" (p. 140). For this reason,

> we must declare the description of human states of mind to be the fundamental dogmatic form; while propositions of the second and third forms [statements about God or the world as they appear in the self-consciousness] are permissible only in so far as they can be developed out of propositions of the first form; for only on this condition can they be really authenticated as expressions of religious emotions. (pp. 125-26)

Because of the double constitution of self-consciousness, all descriptions of human states of mind must account for both elements (constant and variable) in the self-consciousness, as well as their relational unity. This relationality marks the horizon of theological knowledge.

In this sense the principle of reciprocal relationality functions regulatively for Schleiermacher's theology. I would like to point briefly to two key examples: the doctrine of God and Christology. In reference to the former, it is helpful to begin with the debate between Schleiermacher and Hegel. There is general agreement among scholars that the core issue of their debate centered on the problem of immediate knowledge.[19] This bears on the metaphysical question because, as Schleiermacher argues in his *Dialektik*, all speculative questions can be reduced to the question of the relationship between God and the world. According to Spiegler, although "God" and "world" were nearly equivalent terms in the 1811 edition of the *Dialektik*, Schleiermacher's theological concern led him to reject this identification in the 1814 draft. But this resulted in the "assertion of a relationship between, in principle, unrelatable terms. Schleiermacher had returned to the conception of a duplex division of reality."[20] For Vance, the problem in his view of feeling is due to the fact that "it must be located in a relative realm of continuous dialectical existence, but that it must exposit a non-dialectical conjunction of relative world and absolute God which together constitute its essential determination."[21]

Robert Williams, who describes Schleiermacher's conception of the relation of God and world as "non-reciprocal," has written extensively on Schleiermacher's doctrine of God.[22] Williams provides us with a detailed description of an alleged methodological inconsistency in his treatment of the divine attributes of love and wisdom. He starts with the distinction between Hegel and Schleiermacher. For Williams, the central difference is the way they dealt with "the problem of mediation between formal universal structures and particular Christian fact."[23] Hegel saw Schleiermacher's retreat into feeling as no better than Kant's critical formalism. The reliance on "immediate self-consciousness" empties theological statements of all substance and content, according to Hegel. Williams interprets Hegel's own response

19. Cf. R. Crouter, "Hegel and Schleiermacher at Berlin: A Many-sided Debate," *JAAR* 48 (1980): 19-43; and H. Dembrowski "Schleiermacher und Hegel: Ein Gegensatz," in *Neues Testament und christliche Existenz*, ed. H. Betz (Tübingen: Mohr, 1973), 115-41.

20. Spiegler, "Theological Tensions," 21; cf. 15.

21. Vance, "Sin and Consciousness," 261.

22. Robert Williams, "Schleiermacher, Hegel and the Problem of Concrete Universality," *JAAR* 56 (1988): 488. See his *Schleiermacher the Theologian: The Construction of the Doctrine of God* (Philadelphia: Fortress, 1978); and "Hegel and Schleiermacher on Theological Truth," in *Meaning, Truth and God*, ed. L. S. Rouner (Notre Dame, Ind.: University of Notre Dame Press, 1982), 52-69.

23. Williams, "Concrete Universality," 481.

to the collapse of onto-theology as the development of an "ontology of positivity," which allowed him to formulate concrete universals, involving change in the universal.

However, Williams argues that Schleiermacher too had a "hidden" principle of positivity, though he never made it thematic and did not follow it consistently. Indeed, according to Williams, Schleiermacher followed this principle only in the cases of the divine attributes of love and wisdom. On Williams's hypothesis, "the argument of the *Glaubenslehre* is incomplete on its own terms because Schleiermacher fails to show the modification and transformation of the generic universals into concrete universals. He does this only in the case of divine wisdom and love."[24] Williams notes the tension in his own interpretation. He quotes Schleiermacher's explicit statement that the divine attributes "refer to nothing special in God" (*CF*, p. 194), but believes that this proposition does not reflect his actual method. According to Williams, Schleiermacher "did himself considerable injustice in the above proposition."[25]

More than "doing himself considerable injustice," if Williams is right we would have to say Schleiermacher is blatantly contradicting himself, for he says explicitly that we must not "subject God to the antithesis of *abstract and concrete*, or *universal and particular*" (*CF*, p. 501) and that "we have no formula for the being of God in Himself as distinct from the being of God in the world" (p. 748). Given the powerful coherence evinced throughout Schleiermacher's writings, and his own warning that statements about the divine attributes are "based proximately on the poetical" (p. 141) and more dangerous than the fundamental form of dogmatic propositions (i.e., human states of mind, p. 140), I believe we should at least try to understand his treatment of the divine attributes in light of his broader methodological program rather than vice versa.

My argument is that interpreting the attributes of love and wisdom as facts of the pious self-consciousness that are reciprocally related reveals that there is no inconsistency. Note carefully how the vocabulary of reciprocal relationality (terms like "more/less," "sphere," etc.) pervades Schleiermacher's language in §§164-69 on love and wis-

24. Ibid., 480.
25. Williams, *Schleiermacher the Theologian*, 81.

dom. First, it is important to recognize that these attributes are treated in the overall context of "divine causality"; we are dealing with the "sphere of the divine self-impartation" (p. 728). "Now in all human causality we distinguish between the underlying temper or disposition and the more or less corresponding form in which it is given effect.... [Love and wisdom are] conceived on the lines of this human distinction" (p. 726). Here we see again the self-identical element (underlying disposition) and the determined element (more or less). Love, which is the "impulse to unite," represents the underlying disposition; wisdom represents the "more or less" element in the "sphere of redemption," regarded in its "manifold characteristics and in the whole round of their reciprocal relations" (p. 727).

"Love" is attributed to God because of the feeling in the pious self-consciousness of "the union of the Divine Essence with human nature." But this is nothing new to the *Glaubenslehre*. Schleiermacher already explained this to us in the Introduction, §4: "the self-identical essence of piety, is this: the consciousness of being absolutely dependent, or, which is the same thing, of being in relation with God" (p. 12). The essence of the divine love is that the Supreme Being "imparts himself" (p. 727). But what is this impartation? It is the causality "whereby the God-consciousness is renewed and made perfect" (p. 728). §166 tells us that "the divine love . . . is seen in the work of redemption." But redemption for Scheliermacher, as we will see below, is nothing more than the completion of creation, which involves the increase of God-consciousness. Referring to God as "Love" is another way of saying "Whence" or "Determinant," that is, of referring to the causality of the feeling of absolute dependence.

"Love" and "wisdom" are two terms that can also be charted as reciprocal relations, that is, facts of the pious self-consciousness. As such, they are analogous to the two doctrines that are the original expression of that self-consciousness: creation and preservation:

| Love | ↔ | Wisdom |
| Creation | ↔ | Preservation |

Love alone, however, "is made the equivalent of the divine being or essence of God" (p. 730). This makes perfect sense when we recognize that "love" is in the left column, representing the self-identical element of pious self-consciousness. It alone enters our consciousness directly as "feeling," while wisdom represents the determined element. "If we look at the way in which we become aware of the two attributes respectively, it turns out that we have the sense of divine love directly in the consciousness of redemption, and as this is the basis on which all the rest of our God-consciousness is built up, it of course represents to us the essence of God" (p. 732). With the phrase "divine love" Schleiermacher points to the causality of the feeling of absolute dependence. This is exactly what he told us he was going to do on p. 198: "all the divine attributes to be dealt with in Christian Dogmatics must somehow go back to the divine causality, since they are *only meant to explain the feeling of absolute dependence.*"

Like Pannenberg, Williams seems to interpret the two elements of Schleiermacher's pious self-consciousness as united through a fusion; for example, Williams speaks of a "synthesis" of two elements.[26] But I am arguing that the attributes of love and wisdom are an expression of two reciprocally related elements in the pious self-consciousness. This is completely consistent with Schleiermacher's methodological insistence that divine attributes can be described only as they appear in the pious self-consciousness, and should not be taken as referring to "something special in God." I do not think it is necessary to call in Husserl, Hartshorne, or Hegel (as several scholars have done) to rescue Schleiermacher. Nor should we follow other scholars who try to save Schleiermacher from his alleged inconsistency by calling in the cavalry of structuralism, phenomenology, or transcendental philosophy.[27] The extent to which he influenced or was influenced by these forces is not the issue; the key to understanding him is laid out in his own Introduction, and consistently followed throughout the *Glaubenslehre*: reciprocal relationality in the pious self-consciousness.

Finally, it is helpful to examine Christology as an example of my

---

26. "Concrete Universality," 476.

27. See, respectively, Jean-Pierre Wils, *Sittlichkeit und Subjektivität: Zur Ortsbestimmung der Ethik im Strukturalismus, in der Subjektivitätsphilosophie und bei Schleiermacher* (Freiburg: Herder, 1987); E. Mendieta, "Metaphysics of Subjectivity and the Theology of Subjectivity: Schleiermacher's Anthropological Theology," *Philosophy and Theology* 6, no. 3 (1992): 276-89; S. Sorrentino, "Schleiermachers Philosophie und der Ansatz der transzendentalen Philosophie," in *Schleiermacher in Context*, ed. Richardson, 227-41.

thesis on the regulative principle of relationality in Schleiermacher's theology. This is an appropriate doctrine to explore, because of the centrality of "redemption" in his dogmatics. Several scholars have argued that his Christology is inconsistent with or divorced from his Introduction.[28] But I would like to focus on the work of Junker-Kenny because she explicitly treats the connection between redemption, the divine attributes, and the completion of creation. She recognizes the transcendental turn in the second edition of the *Glaubenslehre,* but thinks that this makes his Christology inconsistent with the method of the new introduction. The second edition "made the whole Introduction more scholarly. But the result, unforeseen by Schleiermacher, was also to change its relationship to the dogmatics. . . . For if the relationship with God is not only demonstrated to be a feeling which in fact exists but rather is grounded transcendentally, then the Introduction acquires a foundational significance that any christology can scarcely counterbalance."[29]

Junker-Kenny later argues (rightly) that redemption is reduced to creation/preservation in Schleiermacher, but I believe that he did foresee the impact of his new Introduction on dogmatics. Christology is not intended to counterbalance the transcendent ground of the feeling of absolute dependence. Rather, it is the central test case for the regulative function of reciprocal relationality: statements about the antithesis of sin and grace in the "more or less" sphere of redemption are reciprocally related, but do not modify the feeling of absolute dependence, or God-consciousness. The latter clearly has conceptual priority, for

> The term itself [redemption] is in this realm merely figurative, and signifies in general a passage from an evil condition, which is represented as a state of captivity or constraint [of the God-consciousness], into a better condition. . . . This certainly makes it

28. E.g., R. Muller, "The Christological Problem as Addressed by Friedrich Schleiermacher: A Dogmatic Query," in *Perspectives on Christology: Essays in Honor of Paul K. Jewett,* ed. M. Shuster and R. Muller (Grand Rapids: Zondervan, 1991); and H. Richard Niebuhr, "Christ, Nature, and Consciousness: Reflections on Schleiermacher in the Light of Barth's Early Criticisms," in *Barth and Schleiermacher: Beyond the Impasse?* ed. James O. Duke and Robert F. Streetman (Philadelphia: Fortress, 1988), 23-42.

29. "Transcendental Turn," 33.

seem as if these two conditions, that which exists before redemption and that which is to be brought about by redemption, could only be distinguished in an indefinite way, as a more and a less (*CF*, p. 54).

The sphere of redemption represents the "determined" element in the pious self-consciousness, participating in the "more or less" antithesis of sin and grace. In fact, the term "Redemption" is ultimately deemed "not suitable for this new communication of a powerful God-consciousness," for the work of Christ should be regarded "as the completion, only now accomplished, of the creation of human nature" (p. 365).

It is clear that Christology does not "counterbalance" the method Schleiermacher set out in the Introduction when we think through the implications of his reduction of redemption to creation/preservation. "And we know no divine activity except that of creation, which includes preservation, or conversely, that of preservation, which includes that of creation. . . . And thus the total effective influence of Christ is only the continuation of the creative divine activity out of which the Person of Christ arose" (pp. 426-27). Schleiermacher even calls the assertion of the completion of creation through Christ "an all-round test in scrutinizing Church formulae" (p. 437). He holds on to this equation and works out its implications consistently in the *Glaubenslehre* (e.g., pp. 501, 728). This suggests he was aware of the impact of his method, with its "rule of equivalence," as subtended by "more or less" reciprocal relationality, on his christological statements; for this very reason he labored to render the doctrine of redemption totally consistent with the "original expression" of the feeling of absolute dependence as determined in the pious self-consciousness, viz., the doctrine of creation/preservation.

Conclusion

Schleiermacher acknowledged that if any case could be found in which a real qualitative antithesis could be identified in any sphere, then the feeling of absolute dependence would be contradicted. An opposition that was more than merely "greatest and least" in a single province would imply that the poles of the antithesis are not equivalently absolutely dependent on God; the doctrine would "fall to the ground" (p. 193). If the nature-system exists in absolute dependence on God, this demands that every aspect of the system be dependent equivalently (for "absoluteness" allows no gradations). On the basis of his methodological insistence that dogmatics must never make this fatal mistake, he consistently avoids it by formulating every Christian doctrine in terms of a "more or less," presupposing the relation of this "determined" element to the "self-identical" element in the self-consciousness. By holding together the unity of self-consciousness with a reciprocal relationality, which is more than a juxtaposition but less than a fusion, he is able to protect the feeling of absolute dependence. One could also show this regulative function in his ecclesiology, eschatology, and other doctrines. But, having examined his view of the human self, the divine attributes, and redemption, we might borrow a phrase from Schleiermacher himself: "beyond these there are no difficult cases to consider" (p. 193).

I have tried to show the constructive and regulative role of Schleiermacher's reciprocal relationality in his theology. I have argued that a failure to grasp this underlying dimension of his thought has led to much misunderstanding. This suggests a critical insight for contemporary theological method. It is important for us to render thematic our own tacit understandings of the structural relationality that constitutes the self and regulates the boundaries of knowledge, for, as my analysis of Schleiermacher has shown, this inevitably shapes epistemological assumptions and pervades doctrinal formulation. In the next two chapters, I explore some additional historical examples of the hermeneutical reciprocity between anthropology and theology, paving the way for a fresh analysis of the role of relationality in the articulation of the themes of Christian anthropology in late modernity.

Anthropology and Trinity: Constitutive Relationality in Barth and Pannenberg

Both Karl Barth and Wolfhart Pannenberg assert that human being is essentially constituted by a specific form of relationality, and both develop models of the *imago Dei* in which the relationality that constitutes humanity is structurally analogous to the constitutive relations of the triune God. Materially and methodologically, however, the differences between them are significant and in some cases extreme. The purpose of this chapter is to compare and contrast the constitutive relationality proposed by each theologian and to explore how the different structural patterns shape their respective doctrines of the *imago Dei*. From the perspective of systematic theology, we will observe the reciprocity that characterizes the internal shaping of their doctrinal formulations of the nature of divinity and humanity. From the perspective of philosophical theology, our interest will be in the methodological reciprocity that characterizes their understanding of the relation between the disciplines of anthropology and theology. In a broad sense, it is a study in the mutual influence of anthropology, theology, and methodology — a reciprocity that I believe could be traced in most major theologians.[1]

In addition to asking how methodology shapes anthropology, we will explore the degree to which material anthropological and trinitar-

1. For example, Colin Gunton has argued that the Christian doctrine of the triune Creator discloses that "of both God and man it must be said that they have their being in their personal relatedness: their free relation-in-otherness" (*The One, the Three, and the Many: God, Creation, and the Culture of Modernity* [Cambridge: Cambridge University Press, 1993], 229). He further suggests that the conceiving and practicing of relationality as characterized by the dynamic of "gift and reception" is a critical task for theology.

ian statements (embedded in the doctrine of *imago Dei*) not only illustrate but also uphold and support each theologian's methodological assumptions about the terminus a quo for theological knowing. In other words, how does anthropology shape methodology? Placing Barth and Pannenberg side by side in this chapter is intended as a heuristic device to draw out and clarify the salient factors of constitutive relationality that function regulatively in their methods.

Barth proposed "I-Thou encounter" as the content of the analogy between humanity and God. What is the basis for our knowledge of this correspondence? For the early Barth, the shaping influence between the doctrine of God and the doctrine of humanity is one-directional, flowing only from the revelation of the triune God, through the incarnation of Jesus Christ, to a disclosure of the reality of human nature in him. This methodological move was severely criticized by Pannenberg: "[Barth's] very *rejection* of anthropology was a form of *dependence* on anthropological suppositions. That is, when Barth, instead of justifying his position, simply decided to begin with God himself, he unwittingly adopted the most extreme form of theological subjectivism."[2] The implication here is that Barth, without realizing it, started with a quasi-Buberian anthropology of I-Thou personalism, and then projected it onto God.[3] In light of this fundamental criticism, Pannenberg takes a very different approach to relating anthropology to theology, often explicitly contrasting his method to that of Barth. Pannenberg suggests that it is "exocentric" relationality that constitutes both human and divine being. For him, it is the individual person's determination as a self, specifically in the tension between the central organization of the self and the self-transcendent presence to what is other than the self, that defines the identity of a human being.

I offer a more detailed exposition of these views below. My initial task in the first section, however, is to provide a brief overview of each

2. *ATP*, 16.

3. Pannenberg addresses the issue of Buber's influence on Barth in his *Problemgeschichte der neueren evangelischen Theologie in Deutschland* (Göttingen: Vandenhoeck & Ruprecht, 1997), especially 197, 251. I say "quasi-Buberian" because Pannenberg recognizes other influences on Barth's anthropology, especially Hegel, in "Die Subjektivität Gottes und die Trinitätslehre: Ein Beitrag zur Beziehung zwischen Karl Barth und der Philosophie Hegels" (1977), reprinted in *Grundfragen systematischer Theologie*, vol. 2 (Göttingen: Vandenhoeck & Ruprecht, 1980), 96-111.

theologian's general methodological approach to dealing with anthropology in relation to theology. Section two then outlines Barth's "I-Thou relationality" in regard to its implications for both terms of the analogy between God and humanity, and identifies the way in which this *tertium comparationis* itself functions regulatively in the formal and material development of the doctrine of *imago Dei*. Section three engages in a similar analysis of Pannenberg's "exocentric relationality." Throughout this process, as I compare and contrast Barth and Pannenberg, I also suggest some possible interpretations of the way in which anthropology has shaped their broader methodologies.

The Methodological Shaping of Anthropology

Barth was not shy about his rejection of speculative anthropology, which follows from his general methodological grounding of dogmatic statements in the revelation of the Word of God. In some ways anthropology served as a lightning rod (especially in his debates with Brunner) for all of Barth's polemic against the *analogia entis*, which he viewed as trying to provide true theological knowledge apart from and without relying on revelation. Barth's use of the concept *analogia fidei* provides the background for understanding the mutual shaping of his methodology and his anthropology as illustrated in the *imago Dei*.[4] For Barth, "when and where the Word of God is really known by men the manner of this knowing corresponds to that of the Word of God itself. . . . We have to think of man in the event of real faith as, so to speak, opened up from above. From above, not from below!" (*CD*, I/1, 242). This applies to theological knowledge of true humanity as well, which is known only by the revelation of the Word of God.

In the first volume of the *Church Dogmatics*, Barth exclaims, "from above, not from below!" But in the last fragment volume, speaking of

---

4. While *analogia fidei* is not itself a "method," it certainly has methodological implications, as B. McCormack notes, *Karl Barth's Critically Realistic Dialectical Theology* (Oxford: Clarendon, 1995), 19. What some of these implications are is the topic of the next section. I would suggest (more strongly than McCormack), however, that the *analogia fidei* has not only implications but also ramifications for method so that Barth may at times treat *analogia fidei* in such a way that it becomes almost hypostatized into a method.

baptism, he states that "the matter explains itself, not only from above downwards, but also from below upwards" (IV/4, 22). In the *Festschrift* for his brother Heinrich, Barth speaks of a "counter-movement from below to above [in theological formulation], which becomes possible and real as motivated wholly by the power of the primordial movement from above to below,"[5] emphasizing the irreversibility of this priority in the movements. It seems that Barth's main concern in using the term "from above" is to protect the sovereignty of God's revelation, and to deny any control over it by the human subject. In *CD*, IV/4 (p. 23), he warns against both a "subjectivism from below" (anthropomonism) *and* a "subjectivism from above" (christomonism). So it appears that (for the later Barth at least) his real focus is on avoiding subjectivism in his method.

It is important to distinguish between the roles of the divine and the human subjects (1) in revelation, and (2) in understanding and explaining revelation. Barth and Pannenberg agree that revelation is "from above." The question is whether our explanatory task begins "from below" or "from above." Barth argues for the latter through his use of the term *analogia fidei*, insisting that knowledge of the Word of God corresponds to itself in the event of faith.

Inherently related to the *analogia fidei* is a second aspect of Barth's methodology that shapes his anthropology, viz., his christocentrism. This is especially clear in *CD*, III/2, where he starts each main section with a description of God's self-revelation in Jesus Christ, emphasizing that theology must eschew all speculative anthropology that tries to describe the essence and nature of humanity apart from the Word of God. For Barth, we cannot speak appropriately about human being generally until we first see that the humanity of "this man" Jesus Christ reveals the real essence of humanity. Earlier in the same volume, he explained that this criterion is not only the basis but also the appropriate limit for theological anthropology:

> Man is made an object of theological knowledge by the fact that his relationship to God is revealed to us in the Word of God. . . . Anthro-

5. Originally published in 1960. Reprinted as "Philosophy and Theology," in *The Way of Theology in Karl Barth: Essays and Comments*, ed. H. Martin Rumscheidt (Allison Park, Pa.: Pickwick, 1986), 84.

pology confines its enquiry to the human creatureliness presupposed in this relationship and made known by it, i.e., by its revelation and biblical attestation. It asks what kind of a being it is which
stands in this relationship with God. Its attention is wholly concen-
trated on the relationship. Thus it does not try to look beyond it or
behind it . . . abstracting from this relationship. (III/2, 19)

In accordance with the overarching theme of the relationship introduced in *CD,* III/1, between "Creation and Covenant," Barth's approach in III/2 is first to treat the human being "as the creature of
God" (§44) and then "as the covenant-partner of God" (§45).[6] In each
of these sections he starts with an exposition of Jesus as the one who
reveals that true humanity is to be "for God" (§44.1) and "for other
men" (§45.1). In the second subsection of each section, he derives from
revelation that we must presuppose that humans generally are "with
God" (§44.2) and "with the other" (§45.2). The third subsection in each
case then treats human being as an object of theological knowledge vis-
à-vis Jesus Christ, focusing first on the sphere of creation (§44.3, "real
man") and then on the sphere of the covenant (§45.3, encounter as
"likeness and hope" in him). Throughout these pages, Barth continuously reminds us that "our criterion in answering this question [of the
basic form of humanity] is the humanity of the man Jesus. . . . That
which is incompatible with this similarity is *ipso facto* non-human. . . . If
we see man in and for himself, and therefore without his fellows, we do
not see him at all" (III/2, 226). In summary, Barth's anthropology is
shaped by his christocentric form of "from above" methodology, which
is rooted in the *analogia fidei.*

In the introduction to this chapter, I quoted Pannenberg's harsh
rejection of this method of theology "from above." In his earlier years,
Pannenberg's "from below" approach stood in strong contrast to
Barth.[7] In his later writings and particularly in the *Systematics,* however,

---

6. §46 treats "man as soul and body," and §47 treats "man in his time." Although
both of these sections are critical for understanding Barth's anthropology, for the sake
of space I limit the discussion to §§44 and 45, where he lays out most clearly the aspects
of the correspondence between anthropology and Trinity in terms of the *imago Dei.*

7. Especially in *Jesus — God and Man,* trans. L. Wilkins and D. Priebe, 2d ed. (Philadelphia: Westminster, 1977), 34-35. The original was published in 1964 as *Grundzüge der
Christologie* (Gütersloh: Mohn); see 26-27. Even then, however, Pannenberg accepted a

he offers a more nuanced way to relate both approaches. What he rejects strongly is starting *only* with "from above." In *Anthropology in Theological Perspective*, Pannenberg begins with the data of human existence, which he believes cannot be explained without the "religious thematic" of openness to the Infinite. Thus anthropology is the basis (in the sense of starting point) for the methodological approach he has called a "theology of religion."[8] This does not mean that anthropology is the material basis of theology; Pannenberg makes clear that the doctrine of God holds this central position. In volume 2 of his *Systematic Theology*, he maintains this method. He presupposes

> first, that religion is not dispensable in the search for a proper understanding of human reality, that it is not a relic of a past age, but that it is constitutive of our being as humans. Second, it is presupposed that there are sufficient reasons for regarding the God of the Bible as the definitive revelation of the reality of God that is otherwise hidden in the unsearchable depths of the world and of human life.[9]

The first presupposition of a religious thematic in human life is dealt with extensively in his *Anthropology*. Here he argues that it is rooted in the tension between human centrality (which we have in common with animals) and human exocentricity, or "openness to world." The second presupposition is then worked out in volume 2 of his *Systematics*. Whereas Barth rejected theology "from below," Pannenberg argues that both "from below" and "from above" are necessary and complement each other. He asserts that "we have here a relation of real mutual conditioning between an idea of God and a human self-understanding."[10]

A second aspect of Pannenberg's method that shapes his anthropology is his emphasis on human anticipation of the consummation of

---

"relative justification" for the approach "from above," which he also emphasized in the "Afterword" to the 5th edition (1976).

8. Pannenberg, *Theology and the Philosophy of Science*, trans. Francis McDonagh (Philadelphia: Westminster, 1976), 368-71. In vol. 1 of his *Systematic Theology*, trans. G. W. Bromiley (Grand Rapids: Eerdmans, 1991), he reaffirms his contention that anthropology has "fundamental theological rank" as a basis for a theology of religion (158).

9. *ST*, 2:225.

10. Ibid., 290.

God's historical revelation. This leads to a view of theology as a systematic reconstruction of doctrine involving "theological testing and verification of the truth claims of Christian revelation."[11] Yet he recognizes that theological statements are always provisional and will not be finally verified until the end of history.

> Theological thought has the character of conjecture or, in other words, hypothetical outline, which aims at reconstructions of the contents of faith in its inner coherence and claims to truth, but always with the consciousness of its basic revisability and correctability in view of the superiority of divine truth over human reason.[12]

Here he is consistently following out the implications of his commitment to the ontological priority of the future, and to an idea of God as the power of the future.

The difference from Barth is clear. However, there is also an interesting similarity. Pannenberg too believes that systematic theology begins its task with the witness of Scripture, and specifically with the "discussions that led to the formation of the doctrine of the Trinity."[13] His chapter on "The Trinitarian God" immediately follows his methodological chapters in volume 1. So although in quite a different way from Barth, Pannenberg's theological method is intrinsically wrapped up in the issue of Trinity.[14] How their very different methodological starting points shape their views of constitutive relationality, which in turn function regulatively in the doctrine of *imago Dei*, is the subject of the next two sections.

---

11. *ST,* 1:257.

12. Pannenberg, "Die Rationalität der Theologie," in *Fides quaerens Intellectum: Beiträge zur Fundamentaltheologie,* ed. M. Kessler, W. Pannenberg, and H. J. Pottmeyer (Tübingen: Francke, 1992), 543; my translation. See also idem, "Eine philosophisch-historische Hermeneutik des Christentums," in *Verantwortung für den Glauben,* ed. P. Neuner and H. Wagner (Freiberg: Herder, 1992), 46; idem, "Theological Appropriation of Scientific Understandings," in *Beginning with the End: God, Science and Wolfhart Pannenberg,* ed. C. R. Albright and J. Haugen (Chicago: Open Court, 1997), 438ff.

13. *ST,* 1:257.

14. This was the case for Pannenberg even in his earlier *Theology and the Kingdom of God* (Philadelphia: Westminster, 1969), where he makes trinitarian language central for his view of time and history: "the trinitarian doctrine is the ultimate expression for the one reality of the coming God whose Kingdom Jesus proclaimed" (71).

Barth's "I-Thou" Relationality

In the long history of the development of the concept of "image of God," the idea that it refers to a specific form of relationality is relatively new. Barth traces this development in *CD*, III/1 (183ff.), and builds his own proposal by supplementing the theses of Wilhelm Vischer and Dietrich Bonhoeffer, viz., that the *imago Dei* involves the idea of human relatedness. He explicitly argues that "I-Thou" relationality is constitutive for divine and human being: "the *tertium comparationis,* the analogy between God and man, is simply the existence of the I and the Thou in confrontation. This is first constitutive for God, and then for man created by God" (185).[15] Gilbert Widmer is among those who applaud Barth for his insight into the relational aspect of the image of God.

> Barth's originality consists in his analysis of the christological relation "prototype-copy" without isolating it from its trinitarian foundation. This approach is different from modernist theology with its subjectivism as well as from the theology of Calvin and his followers with its objectivism; thus [Barth] is able to retrieve the original meaning of New Testament thought, which is relational.[16]

However, even if we accept, for the sake of argument, that relationality is an aspect of the *imago Dei,* we are still left with the question: what kind of relationality? Barth and Pannenberg give very different answers. Barth believes that the revelation of the Word of God in Jesus Christ clearly shows that it is an "I-Thou" relationality. But is this self-evident in revelation? Cynthia Campbell asks about the source of the I-Thou pattern to describe humanity: "[Barth's] methodological commitments suggest that it is an outgrowth of an analysis of Jesus' hu-

---

15. George Hunsinger, *How to Read Karl Barth: The Shape of His Theology* (Oxford: Oxford University Press, 1991), calls Barth's view of "I-Thou" relations the most obvious expression of the "motif of personalism." His concern is to show how this motif is the goal of the "objectivist" motif (41) and is structured by the "particularism" motif (195). Although my project in this chapter overlaps Hunsinger's in the sense that we are both inquiring into the underlying thought forms of Barth's theology, my questions are more specific: Why *this* relationality? Where did it come from? Does it regulate Barth's construction of doctrine in ways that he did not recognize?

16. Gilbert Widmer, "L'homme créé à l'image de Dieu chez Calvin et Barth," in *De dignitate hominis,* ed. Holderegger et al. (Vienna: Freiburg, 1987), 229; my translation.

manity. But it appears . . . with very minimal preparation. It *appears*, further, to be the product of Barth's observation of human encounter and interaction."[17] This is not Campbell's main concern so she leaves the question unanswered. But she correctly identifies a tension in his methodology, a tension we should keep in mind as we examine his exposition of the *imago Dei* in terms of I-Thou relationality.

Barth's clearest description of the relationality that is constitutive for human being is in §45.2, "The Basic Form of Humanity." A great deal of the secondary literature on Barth focuses on §45.3 (and §54.1 in III/4), where he posits the relation of male and female as the ultimate expression of the I-Thou encounter, which, as he states explicitly at the end, is the image of God. However, my focus is on the structural relationality that underlies his analysis of male/female, because this seems to be the crux of the matter. Barth himself at the end of §45.2 says: "We have now reached a provisional conclusion in our investigation. What we shall have to say in our third sub-section [re: male/female] will not add anything material to it. All that we can do is to establish a definite and unequivocal form of being in the encounter of I and Thou, namely being in the encounter of man and woman" (III/2, 274). Many authors have provided helpful critiques of Barth by suggesting other alternatives besides the "ordering" of male/female as the definitive form, or by challenging the very idea of "ordering."[18] My focus here, however, is on the prior question about the "basic form" itself.

In §45.2, after a long analysis and rejection of the possibility of starting with the "I am" as the anthropological criterion (which he illustrates negatively in Nietzsche), Barth states his thesis positively: "the humanity of man consists in the determination of his being as a being with the other" (III/2, 243). He then expands on this basic definition: "We describe humanity as a determination of human being . . . as a be-

---

17. Cynthia Campbell, *Imago Trinitatis: An Appraisal of Karl Barth's Doctrine of the Imago Dei in Light of His Doctrine of the Trinity* (Ann Arbor: UMI, 1981), 157n.

18. Cf., e.g., Campbell, *Imago Trinitatis*; Alexander McElway, "Perichoretic Possibilities in Barth's Doctrine of Male and Female," *Princeton Seminary Bulletin* 7/2 (1986): 231-43; Elizabeth Frykberg, *Karl Barth's Theological Anthropology: An Analogical Critique Regarding Gender Relations*, Studies in Reformed Theology and History 1/3 (Princeton: Princeton Theological Seminary, 1993); Paul Jewett, *Man as Male and Female* (Grand Rapids: Eerdmans, 1975); Daniel Migliore, *Faith Seeking Understanding: An Introduction to Christian Theology* (Grand Rapids: Eerdmans, 1991), 127-28.

ing of man with others . . . as a being of the one man with the other."
This basic form persists "where one is with many, or many with one, or
many with many" (244), but not in the individual alone.

> I am in encounter. . . . At the very root of my being and from the very
> first I am in encounter with the being of the Thou, under his claim
> and with my own being constituting a claim upon him. And the hu-
> manity of human being is this total determination as being in en-
> counter with the being of the Thou, as being with the fellow-man, as
> fellow-humanity. . . . The basic formula to describe it must be as fol-
> lows: 'I am as Thou art' . . . [which] tells us that the encounter be-
> tween I and Thou is not arbitrary or accidental, that it is not inciden-
> tally but essentially proper to the concept of man. (III/2, 247-48)

Before examining some of the ways in which I-Thou relationality
functions regulatively in Barth's theology, I will show briefly how this
relationality is attributed to the divine term in the analogy. To what extent does the relationality constitutive of human being correspond to
relationality in the triune God? Barth answers the question explicitly in
CD, III/1. The fact that humans are created in the divine image means
that there is a self-grounded prototype to which human being corresponds.

> In God's own being and sphere there is a counterpart: a genuine but
> harmonious self-encounter and self-discovery; a free co-existence
> and co-operation; an open confrontation and reciprocity. Man is the
> repetition of this divine form of life; its copy and reflection. He is
> this first in the fact that he is the counterpart of God, the encounter
> and discovery in God Himself being copied and imitated in God's re-
> lation to man. But he is it also in the fact that he is himself the coun-
> terpart of his fellows and has in them a counterpart, the co-existence
> and co-operation in God Himself being repeated in the relation of
> man to man. Thus the *tertium comparationis*, the analogy between
> God and man, is simply the existence of the I and the Thou in con-
> frontation. This is first constitutive for God, and then for man cre-
> ated by God. . . . God wills and creates man when He wills and creates
> the being between which and Himself there exists this *tertium
> comparationis*, this analogy; the analogy of free differentiation and re-
> lation. (III/1, 185)

Barth believed that the "Let us" of the creation saga attests to a differentiation and relationship, an I and Thou, which are antecedently in God. Here we have a witness to the *analogia relationis* between God and "the being of man, male and female." However, this relationality in God is always held in check by the oneness of God through Barth's emphasis on the sovereign Lordship. When speaking about the Trinity, he reserves for the one Lord the term "person," which he defines as "an I existing in and for itself with its own thought and will" (CD I/1, 358). This is how God meets us in revelation, thinks Barth, and so this defines the idea of person. Barth continues to hold this view in IV/1, where he qualifies the names of Father, Son, and Spirit, as speaking of "the one 'personality' of God, the one active and speaking divine Ego" (205).

For Barth, the image of God is the fellowship of I and Thou: "God exists in relationship and fellowship. As the Father of the Son and the Son of the Father He is Himself I and Thou, confronting Himself and yet always one and the same in the Holy Ghost. God created man in His own image, in correspondence with His own being and essence. . . . God is in relationship, and so too is the man created by Him. This is his divine likeness" (III/2, 324). In accordance with his christocentric method, Barth emphasizes that our knowledge of the fact that the *imago Dei* is this constitutive relationality cannot be read off the "phenomenon of the human." It is revealed only in Jesus Christ, who alone is directly the image of God.

> If "God for man" is the eternal covenant revealed and effective in time in the humanity of Jesus, in this decision of the Creator for the creature there arises a relationship which is not alien to the Creator, to God as God, but we might almost say appropriate and natural to Him. God repeats in this relationship *ad extra* a relationship proper to Himself in His inner divine essence. . . . The humanity of Jesus is not merely the repetition and reflection of His divinity, or of God's controlling will; it is the repetition and reflection of God Himself, no more and no less. It is the image of God, the *imago Dei*. (III/2, 218)

Here we can begin to see the regulative function of I-Thou relationality for the *imago Dei*. Several theologians have observed that Barth's view of the image of God posits a reality that is apparently separate from or external to the humanity we experience here and now.

127

Barth seems to put the "image" so deeply into Jesus that it is separated completely from the "real man" that needs salvation. Emil Brunner expressed concern about this as early as 1951: "Either 'real man' means man whom Jesus Christ delivers, man, that is, who is not doing the will of God, or else this 'real man' is not the man we in fact are."[19] More recently, Paul Stroble has concluded that "Barth's mature theology does not sufficiently account for the factical human existence in its accomplishment of self-becoming and in its meeting the Other as Other."[20] More detailed objections to Barth's view are brought out by G. C. Berkouwer. He sees Barth as implying that "our participation in the history of Adam has no independent meaning but is indirectly a witness to the reality of Christ."[21] In a later work, Berkouwer identifies a tension between two motifs in Barth's analyses, the "Christological" motif and the motif of "total dependence" of the human on God.

> This tension becomes understandable when we realize that from the Christological motif alone — Immanuel, God with us, as man's true nature — there is no way to arrive consistently at a critique of other forms of anthropology. Barth does indeed give us such a critique . . . but this is only possible for him because he uses another motif than the Christological as the basis for his critical argument: namely, the motif of the total dependence of the whole man on God. Nevertheless, Barth's own sympathies manifestly lean more to the Christological emphasis, and that taken not only noetically but also ontologically. We *participate* in Jesus' nature; not He in ours, but we in His. The positiveness with which this is said is all the more striking when we consider that the Biblical reference to the Incarnation takes the form of saying that Jesus *became like* us.[22]

There is no way to enter a dialogue with anthropological disciplines using only the christological motif. If Barth is really moving

19. Emil Brunner, "The New Barth: Observations on Karl Barth's *Doctrine of Man*" (trans. John C. Campbell), *Scottish Journal of Theology* 4 (1951): 130.

20. Paul E. Stroble, *The Social Ontology of Karl Barth* (San Franscisco: Christian Universities Press, 1994), 129.

21. G. C. Berkouwer, *The Triumph of Grace in the Theology of Karl Barth,* trans. Harry R. Boer (Grand Rapids: Eerdmans, 1956), 86.

22. Berkouwer, *Man: The Image of God,* trans. Dirk W. Jellema (Grand Rapids: Eerdmans, 1962), 95.

back and forth between these motifs, he would seem to be contradicting his "from above" methodology, and his stated intention to stick to
the subject matter of the Word of God, even in anthropology (III/2, 23).
If Barth has severed (as Brunner puts it) "the bond between the
humanum and man's relation with God,"[23] then it is unclear on what
basis he can attribute "I-Thou encounter" to both God and humanity.
Barth's response might be that we need "only to read the truth about
both [God and man] where it resides, namely . . . in Jesus Christ."[24] But
is it that simple to "read" off of revelation that both are constituted by
"I-Thou" relationality? Is this self-evident to faith? Is it obvious from
Scripture? Unless it is, Barth seems open to the criticism that his un-
recognized anthropological assumptions about "I-Thou" relationality
are regulating his dogmatic statements.[25]

We saw above that, for Barth, Jesus Christ as the *imago Dei* reveals
the free differentiation and relation that constitutes God's triunity in
one "individual," and that is reflected in the free differentiation and relationship between human individuals in I-Thou encounter. The critical dissimilarity within the similarity is, of course, that the free differentiation and relationship between I and Thou in humanity takes place
"between two different individuals, whereas in the case of God they are
included in the one individual . . . the I-Thou relationship is the only
genuine distinction in the one divine being" (III/1, 196). In III/2, however, Barth attacks Fichte's anthropology, which he believes is vitiated
by "the fundamental lack of a counterpart, the absolute subjectivity to
which his man was condemned from the very first. Because this un-
happy man must be absolutely subjective . . . his being cannot be regarded as free" (108). These problems are inevitable because "Fichtean
man is both subject and object, both I and Thou." But if a being that is
I-Thou in itself (and God fits this description for Barth) cannot be free,
how does this affect God's freedom?

This leads us to Jürgen Moltmann's charge that Barth projected the

23. Emil Brunner, *Man in Revolt: A Christian Anthropology*, trans. Olive Wyon (Philadelphia: Westminster, 1939), 95.

24. Karl Barth, *The Humanity of God* (Richmond: John Knox, 1960), 47.

25. For an analysis of Barth's unacknowledged reliance on Martin Buber's "I-Thou"
personalism, see Dieter Becker, *Karl Barth und Martin Buber: Denker in dialogischer
Nachbarschaft? Zur Bedeutung Martin Bubers für die Anthropologie Karl Barths* (Göttingen:
Vandenhoeck & Ruprecht, 1982).

reflection logic of Idealism onto God, resulting in an Absolute Subject. "Barth's idealist heritage finally betrays itself in the use of the reflection structure to secure God's subjectivity, sovereignty, selfhood and personality . . . this idea of the revelation of the God who reveals himself was developed out of that reflection logic."[26] Catherine LaCugna concurs, although she places Barth's heritage further back historically to "the extreme individualism of the Cartesian center of consciousness."[27] The concern that both theologians have in common is that Barth's theological method is undermined by anthropological and philosophical assumptions, which have crept in unchallenged. Barth's belief that he, as a theologian, could operate without a worldview (e.g., III/2, 12) may have allowed for a surreptitious shaping of some of his theological statements by elements of his worldview, elements that are granted immunity from critique by their alleged nonexistence.

Another instance of the regulative function of "I-Thou" relationality in the *imago Dei* is seen in Barth's treatment of soul and body. We might have expected to find the structural constitutive relation of humanity in this dyad. However, neither Barth nor Pannenberg sees this as what makes us human; it is something we hold in common with the animals. Nevertheless, for Barth the ordering of the soul over body has a "similitude" to the ordering of Christ and church, man and woman. Although it was "not by accident that God the Creator and Reconciler [note that he omits God the Redeemer] . . . ordained as His partner and covenant associate the man who exists as ruling soul of his serving body" (III/2, 427), Barth stops short of saying this relationality has to do with the image of God, which corresponds to a relationality in God. Why was Barth unwilling to push this analogy farther to point to a correspondence within God, when he does describe soul and body as corresponding with the relations of Christ and church, and so on, which elsewhere are brought into such an analogy? I believe it is because the soul-body relationality is incapable of being formulated in terms of an "I-Thou" encounter,[28] once again showing the regulative function of

26. J. Moltmann, *The Trinity and the Kingdom,* trans. Margaret Kohl (Minneapolis: Fortress, 1993), 142.

27. C. LaCugna, *God for Us: The Trinity and Christian Life* (San Francisco: Harper-Collins, 1991), 254.

28. Stuart McLean, "Creation and Anthropology," in *Theology Beyond Christendom: Essays on the Centenary of the Birth of Karl Barth,* ed. John Thompson (Allison Park, Pa.:

the latter. Barth correlates various relationalities in §46 in the following way:

Soul	Will	Thought	God "for us"	Man	Christ
↓	↓	↓	↓	↓	↓
Body	Desire	Awareness	God "in us"	Woman	Church

Notice that the other relationalities are grounded in God's act of election, which has to do primarily with the Father and the Son, while soul/body relationality is constituted by the act of the Spirit as the source of the life of the soul and body (III/2, 395). Only the last two pairs, man-woman and Christ-Church, are ever explicitly brought into the scope of the *imago Dei*. Barth seems to reserve this privilege for relations that are capable of serving as analogies of the Father-Son relationship (i.e., "I-Thou"), and to exclude all analogies that involve (primarily) an action of the Holy Spirit, as do the first four pairs. This interpretation is supported by the fact that he excludes the "Redeemer" (which is the "mode" of revelation Barth links to the Holy Spirit) from his discussion of the similitude of soul-body to the covenantal relations (III/2, 427). Many scholars have criticized Barth's doctrine of the Holy Spirit, suggesting that he downplays the importance of the third person of the Trinity.[29] This question is beyond the scope of this chapter. The point to be made here is that in the treatment of soul-body, we seem to have another case in which Barth's "I-Thou" relationality, with its tendency to privilege Father and Son over the Holy Spirit, is covertly shaping the development of doctrine.

Pickwick, 1986), 111-42, misses this point in his treatment of the soul-body relation in Barth. His use of the term "dialectical-dialogical" to describe Barth's method certainly breaks down here. To my knowledge, Barth never describes himself as dialogical, and probably would resist the label. While it may work in application to relations like God-man, Christ-church, etc., it does not work with soul-body, which are not in "dialogical" relation.

29. For example, Philip J. Rosato, S.J., *The Spirit as Lord: The Pneumatology of Karl Barth* (Edinburgh: T&T Clark, 1981). Although Rosato highly values Barth's contributions, he nevertheless concludes that "Barth's 'second article' pneumatology seems to leave the Father and the Spirit somewhat inhibited from action, and man decidedly sheltered from responsibility, by the Son" (188).

Pannenberg's "Exocentric" Relationality

Pannenberg has formulated his own understanding of the relationality that constitutes human and divine nature, and in his case too we look for signs of its influence in shaping his doctrine of *imago Dei*. I follow a similar approach to that I used in analyzing Barth. First, I describe Pannenberg's concept of "exocentricity" as a constitutive relationality for human nature.[30] Second, I attempt to show that this same relational structure is, mutatis mutandis, also constitutive for divine nature. Although he does not use the term "exocentric" (which he borrows from philosophical anthropology) to refer to God, Pannenberg clearly describes the identity of the three persons of the Godhead in similar ways, and affirms a "correspondence between the image of God in human beings and the Trinitarian life of God."[31] As I move through this exposition, I try to identify ways in which this relationality functions regulatively for his view of the *imago Dei*.

For Pannenberg, "exocentricity" is a tensional relation grounded in our biological nature, and its effects point ultimately to the "religious thematic" of human life.

> The opposition between the striving for pleasure and the objectivity of the human relation to the world . . . may now be described as a conflict between basic factors in the structure of human existence, as an expression of a tension between the centralized organization of human beings and their exocentricity. . . . In its exocentric self-transcendence the ego is originally present to what is other than its body, but it is in knowing the otherness of the other, which is identical with its body, as distinct from all else, that it knows itself to be distinct from itself. . . . This exocentric self-transcendence, this being present to what is other than the self, . . . constitutes the ego or per-

---

30. For good summaries of Pannenberg's anthropology, with special reference to the *imago Dei* and the concept of exocentricity, see Reginald Nnamdi, *Offenbarung und Geschichte: Zur hermeneutischen Bestimmung der Theologie Wolfhart Pannenbergs* (Frankfurt am Main: Peter Lang, 1993), 141-75; Elisabeth Dieckmann, *Personalität Gottes — Personalität des Menschen: Ihre Deutung im theologischen Denken Wolfhart Pannenbergs* (Altenberge: Oros, 1995); M. W. Worthing, *Foundations and Functions of Theology as Universal Science: Theological Method and Apologetic Praxis in Wolfhart Pannenberg and Karl Rahner* (Frankfurt am Main: Peter Lang, 1996), 178-88.

31. *ATP*, 531.

son. At the same time, however, the ego, in its identity with "itself," also places itself over against the other.[32]

Human beings are peculiar because (unlike the other animals) their identity may be clarified "in terms of the twofold reference of human self-consciousness that corresponds to the tension between centrality and exocentricity."[33] In a sense, this relationality offers a broader view of the other-relatedness of human being than Barth's position, because it is not limited to "Thous." In his *imago Dei* doctrine, however, Pannenberg places more emphasis on the individual person than does Barth. The image of God is predicated of particular individuals, not of encounters between individuals, although Pannenberg emphasizes that human identity is socially mediated.

For Pannenberg, the constitutive relationality of exocentric centrality points only to the religious theme of human life, that is, its inherent openness to the Infinite.[34] He takes the next move in his *Systematics*, where he argues that the biblical revelation in Jesus of Nazareth best explains this data. It is at this point that he exposits the Christian doctrine of *imago Dei* as the exocentric destiny of human beings for fellowship with God.[35] Also in this context he explicitly critiques Barth, whom he characterizes as describing fellowship with God "as a purpose for us creatures that is external to our essential nature."[36] Already in his *Anthropology*, he had identified this concern, in contrasting Barth to

---

32. Ibid., 84-85.

33. Ibid., 105. In *Theologie und Philosophie* (Göttingen: Vandenhoeck & Ruprecht, 1996), Pannenberg places the concept of *Exzentrizität*, or openness to the world, which was developed by H. Plessner and M. Scheler, into the broader philosophical context of the "Wendung zur Anthropologie," 337-45. The way in which Pannenberg's whole theological method is shaped by his view of the relation to God (implied by exocentricity) is described in my *The Postfoundationalist Task of Theology* (Grand Rapids: Eerdmans, 1999), chap. 3.

34. In his earlier works, Pannenberg was already placing great emphasis on the idea of "openness to the world" for anthropology. For example, *What Is Man?* trans. Duane A. Priebe (Philadelphia: Fortress, 1970), 3ff., originally published as *Was ist der Mensch?* (Göttingen: Vandenhoeck & Ruprecht, 1962). In *The Idea of God and Human Freedom* (Philadelphia: Westminster, 1971), he described this idea as "the outer aspect of the freedom, the inner aspect of which is the theme of the problems of subjectivity" (93).

35. *ST*, 2:220.

36. Ibid., 226.

Herder. For Herder, humans are involved in the question of their destination, so

> it is not possible that this destination, though grounded in the divine creative intention, should remain purely external to them; rather, their being must be understood as constituted by the divine creative intention. Otherwise the intention would remain ineffectual and would therefore not be understood as a true intention of God in his creative activity. . . . in Barth's theology the externality of God's creative intention in relation to "the phenomenon of the human" prevents the divine creative intention from showing itself, to the same extent as in Herder, as determining the entire range of natural human dispositions and existential conditions and thus as an *effective* creative action.[37]

Pannenberg believes that Barth's emphasis on the concealment of this human determination (cf. *CD*, III/2, 321) implies that our creaturely reality is not of itself oriented to God and to being with God. He argues that Barth's use of cohumanity as the parable of the *imago Dei* renders the original act of creation impotent in "setting this work in motion toward the appointed goal."[38] Pannenberg attempts to avoid this problem of externality by systematically linking his description of constitutive (natural) anthropological relationality as exocentricity to the corresponding doctrine of the image of God as exocentric destiny. As self-conscious beings, we are centered outside ourselves; our self-identity is mediated through knowledge of the other as other. The Creator's goal for this natural tensional structure in the creature is

37. *ATP,* 59-60.
38. *ST,* 2:227. Pannenberg's critique of Barth is convincing here, and may be strengthened by the following observations. In *CD*, III/1, Barth argued that the *humanum*, "and therefore the true creaturely image of God," is the principle of differentiation and relationship (186). But at the end of §45.2 (III/2, 276), he says that "there are two determinations of man which do not belong at all to his creatureliness and therefore to his nature." These are humanity's determination by the inconceivable acts of sin and mercy. For Barth, the basic form of humanity, the image of God, the *humanum*, is not lost after the fall (III/2, 324); it is "unbroken by sin" (III/2, 43). These statements certainly imply an "image of God" that is somehow ontologically quarantined from current human existence. That is, "sin and mercy" are something that happens externally to who we really are.

achieved when we find our true identity as centered outside ourselves in Christ, that is, *extra se in Christo* (Luther).

We saw above that Barth has a view of "free differentiation and relation" (as definitive for the *imago Dei*) that he locates interindividually, so to speak, when referring to the human term of the analogy. Pannenberg, on the other hand, attributes free differentiation and relation to a single human individual by taking into account the exocentricity discussed above. I already noted the concerns of Berkouwer and others who thought that Barth leaned too heavily toward a view of "real man" that was untouched by sin. Pannenberg's reading of constitutive relationality as the exocentricity of the individual recognizes sin as a real brokenness of the structure of existence. This has the positive benefit of an understanding of sin as really affecting the *humanum*. For Barth, we know what sin is only when it is revealed to us in Jesus. Pannenberg thinks this renounces any "connection between Christian statements about human sinfulness and empirical data which no human observer can deny. . . . This means that those who refuse to believe in Christ can no longer be expected to have any realization of the brokenness that characterizes the human mode of existence."[39] Pannenberg implies that Barth "saw as irrelevant any and every consideration of the experience that human beings have of their brokenness." At any rate, it is clear that there is a tension in Barth's method that leads to an apparent ontological chasm between normal human experience and redemption (a chasm Barth may have both recognized and welcomed).

Pannenberg also differs radically from Barth in his view of the constitutive trinitarian relations, taking a position Barth would probably consider tritheistic: "If the trinitarian relations among the Father, Son, and Spirit have the form of mutual self-distinction, they must be understood not merely as different modes of being of the one divine subject but as living realizations of separate centers of action."[40] The monarchy of the Father, for example, is established and acquires its material definition through the mediation of the Son and Spirit. This is true not only for our knowledge of revelation (economic trinity), but also for the "inner life" of the triune God. "The relations between the per-

39. *ATP,* 91-92.
40. *ST,* 1:319.

sons are constitutive not merely for their distinctions but also for their deity."[41] As early as 1976, Pannenberg explicitly drew an analogy between the relation of a human person to his or her human essence and the relation of a divine person to the divine essence: "As an individual human finds her relation to her destiny as a human being, to her human essence and subsistence as a self, only through relation to other human beings, so also the Son has his relation to his divine essence, his deity, only through the relation to the Father, and vice versa."[42]

For Pannenberg, human self-consciousness (and "reason" in particular) participates in both the differentiation of the Logos and the unifying relational function of the Spirit:

> in a rational distinction of each finite thing from every other, and of all finite things, including ourselves, from the infinite, the divine Logos is at work, who creates and rules all creaturely existence in its individuality. In spite of all the perversion due to sin . . . human intelligence in its perception of the otherness of the other participates in the self-distinction of the eternal Son from the Father by which he is not merely united to the Father but is also the principle of all creaturely existence in its individuality. . . . As the Son, in his self-distinction from the Father, is united with him by the Spirit in the unity of the divine life, and as, in his creative activity, he unites what is distinct by the power of the Spirit, so the differentiating activity of human reason needs the Spirit who enables it, by mediating the imagination, to name each thing in its particularity, and in all the distinction to be aware of the unity that holds together what is different.[43]

Both aspects of this "participation" are related to Pannenberg's view of the *imago Dei* as our exocentric destiny, for they make possible human self-distinction, which is a prerequisite for true fellowship with God.

I would like to focus here on the fact that Pannenberg, like Barth, maintains a structural similarity between the constitutive relationality of human and divine persons. For Barth, the constitutive I-Thou *divine*

---

41. Ibid., 323.
42. Pannenberg, "Person und Subjekt," reprinted in *Grundfragen systematischer Theologie*, 2:92-93; my translation.
43. *ST*, 2:196-97.

relationality adheres in a single individual, while the constitutive I-Thou *anthropological* relationality obtains between or among different individuals. In Pannenberg's case, "exocentric" relationality obtains between and among the different persons of the Trinity, while it may be attributed directly to a single human person (whose identity is mediated through the relations with other individuals). This inversion from intra-personal to inter-personal (or vice versa) when transposing the predication of constitutive relationality from divine to human persons (or vice versa) may be evidence of the regulative function of relationality in both theologians. In Pannenberg's doctrine of the *imago Dei*, exocentric dynamics describe both human and divine persons, although not in exactly the same way.

As Ted Peters points out in his summary of Pannenberg, there is a significant difference between human personhood and divine personhood. The former involves a split between the ego and the self.[44] Each of the three persons of the Trinity undergoes no such split, so they do not have the pain that derives from it. It seems plausible to argue that Pannenberg is restricted from attributing "personhood" to the Godhead as a whole (as one individual) because, given his view of constitutive relationality as exocentricity, such an attribution would inevitably deny the true Infinity of God or entail a form of modalism involving an Absolute Subject. The latter is exactly what he critiqued in Barth.

> The *Church Dogmatics* does not develop the doctrine of the trinitarian God from the data of the historical revelation of God as Father, Son, and Spirit, but from the formal concept of revelation as self-revelation, which, as Barth sees it, entails a subject of revelation, an object, and revelation itself, all of which are one and the same. This

---

44. Ted Peters, *God as Trinity: Relationality and Temporality in Divine Life* (Louisville: Westminster/John Knox, 1993), 139. Unfortunately, Peters misreads Pannenberg on the specific issue of the emergence of the ego. Peters summarizes Pannenberg's position thus: "The ego is not mediated through social relations, whereas the self includes the summary of the picture others have of each of us" (139). But this is G. H. Mead's position, which Pannenberg explicitly criticizes and rejects: "contrary to Mead's claim, not only the self but also the ego is always mediated to itself through social relations" (*ATP*, 189). Nevertheless, this does not affect Peters's correct statement that divine personhood does not involve a split between self and ego.

model of a Trinity of revelation is easily seen to be structurally identical with that of the self-conscious Absolute, especially when God's revelation has to be viewed primarily as a self-revelation. The subject of the revelation is only one. Barth could thus think of the doctrine of the Trinity as an exposition of the subjectivity of God in his revelation. This being so, there is no room for a plurality of persons in the one God but only for different modes of being in the one divine subjectivity.[45]

In Pannenberg's own exposition of the *imago Dei*, he emphasizes that we are called to accept our finitude with God: "we must be fashioned into the image of the Son, of his self-distinction from the Father. We participate thus in the fellowship of the Son with the Father."[46] Pannenberg believes both that we are the image of God (exocentric structure of existence) and that we must anticipate a final consummation in which we will become the image of God (exocentric destiny).

> Here an eschatological turn is given to the fellowship with God that Jewish wisdom viewed as the deeper meaning of the divine image and likeness of Adam before the fall. It is reinterpreted as our final destiny, which is manifested already in Jesus Christ and in which believers share already through the power of the Spirit, who is already effecting the eschatological reality of the new man in them.[47]

This view of the *imago Dei* raises interesting questions about the possible regulative function of exocentric relationality in Pannenberg's theology. For Pannenberg, relationality is constitutive for both human and divine persons. However, the *imago Dei* is not a static likeness between two substances but a dynamic longing that constitutes creaturely personhood, a longing for participation in the peaceful life of the eternal trinitarian God. The exocentricity of this relationality regulates his theological statements in the sense that his systematic recon-

---

45. *ST*, 1:296. In "Die Subjektivität Gottes und die Trinitätslehre," Pannenberg offered a more extensive critique along these lines, with special attention to the influence of I. A. Dorner on Barth.

46. *ST*, 2:230.

47. Ibid., 220.

structions in both anthropological or trinitarian doctrine are guided by the structural dynamics of this relationality.[48]

Conclusion

For both Barth and Pannenberg the doctrine of *imago Dei* plays a central role in expositing the correspondence between the constitutive relationality of human and divine being. I have illustrated how some of the material and formal differences between these theologians are rooted in prior anthropological and methodological decisions. I also tried to show how the relational conceptualization of the structure of human and divine personhood (whether "I-Thou" or "exocentric") functions regulatively in the construction of doctrinal formulations for both Barth and Pannenberg. By comparing and contrasting the material ramifications of each approach, I have attempted to draw out and thematize the reciprocal influence of theological method and constitutive relationality. The final chapter of part II explores a similar reciprocity between relationality in anthropology and in Christology, with special attention on the relation between the divine and human in Jesus Christ. I trace this hermeneutical influence by examining the historical development and significance of a specific formulation in the tradition. As we will see in part III, evidence of this reciprocity appears throughout church history, which suggests that we too should be aware of these dynamics as we reform theological anthropology in our own contexts.

48. The regulative function of exocentric relationality and destiny can be seen as operative in Pannenberg's thought beyond the doctrine of the *imago Dei* as well. For example, in his proposal for a new metaphysics of the Absolute, he calls for a starting point "that encompasses worldly experience, self-consciousness, and their reciprocal mediation . . . it is crucial that a newly rethought metaphysics must conceive the Absolute as the source and goal of finite subjectivity" (*Metaphysics and the Idea of God*, trans. Philip Clayton [Grand Rapids: Eerdmans, 1990], 62).

Anthropology and Christology:
The *Anhypostasis-Enhypostasis* Formula

This chapter illustrates the reciprocity between anthropological and theological relationality through an analysis of the dual formula of *anhypostasis-enhypostasis,* which has become an increasingly popular way of describing the relation of the human and divine natures of Jesus Christ. The formula aims to express the doctrine that the human nature of Jesus has no subsistence *(anhypostasis)* apart from the union with the Logos, but that it has its being only "in" the subsistence *(enhypostasis)* of the incarnate Son of God. The use of this formula is especially prevalent among theologians influenced by Karl Barth, who in adopting the terms appealed to "the older dogmatics — using the language of later Greek philosophy."[1] Unfortunately, Barth's appropriation of the terms and his dialectical reconstruction of the formula are problematic in several ways, especially since in fact this is in no way the "language of later Greek philosophy," but an invention of Protestant Scholasticism.

This chapter argues further that this innovative usage by the Scholastics was in serious conflict with the use of the terms in patristic Christology, and that the uncritical acceptance of the words by modern theologians has obfuscated their original meaning. My goal is to trace the genesis and development of these terms from Leontius of Byzantium to Karl Barth in order to show the fateful moves that led to a radical misreading of Leontius. What is at stake christologically is nothing less than the clarity of the Christian confession that Jesus Christ is fully divine and fully human in one person.

1. *CD,* IV/2, 49.

This modern interpretation of the Christology of Leontius of Byzantium is centered around that sixth-century monk's alleged redefinition of the term *enypostaton* (the adjectival form of *hypostasis*) to signify a nature that has its existence not in its own hypostasis but *in* the hypostasis of another nature. Dominating scholarly opinion for well over a century, this interpretation assumes that Leontius introduced a philosophical theory, with the aid of a new meaning for *enypostaton,* to help explain how two natures can be in a single hypostasis. This reading has recently been convincingly challenged through the work of two Catholic writers, Aloys Grillmeier, S.J., and Brian E. Daley, S.J.,[2] who trace the theory to the influential treatment of Leontius by Friedrich Loofs in 1887.[3]

The roots of this misunderstanding of Leontius, however, appear to go all the way back to certain seventeenth-century Protestant Scholastics. By examining Leontius's original texts, which have not been translated fully into English, I hope to reveal additional fallacies in the "enhypostasis theory." The negative impact of this misinterpretation of Leontius has perhaps been stronger in some Protestant theology, where it continues to exert a powerful influence. For example, Bruce McCormack has argued that when Barth adopted the *anhypostasis-enhypostasis* formula in 1924, it "provided the material conditions needed to set free the elaboration of the *analogia fidei,*"[4] from which his whole methodol-

2. Aloys Grillmeier, S.J., "Die anthropologisch-christologische Sprache des Leontius von Byzanz und ihre Beziehung zu den Symmikta *Zētēmata* des Neuplatonikers Porphyrius," in *Hermeneumata: Festschrift für Hadwig Horner,* ed. H. Eisenberger (Heidelberg: Carl Winter Universitätsverlag, 1990), 61-72; idem, "The Understanding of the Christological Definitions of Both (Oriental Orthodox and Roman Catholic) Traditions in the Light of the Post-Chalcedonian Theology (Analysis of Terminologies in a Conceptual Framework)," in *Christ in East and West,* ed. P. Fries (Macon, Ga.: Mercer University Press, 1987), 65-82; Brian E. Daley, S.J., "A Richer Union: Leontius of Byzantium and the Relationship of Human and Divine in Christ," in *Studia patristica* 24, ed. E. Livingstone (1993), 239-65. Note that while I consistently use the spelling *enypostaton* in the following exposition, both Daley and Grillmeier follow the traditional transliteration of *enhypostaton* (with an *h*). In the adjectival form, the *n* (Greek *nu*) is added as a glide to ease pronunciation, separating the *epsilon* and the *ypsilon.* The *h* sound disappears with the addition of the *en* prefix, so *enypostaton* is more accurate.

3. Friedrich Loofs, "Leontius von Byzanz und die gleichnamigen Schriftsteller der griechischen Kirke," in *Texte und Untersuchungen* 3, ed. O. Von Gebhardt and A. Harnack (Leipzig, 1887), 1-317.

4. Bruce L. McCormack, *Karl Barth's Critically Realistic Dialectical Theology: Its Genesis and Development, 1909-1936* (Oxford: Clarendon, 1995), 19.

ogy flowed. This suggests that the misreading of Leontius, exemplified and hardened by Loofs, has deeply permeated some strands of Protestant theology and may be difficult to disentangle.

The first step is to examine Leontius's use of the terms *enypostaton* and *anypostaton* in book 3 of *Contra Nestorianos et Eutychianos*, written around 540 c.e.[5] By identifying the precise function of these words in the context of the christological exigency to which he was responding, I will show that he was not using them in a radically new way. Next I summarize and expand on the analyses of Grillmeier and Daley, who introduced the critique of the modern consensus, in order to show that the putative belief that Leontius intended for *enypostaton* to refer to a nature that has its hypostasis *in* the hypostasis of another nature is false. My thesis is that a commonsense translation of *enypostaton* as simply "subsistent" has the advantages of reflecting the normal usage of the term during the first eight centuries of Christian theology and of making more sense of Leontius's Christology, which indisputably played an important role in the post-Chalcedonian development of christological doctrine. In the second major section, I trace the emergence of the terms *anhypostasia* and *enhypostasia*, which do not appear at all in Leontius or the other early fathers, to the late sixteenth- and seventeenth-century Protestant Scholastics. Finally, I assess Barth's dialectical appropriation of the dual christological formula and explore briefly what implications this analysis may have for the contemporary task of theology.

Before I begin, let me emphasize the importance of distinguishing between the following two propositions: (1) The human nature of Jesus does not subsist except in its union with the Logos in the one person of Christ, and (2) the early modern way of using the terms *enhypostasis* and *anhypostasis* provides an adequate model for describing this claim about the human nature of Jesus. Most of the players in this theological drama (certainly Leontius, most of the Protestant Scholastics, and Barth) do in fact affirm the first proposition. Although the formula under discussion has been wed to this doctrine for the last four hun-

5. The title *Contra Nestorianos et Eutychianos* is a misnomer; the three books that make up the document we call by that name were actually written years apart and deal with different issues. Only book 1 actually treats Nestorianism and Eutychianism directly. My concern is only with book 3, and generic references to the title are meant in this essay to refer to book 3.

dred years in much of Protestant theology, it is not necessary to assert the second in order to affirm the first. Therefore, if my analysis of Leontius and other patristic writers gives us reason to doubt the second proposition, this does not have to shake our faith in the first. Rather, we simply need to look for better ways of stating this Christian intuition. At the very least, those who decide to continue using the formula should be aware of the pertinent grammatical problems involved and of the philosophical issues that shaped its early modern formulation. The epistemic and methodological factors that led to the affirmation of the second proposition need to be appreciated so that any new reconstructive formulations will not repeat the errors of the past. The first step is to understand the context of the allegedly new definitions of the terms in question.

Leontius of Byzantium

That several persons with the name Leontius were producing theological treatises in the sixth century has often led to confusion.[6] For our purposes, it is important only to note that most scholars link our Leontius, that is, the author of *Contra Nestorianos et Eutychianos,* with the Leontius of Byzantium about whom Cyril of Scythopolis wrote in his *Vita Sabae.* This is relevant because this Leontius was a Palestinian monk who led an "Origenist" party that caused considerable political trouble, apparently even taking up garden implements as weapons at one point. Virtually all scholars now agree that we are dealing here with one and the same Leontius. This is enigmatic, for in what sense may our Leontius, whose Christology seems to support Chalcedonian orthodoxy, be labeled an Origenist?

In 1970 David Evans went against the received wisdom of affirming Leontius's orthodoxy. For Evans the "Origenism" of our Leontius is indeed doctrinal. In order to make his case, however, Evans has to admit that Leontius never actually says anything christologically Origenistic,

---

6. For example, Migne in *PG* 86 mistakenly attributes *Adversus Nestorianos* to Leontius of Byzantium; we now know it was written by Leontius of Jerusalem, his contemporary. For a summary of the issues on Leontian scholarship, see Brian Daley, S.J., "The Origenism of Leontius of Byzantium," *JTS* 27 (1976): 333-69.

but that it is "hidden" behind the arguments. In fact, Evans posits that Leontius consciously went to extensive effort to hide it so he would not be persecuted. He concludes "that the Jesus Christ of Leontius is the *nous* Jesus Christ [a created preexistent being] of the Origenist Evagrius of Pontus."[7] Because of Evans's exhaustive analysis and creativity, this reading held sway for a few years. But after the appearance of two articles in the mid-1970s, Evans's thesis lost its popularity. The first article is by John J. Lynch, who argues that Leontius was in fact a Cyrillian when it came to Christology,[8] an analysis that has explicit textual evidence. The second critique is provided by Brian Daley, who shows that the Origenism of monks in the sixth century was more of an attitude (of openness to metaphysical speculation) toward theology than a doctrinal system. Indeed, Daley points out several areas where Leontius's Christology is clearly anti-Origenistic.[9] Leontius did engage the tradition in a critical way. For example, although he follows Cyril most of the time in his attack on Nestorius, there are some important differences of emphasis, as noted by John of Damascus two centuries later.[10] Nevertheless, Leontius clearly desired to follow the teaching of the holy fathers, as we can see from his florilegium. Let us assume, then, that Leontius was not a closet heretic, but meant to remain in the orthodox tradition. Was his use of *enypostaton* radically new or was it a restatement of Chalcedon?

Leontius's goal in book 3 of *Contra Nestorianos et Eutychianos* was to fight the Monophysites, who were gaining strength in the sixth century (and would be anathematized at the Second Council of Constantinople, 553), without falling into the opposite extreme of the Nestorians (who had been condemned at Chalcedon, 451). He explicitly states his purpose in the prologue: "[Since] the definition of [the terms] hypostasis and ousia . . . remains confused and vague among those now counted wise, I have undertaken to elucidate and clarify [them]."[11] This

7. David Evans, *Leontius of Byzantium: An Origenist Christology* (Washington, D.C.: Dumbarton Oaks, 1970), 143.

8. John J. Lynch, "Leontius of Byzantium: A Cyrillian Christology," *TS* 36 (1975): 455-71.

9. Daley, "Origenism of Leontius," 355-60.

10. John of Damascus, *De Fide Orthodoxa* 3.3-9 (*PG* 94:987B-1017B). Translated as "Exposition of the Christian Faith," NPNF² 9:47ff.

11. *PG* 86:1273A 1-5. Translation by Evans, *Leontius of Byzantium*, 15.

is the christological exigency that Leontius addresses. A brief summary suffices to give a sense of the argument. The book is comprised of a brief prologue, seven chapters, and an epilogue that introduces a long florilegium. Each of the seven chapters begins with a *dubitatio* or objection set forth by Leontius's adversaries, to which he then responds.[12]

Summary of *Contra Nestorianos et Eutychianos*

Chapter 1 (*PG* 86:1276D 5–1280B 10) stands by itself as the first step in the argument. It is primarily here that he uses the term *enypostaton*. He first asserts that both the Nestorians and the Monophysites (represented metonymically by Eutyches) share in a common fallacy. Both offer the following *dubitatio:* "If you posit two natures of the one Christ, but if there is no nature without hypostasis, then there will be [in him] two hypostases, too." Our task is to understand how Leontius responded to this objection, and how his view of substantial and hypostatic relationality registered its effect on his anthropology and Christology.

However, the famous section using the term *enypostaton* in chapter 1 cannot be understood fully apart from the general flow of his broader argument. The next five chapters are conceptually unified by Leontius's argument that the paradigmatic analogy for understanding the two natures of Christ is the union of soul and body, which he introduces in the last sentence of chapter 1 (1280B 7-10). His own view of this union of body and soul is rooted in an anthropology that first divides the soul into *ousia logikē* and *poiotēs asōmatos,* and then divides the latter "immaterial quality" into three faculties: appetitive, spirited, and cognitive. These five chapters are Leontius's responses to further *dubitationes;* chapters 2-4 are against the Nestorians (who reject this analogy), 5-6 are against the Monophysites (who misrepresent it to buttress their heretical teachings).

Chapter 7 stands alone as a summary and conclusion. Although Leontius formally maintains the style of *dubitatio,* in reality he has left it; here his imaginary interlocutors simply ask him to summarize the issues and his position. This he does by discussing the *tropos tēs henōseōs.* He attacks both the Nestorian *kat' axian* and the Monophysite misun-

---

12. I am indebted to the analysis of Evans in the following summary.

derstanding of *kat' ousian*. Leontius summarizes his analysis of being that he has developed to make comprehensible the type of union he wants to predicate of the two natures of Christ. For Leontius, all beings are defined by simultaneous modes of union and distinction. So (in 1301D) he says there are things united by species but distinguished by hypostases (class I) and things distinguished by species but united by hypostases (class II). As Evans puts it, these can be thought of as beings in their mode of nature and in their mode of union, respectively.[13] Class I beings may be further divided in two ways. First, they possess their union and distinction either as simple or as composite. Second, when considering class I beings that are in a union *kat' ousian*, we may also distinguish between those that do not preserve the integrity of the definition of their being (in the union) and those that do. For Leontius, both the "Word" and the "flesh" are beings that fall into this latter subdivision in their union *kat' ousian*. Other examples of the union of such beings include fire and wood in one torch, and body and soul in one person.

My main concern is how (or whether) Leontius meant the term *enypostaton* to serve as a solution to the *dubitatio* of the first chapter. One can reconstruct it in the form of a syllogism. For Leontius's adversaries, the conjunction of A and B entails C.

A. Jesus Christ has two natures *(dyo physeis epi tou henos Christou)*
B. There is no nature without hypostasis *(ouk esti physis anypostatos)*
C. Jesus Christ has two hypostases *(dyo ara an eien kai hai hypostaseis)*

The Monophysites avoid C by rejecting premise A, and argue instead for one nature (at least "after the union," following Eutyches). The Nestorians bite the bullet and accept C, or at least put a division between hypostases. Leontius, on the other hand, rejects the validity of the syllogism by attacking the elliptical premise of his enemies that would be required for the entailment relation to hold, viz., that two natures cannot be united in one hypostasis. This was the whole point of his extensive analysis of being, which he summarized in chapter 7. The early modern reading of Leontius claimed that the way he critiqued this el-

---

13. Evans, *Leontius of Byzantium*, especially 33ff. Evans introduced the terms "class I" and "class II" for easy reference in his argument.

liptical premise was to give the term "enhypostasized" a new specific and nontraditional metaphysical meaning, which enabled him to avoid the heresy of C. This modern interpretation is now commonly attributed to the influence of Loofs.

The Modern Interpretation of Leontius

Loofs suggested that Leontius invented the idea of something having its *hypostasis* not in itself, but *in* the hypostasis of another nature, and that this conception played a special role in the development of doctrine. This reading certainly has a prima facie tenability to it, and has been accepted almost unanimously. Apart from the recent writings of Grillmeier and Daley (examined below), one finds in the textbook analyses of Leontius near unanimity in ascribing to him a new use of the term *enypostaton*. Two examples will suffice. R. V. Sellers explains that Leontius responded to the enemies of orthodoxy by bringing "forward his theory of *enhypostasia*."[14] Hans Stickelberger asserts, in the context of describing the union of the natures in "the hypostasis of the Christ-Logos," that Leontius "called this relation the *enhypostasis* of the human nature."[15] As I hope to show, Leontius did no such thing. There are compelling reasons for rejecting the consensus view.

According to Loofs, Leontius's original contribution was the "theory of the *enhypostasis*" of the human nature of Christ. He argues that, for Leontius, "The human nature in Christ is not *anypostatos,* nor itself an *hypostasis,* but *enypostatos* (1277D), that is, it has its *hypostēnai en tō logō* (1944C)."[16] Loofs here makes a connection between Leontius's use of *enypostatos* in *Contra Nestorianos et Eutychianos* (1277D) and a second quotation from a separate text attributed to Leontius, *Solutio argumentorum a Severo objectorum* (PG 86 1944C).

14. R. V. Sellers, *The Council of Chalcedon* (London: SPCK, 1961), 304.

15. Hans Stickelberger, "Substanz und Akzidens bei Leontius von Byzanz," *TZ* 36 (1980): 159; my translation.

16. Friedrich Loofs, "Leontius von Byzanz," 65; my translation. Note that Loofs recognizes that Leontius would not predicate *anypostaton* of the human nature of Jesus. This will be important for the argument below. Some of the Protestant Scholastics do predicate the term of the human nature. For now, the focus is on whether Leontius predicated *enypostaton* of the human nature in any special way.

However, there are several problems with Loofs's analysis. It is clear that in *Contra Nestorianos et Eutychianos* itself Leontius does *not* say that the human nature is *in* the *hypostasis* of the Logos; thus the onus of proof is on Loofs. He is forced to appeal to *Solutio argumentorum,* which was written at a different time and against a different adversary. But a closer examination of the passage he quotes invalidates his appeal. First, Loofs changes the word order of the original text, putting *hypostēnai* before *en tō logō,* to strengthen his argument (cf. 1944C 4). Second, he twists the grammar: the verb form is passive infinitive and does not fit "it has its" *(sie hat ihr).* To cap it off, the text quoted by Loofs is one Leontius puts in the mouths of his enemies! The context of the quotation in *Solutio argumentorum* is an argument that such statements (like *en tō logō hypostēnai*) about the nonpreexistence of the human nature do not guarantee a single hypostasis. Therefore, Leontius wants to argue for one hypostasis on stronger grounds. But the critical thing to note is that even if Leontius conceded this point to his Cyrillian interlocutors, this has no relevance for the crucial question of the meaning of *enypostaton,* because the word *enypostaton* appears nowhere in the *Solutio argumentorum* passage.

Finally, Loofs misunderstands the word *enypostaton* itself. As Daley notes: "One of Loofs' most influential mistakes was to take the word *enhypostaton . . .* not to mean 'hypostatic,' 'having a concrete existence,' as in fact it does, but to mean 'hypostasized' or 'existent *within*' something else: to take the en- in the term, in other words, as a localizing prefix rather than simply the opposite of an alpha privative."[17] If *enypostaton* just means "subsisting," and does not carry the metaphysical implications proposed by Loofs, then Leontius can be seen as a creative systematizer of Chalcedon, rather than a radical innovator or neologist.

Grillmeier comes to a similar conclusion: "Chalcedon speaks of one *hypostasis* only. It seems that contrary to an *opinio communis* Leontius of Byzantium has not advanced much further. It was believed [wrongly] that Leontius had found another meaning of *hypostasis* which went well beyond the one given here."[18] In a more detailed treatment of Leontius, Grillmeier explains: "that which is *enhypostaton* has being and

17. Daley, "Richer Union," 241.
18. Grillmeier, "Understanding," 80.

actuality in itself. Thereby it is also shown that the prefix *en* in the compound word *enhypostaton* has been falsely interpreted. It is the opposite of an *alpha privatum* (e.g., a-hypostaton) and means precisely the possession of that property which was denied by the negation. *Enhypostaton* thus means nothing other than 'to have a concrete existence,' 'to have actuality.'"[19]

Other church fathers throughout the first millennium of Christian theology use the terms *enypostaton* and *anypostaton* simply to mean "subsisting" and "not subsisting," respectively. Let us look at a few examples of this common usage before, during, and after the time of Leontius. Because he quotes them extensively as authorities in the florilegium of *Contra Nestorianos et Eutychianos,* it is appropriate to start with the Cappadocians. In a letter to Count Terentius, St. Basil explains that because "*ousia* bears the same relation to *hypostasis* as the common does to the particular (. . .) it makes no sense for them to say that the persons are without *hypostasis* [*anypostata*],"[20] for of course the persons are not merely abstract essences but truly exist. In chapter 2 of *Oratio Catechetica,* St. Gregory of Nyssa argues that the Word of God is not *anypostaton,* that is, it is not "without subsistence."[21] In his Catechetical Lectures (17.5), St. Cyril of Jerusalem refers to the Holy Spirit as "not diffused throughout the air, but having actual subsistence [*enypostaton*]."[22] Leontius of Jerusalem (a contemporary of our Leontius) uses *enypostatos* to mean just "existing" in his arguments with the Dyophysites; for him, all natures are *enypostaton.*[23] John of Damascus in the eighth century used the terms in this straightforward way in his treatment of Cyril and Leontius of Byzantium in *De Fide Orthodoxa* 3.9. He refers directly to Leontius's argument in chapter 1 of *Contra Nestorianos et Eutychianos,* and asserts that the flesh and the Word have one and the same subsistence. Therefore, the Damascene argues, we cannot speak of either of them as *anypostaton.*[24] Since Leontius was consciously try-

19. Grillmeier, "Die anthropologisch-christologische Sprache," 68-69.
20. *PG* 32:789A 14-789B 8. For an English translation of the full text, see NPNF[2] 8:254.
21. *PG* 45:17B 5. See NPNF[2] 5:477.
22. *PG* 33:973 2-975A 1. See NPNF[2] 7:125; here the translators render *enypostaton* as "having a real substance."
23. *Adversus Nestorius* (*PG* 86:1561C 3-4). Cf. Evans, *Leontius,* 140.
24. *PG* 94:1017A 9. Later in the same paragraph, he explains that "the flesh of the

ing to follow the earlier fathers, if he had in fact wanted to invent a new meaning for words they all used, it seems he would have been explicit in announcing his intention. Without such an announcement, it makes more sense to assume he used the terms in a way similar to other speakers of this theological language.

A Closer Look at Leontius

To translate the terms as used by Leontius in a common (non-innovative) way does not take away from the importance or the power of his doctrinal presentation of Christ. The critical passage in *Contra Nestorianos et Eutychianos* (PG 86:1277C 13–1280B 10) where Leontius uses the terms *enypostaton* and *anypostaton* has not, to my knowledge, been translated and published in English. Given the importance of this section for understanding the flaws of the "Enhypostasis Theory," I offer the following translation:[25]

> A "subsistence" [*hypostasis*] and "that which subsists" [*enypostaton*] are not the same, no more than a "substance" [*ousia*] and "that which is substantiated" [*enousion*] are the same. "Subsistence" [*hypostasis*] designates the particular individual, but "that which subsists" [*to enypostaton*] refers to the essence. "Hypostasis" defines a person

---

Word . . . did not have a separate *hypostasis* alongside the *hypostasis* of the Word of God, but by subsisting in it [the hypostasis of the Word], it really did come to subsist [*enypostatos*]." See NPNF² 9:53. Notice that this passage does not assert the equivalence of *enypostatos* and "subsisting in another." The ambiguity of this text in John of Damascus makes it a possible locus (the only other likely patristic locus besides Leontius that I know of) for the Protestant Scholastic misreading of the terms, which I analyze below. Since the Damascene refers explicitly to Leontius of Byzantium, however, it still makes the most sense to focus my analysis on the latter. Further research on the sources of the Protestant Scholastics may shed new light on the etiology of the christological formula in its current dual form.

25. Daley is working on a new critical edition of all Leontius's works (see "Richer Union," 239). In producing the translation that follows, I have compared the Migne text to a draft of Daley's currently unpublished critical edition, which he graciously provided. For a German translation (which is sometimes overly determined by the "enhypostasis theory"), see S. Otto, *Person und Subsistenz: Die philosophische Anthropologie des Leontios von Byzanz; Ein Beitrag zur spätantiken Geistesgeschichte* (Munich: Wilhelm Fink, 1968), 192-93.

[*prosōpon*] by means of particular characteristics. "That which subsists" [*to enypostaton*] signifies something that is not an accident; the latter has its being in another and is not seen in itself. It is the case for all such qualities, both those called essential and those called nonessential, that they are not themselves an essence, that is, a subsistent thing, but are perceived always in association with an essence; for example, as cold is in a body and knowledge is in a soul. One speaks truly in saying: "there is no such thing as a nonsubsistent nature [*physis anypostatos*]." But one draws a false conclusion if one infers that a thing is a hypostasis from the assertion that it is not without subsistence [*mē anypostaton*]. Similarly, one can rightly say: "there is no such thing as a body without form [*sōma aschēmatiston*]." But it would be incorrect to conclude that the form is a body; rather, it is only perceived in the body. Certainly, there is no nonsubsistent nature, that is, essence. A nature, however, is not a hypostasis, for there cannot be a reversal here. A hypostasis is also a nature, but a nature is not also a hypostasis. A nature [*physis*] admits of the predication of "being" [*einai*], but a hypostasis may be further defined as that which "is by itself" [*kat' heauton einai*]. The former indicates the character of a universal; the latter identifies a particular within a species. "Nature" designates the peculiarity of that which is held in common; "hypostasis" marks off a particular from the common.

To summarize: things sharing the same essence [*homoousia*], with a common structure of being, are properly said to be of one nature. But one can define as "hypostasis" either [A] things that share a nature but differ in number, or [B] things that are put together from different natures, but that share reciprocally in a common being. By "sharing being" I mean insofar as the nature and essence of each is perceived not by itself but only with the other, with which it has been joined and composited. It is not as if each completed the essence of the other, as in the relation between essences and things essentially predicated of them, which we call their qualities. One finds this "sharing of being" in various things, not least in the relation between soul and body, which have a common hypostasis but individual natures, each with a distinct structure of being.

From this text it is clear that Loofs's interpretation of *enypostaton* as referring explicitly and only to a nature that has its subsistence (or hypostasis) *in* the hypostasis of another nature is doubly wrong. First, the term is not limited, as Loofs apparently thought, to what I have designated as [B] cases, in which there is a union of different natures. *Enypostaton* simply refers to an essence that is in fact subsisting. Second, even when it is predicated of a thing in the category of [B], the hypostasis of that nature is not *in* the hypostasis of another nature; rather, that nature shares a common hypostasis with the other nature. In such hypostatic unions, each individual nature maintains its own distinct structure of being *(logos)*. The paradigm case is the union of soul and body, where the natures share a common subsistence that is constituted by their relationality. Leontius naturally predicates *enypostaton* of both soul and body, for each is subsistent.

Indeed, the translation of the terms in the normal way illustrated above also makes more sense of Leontius's internal argument. If we interpreted the terms consistently through the lens of the Loofsian thesis, it would render Leontius's view problematic on other grounds. Describing the union of two natures of the type fitting the Word and the flesh, Leontius says in chapter 7 that they are perceived "with one another and in one another."[26] Loofs's theory of "enhypostasis" would require that the divine nature was also *in* the hypostasis of the human nature, a conclusion that would have sounded Eutychian to sixth-century ears. If Leontius was using the term *enypostaton* the way everyone else did, however, then it would make sense to predicate it of the Logos too, because the Logos does subsist. As early as 1938, Marcel Richard recognized that for Leontius all natures (substances, *ousia*) are "enhypostatic," but he did not push the logic to show that this contradicts the Loofsian reading.[27] Of course all natures are "enhypostatic," because the latter simply means "hypostatized" or "subsisting"; and, given neo-Aristotelian assumptions, a nature cannot subsist *ante rem* but only *in rebus*.

Why would Loofs make such a terminological mistake, and why was it so readily accepted and dyed into the wool of christological inter-

---

26. *PG* 86:1304B 5: *Met' allēlōn kai en allēlois theōroumenē.* The word *enypostaton* is not used at all in this later section of Leontius's argument. If he had intended to use it in the way Loofs thought he did, we would expect it to be expounded precisely here.

27. Marcel Richard, "Léonce et Pamphile," *Revue des sciences philosophiques et théologiques* 27 (1938): 33. He notes that *enypostatos* is "an essential characteristic of substance."

pretation in the twentieth century? The first clue is Loofs's use of the German noun form *Enhypostasie* (the English form is "enhypostasis"; both translate *enhypostasia*) to refer to the human nature of Christ. But the word *enhypostasia* is not found in *Contra Nestorianos et Eutychianos*. Indeed, one may search the entire corpus Leontianum for it to no avail. Leontius consistently uses the adjectival form *enypostatos* and it means simply "hypostatic." Similarly, there is no such word as *anhypostasia* in Leontius, only the adjective *anypostatos*, which always means simply "without hypostasis" or "not hypostatic." For a nature to be *enypostaton* means for it to have concrete existence. For a nature to be *anypostaton* makes no sense; the latter term cannot be predicated of a nature since both Leontius and his adversaries held to a neo-Aristotelian view of metaphysical categories.

The noun form *enhypostasia* is found nowhere in any of the early fathers, because it is simply not a word in their vocabulary. A search of the *Thesaurus Linguae Graecae* database shows no instances in the Greek fathers of *enypostasia (enhypostasis)* and only one case of *anypostasia*. The latter is found in an obscure author within a seven-word fragment, which is not even a sentence but merely a list of words. Why then did Loofs use these noun forms to describe Leontius's theory? Had theologians ever utilized them prior to Loofs? Indeed, we find these terms side by side in the writings of the Protestant Scholastics of the late sixteenth and seventeenth centuries.

Anhypostasia and *Enhypostasia* in Protestant Scholasticism

If the seeds of the "enhypostasis theory" reading of Leontius were planted during the formative period of Protestant theology and grew alongside other doctrinal developments, then eradicating the terminology of the dual formula as referring to the human nature of Jesus may be more difficult for the Lutheran and Reformed traditions than for Catholic theology.[28] The situation is even more complicated for

---

28. Many (if not most) Catholic Patristic scholars had also accepted the interpretation of Leontius as equating "enhypostatic" with existing in the hypostasis of another. For example, Piet Schoonenberg, *The Christ* (New York: Herder and Herder, 1971), 58. However, Schoonenberg goes on to offer several objections to the Protestant Scholastic theories of *anhypostasia* (59-65). One Catholic author I found who affirms the *anhypos-*

Barth scholarship if in fact the formula was made the material and methodological centerpiece of his whole theology.

When Barth adopted these terms, he clearly thought they represented ancient dogma. But they are not *ancient* theological terms; they are not even words in the vocabulary of the Greek fathers. Barth took them from the theological textbooks of H. Heppe and H. Schmid, who quoted the Protestant Scholastics at length. First, let us look at some representative texts from the Lutheran Schmid. He refers to Hollaz's summation: "To the human nature of Christ there belong certain distinctive characteristics or prerogatives . . . such are (a) *anhypostasia,* the being without a peculiar subsistence, since this is replaced by the divine person *(hypostasis)* of the Son of God, as one far more exalted."[29] Schmid then discusses Quenstedt's clarification of the distinction between "*anhypostasia* and *enhypostasia.*" Finally, he quotes Gerhard: "Relatively, that is said to be *anhypostaton,* which does not subsist in its own, but in the *hypostasis* of another. . . . In this sense, the flesh of Christ is said to be *anhypostatos,* because it is *enhypostatos,* subsisting in the *logos.*"[30]

Apparently the Lutheran Scholastics created the terms *anhypostasia* and *enhypostasia,* since they appear in this noun form for the first time here. Two things are important to note. First, it would be true to their sensibilities to turn the adjectival forms of *enypostatos* and *anypostatos* into nouns. Perhaps the Lutheran Scholastics were influenced here by the nominalism of William of Ockham. With a tendency to eschew the whole discussion of universals and particulars, natures and hypostases, they may have preferred simply to point at a concrete entity (like the humanity of Jesus) and name it something concrete (like *enhypostasia*). This move may have even tacitly provided support for the Lutheran inclusion of the *genus maiestaticum* in the doctrinal debates over *communicatio idiomatum.* Second, whether or not this was the motivation, we have seen that these terms have no basis in the patristic literature. Additionally, I have shown that even if *enhypostasia* had been a word in the early church, it would not have described a nature that has its existence *in* the hypostasis of another nature.

tasis side of the dyad as a "classical" doctrine is John Macken, S.J., *The Autonomy Theme in the "Church Dogmatics"* (New York: Cambridge University Press, 1990), 149.

29. H. Schmid, *The Doctrinal Theology of the Evangelical Lutheran Church,* trans. C. A. Hay and H. E. Jacobs, 3d ed. (1899; reprint Minneapolis: Augsburg, 1961), 300.

30. Ibid., 301.

What about *anhypostasia?* Here the case against the Lutheran Scholastic usage is even stronger. Loofs himself recognized that Leontius referred to the flesh of Christ as "not *anypostaton.*" But the Scholastics quoted above said that the human nature *is anhypostasia.* Even if the latter was in fact a word, this would amount to saying that the flesh of Jesus "is isn't," which makes no sense. Notice that both Leontius and the Lutherans want to affirm what I called proposition 1 in the introduction to this chapter: the human nature does not have an independent subsistence outside the union with the Logos. But Leontius clearly never would have affirmed proposition 2, that is, the *anhypostasis-enhypostasis* formula as a way of expressing this christological doctrine.

Although the Reformed Scholastics may not have used the noun form of these terms, they nevertheless misunderstood the adjectival forms and utilized them in a similar way. Here are two representative Scholastic texts quoted in Heppe. The first is from the Leiden Synopsis: "the Son of God, the second eternal person of the sacrosanct Trinity, assumed into the unity of his person right from the moment of conception not a pre-existent person but one *anhypostatos* of its own hypostasis or devoid of subsistence, and made it belong to himself. [The flesh] subsists in him and is borne and supported by him."[31] The second quote is from J. H. Heidegger: "assuredly there must of necessity be one hypostasis, one subsistent person. Either the divine nature subsists in the human, or the human in the divine. That the divine nature should subsist in and be sustained by the human is opposed to its infinite perfection. So the human is per se *anhypostatos* and becomes *enhypostatos* in the *logos,* who being pre-existent, in fact existent from eternity, has received in time the form of a servant . . . as its shrine and instrument."[32] Loofs (and virtually everyone else) adopted this way of transliterating the terms (i.e., including the *h*), which has had the negative effect of making even the adjectival forms look like nouns. We must conclude that these Protestant Scholastics misappropriated the terms and employed them in a way contradictory to their use by Leontius and the other Greek fathers.

---

31. H. Heppe, *Reformed Dogmatics: Set Out and Illustrated from the Sources,* rev. and ed. Ernst Bizer, trans. G. T. Thompson (1861; reprint London: Allen and Unwin, 1950), 418.
32. Ibid., 428.

The *Anhypostasis-Enhypostasis* Formula in Barth

I have already alluded to the fact that the effects of this interpretation did not stop with the Scholastics. Its ramifications have been particularly evident in the theology of Barth and his followers. In the *Church Dogmatics,* Barth calls the dual formula of *anhypostasis* and *enhypostasis* "the sum and root of all the grace addressed to him," that is, to the human nature of Jesus Christ.[33] While he intended to represent their teaching faithfully, Barth's use of dialectic reshaped the dual formula beyond its character in the Scholastics. He discusses the terms in more detail in the second volume on the Word of God:

> *Anhypostasis* asserts the negative. Since in virtue of the *egeneto*, i.e., in virtue of the *assumptio,* Christ's human nature has its existence — the ancients said, its subsistence — in the existence of God, meaning in the mode of being (*hypostasis,* "person") of the Word, it does not possess it in and for itself, *in abstracto.* Apart from the divine mode of being whose existence it acquires it has none of its own; i.e., apart from its concrete existence in God in the event of the *unio,* it has no existence of its own, it is *anhypostatos. Enhypostasis* asserts the positive. In virtue of the *egeneto,* i.e., in virtue of the *assumptio,* the human nature acquires existence (subsistence) in the existence of God, meaning in the mode of being (*hypostasis,* "person") of the Word. This divine mode of being gives it existence in the event of the *unio,* and in this way it has a concrete existence of its own, it is *enhypostatos.* (*CD,* I/2, 163)

T. F. Torrance, coeditor of the English translation of the *Church Dogmatics,* has followed Barth in this dialectical usage of these terms for expressing the relation of the two natures of Jesus Christ. Torrance goes beyond Barth, however, and presses the dual formula into further service. Explaining the "logic of God," which is revealed in the nature of the incarnate Logos, Torrance argues that "the logic of Grace and the logic of Christ [the two sides of the logic of God] are to be related to one another as the doctrines of *anhypostasia* and *enhypostasia.*"[34] In the context of theological thinking, the former posits the uncondi-

33. Barth, *CD,* IV/2, 91.
34. T. F. Torrance, *Theological Science* (New York: Oxford University Press, 1969), 217.

tional priority of grace, while the latter affirms an unimpaired place for human response. Holding these two together, Torrance suggested, is necessary for "thinking out the interior logic of theological thought."[35] My analysis of the terms *enypostatos* and *anypostatos* in the preceding sections of this essay should at least cause us to pause and consider whether invoking the dual formula is the best way of accomplishing Torrance's goal of describing the logic of theology.

Eberhard Jüngel echoes Barth by incorrectly referring to *enhypostasis* and *anhypostasis* as a "patristic doctrine."[36] Like Torrance, he expands the scope of the formula, arguing that it might also be operative implicitly in Barth's doctrine of election. Interestingly, Jüngel offers an anonymous Greek phrase — *enypostatos tō logō tou theou* — to clarify his argument.[37] Although he gives no reference for this quotation, it is certainly reminiscent of the misquoting of Leontius by Loofs, which I analyzed above. Jüngel even calls for a new formulation of the doctrine of God in these terms: "God's being *ad extra* would be anhypostatic if in this relation there did not take place an *enhypostasis* of the being of God as Father, as Son and as Spirit."[38] John Macken, S.J., has traced Jüngel's further application of the formula to the issue of the autonomy and heteronomy of the human self in relation to Christ. Macken apparently accepted Barth's application of the formula to Christ, but found Jüngel's expansion of the formula to the Christian life too restrictive for a sound distinction between nature and grace.[39]

These authors treat the *anhypostasis-enhypostasis* formula as a single motif in Barth's thought. Bruce McCormack, on the other hand, has argued more strongly that in Barth's 1924 *Göttingen Dogmatics* "the anhypostatic-enhypostatic model had supplanted the time-eternity dialectic as the central parable for expressing the *Realdialektik* of God's veiling and unveiling,"[40] and that the adoption of this formula marked

---

35. Ibid., 218.

36. Eberhard Jüngel, *God's Being Is in Becoming: The Trinitarian Being of God in the Theology of Karl Barth,* trans. John Webster (Grand Rapids: Eerdmans, 2000), 112; cf. p. 96.

37. Ibid., 113.

38. Ibid., 118.

39. Macken, *Autonomy Theme,* 168.

40. McCormack, *Dialectical Theology,* 367. McCormack suggests that Barth's use of the model was "thoroughly Reformed" (371). However, Barth seems to follow the Lutheran Schmid in adopting the noun forms rather than limiting himself to the adjec-

the beginning of a new phase in his theology that continued through the *Church Dogmatics*. It makes sense to think that in 1924 Barth made a theological decision to root dogmatics in the incarnation, as McCormack suggests. But it is less clear that the *anhypostasis-enhypostasis* formula became the central parable for pointing to the *Realdialektik*, because, as Barth himself recognizes both in the *Göttingen Dogmatics* and in the *Church Dogmatics*, the referent of these terms is not God but the human nature of Jesus.[41] One might expect a parable that aims to replace the "time-eternity" dialectic to reach beyond the predicates of the human nature of Jesus. To find such a parable, one might explore, for example, the broader arena of God's revelation "in Christ," which includes for Barth not only Word but also Spirit, not only the objective but also the subjective reality of God's self-revelation. Here too we can find at least the seeds of other parables in §§5-7 of the *Göttingen Dogmatics*.

Despite the fact that Barth refers to the formula only three or four times in *CD*, I/2 and IV/2, it is clearly important for him. This twofold doctrine, which he incorrectly thought was "unanimously sponsored by early theology in its entirety,"[42] is not a superfluous theologoumenon: "this concept [*anhypostasis-enhypostasis*] is quite unavoidable at this point if we are properly to describe the mystery."[43] My preceding analysis of the formula suggests that those who desire to join Barth in affirming the importance of the concept should make an explicit and careful distinction between the concept and the contingency of the linguistic dyad that has come to express it. In any case, by arguing that the dual formula is not necessarily the central parable, and that these terms are not necessary for expressing Barth's view of the *Realdialektik*, we may reject the Protestant Scholastic terminology and its problems without simultaneously rejecting Barth's contributions to the doctrine of revelation.

It is interesting to note that the later Barth refers to "the Church"

tives as in the Reformed Scholastics quoted by Heppe. Barth wrote the preface to the Bizer edition of Heppe's book — there he confesses to a heavy reliance on both Heppe and Schmid in preparing the *Göttingen Dogmatics*. Barth treats the dual formula in *Göttingen Dogmatics*, vol. 1, trans. G. W. Bromiley (Grand Rapids: Eerdmans, 1991), 157.

41. Barth, *CD*, IV/2, 91; *Göttingen Dogmatics*, 157.
42. *CD*, I/2, 163.
43. Ibid., IV/2, 50.

as *anhypostasis* and *enhypostasis* in relation to Christ (*CD*, IV/2, 59), and without using the terms he applies a similar structural apparatus to the experience of awakening to conversion in the individual Christian as well (IV/2, 557-63). That is, the individual is not a "new man" outside the regenerative activity of the divine Spirit, but is a "new man" through that activity. What seems most important to Barth is not the terms but a specific kind of relational unity that maintains the asymmetry of the divine initiative. This suggests that for Barth the critical issue is not the *anhypostasis-enhypostasis* formula, but an insistence on the creature's total reliance on God's grace.

Once again, it is important to distinguish the following claims: (1) The human nature of Jesus does not subsist except in its union with the Logos in the one person of Christ, and (2) *enhypostasis* and *anhypostasis* are good terms to describe this fact about the human nature of Jesus. If we are compelled to reject the second thesis, and the use of the formula in the way meant by the Protestant Scholastics, Loofs, and Barth, this does not mean, of course, that we reject the intuition that they were trying to express by using those terms. Instead, we must search for better ways to state the mystery of the relation between the Logos and the "flesh" of Jesus of Nazareth. What is at issue is the clarity of our confession that Christ is fully divine and fully human in one person.

In the context of the overall argument of this book, the current chapter is intended to demonstrate how powerfully theological anthropology shapes Christology and vice versa. For Leontius, the paradigmatic analogy for the relational unity of the Word and the flesh in Jesus Christ was the relational unity of soul and body in a human person. For the Lutheran Scholastics, it appears that the nominalist avoidance of speaking of a universal human nature led them to misinterpret the terms *enypostaton* and *anypostaton*. Barth's tendency to eschew "speculative" anthropology of any kind (in his polemic against *analogia entis*) led to such a strong emphasis on "from above" in his theological method that he was accused of revelational positivism. While it would be reductionistic to suggest a causal determinism in the relation of anthropology and Christology, the reciprocal influence between them is clear. In part III I will often observe other examples of the reciprocity between the doctrine of God, Christology, and anthropology, not to mention Pneumatology, ecclesiology, eschatology, and

159

other doctrines. Embracing the call to engage our own culture I turn now to an exploration of opportunities in late modernity for reforming theological anthropology after the turn to relationality in philosophy and science.

REFORMING THEOLOGICAL
ANTHROPOLOGY

Relationality and the Doctrine
of Human Nature

In these final three chapters, I explore the ramifications of the turn to relationality on the three traditional loci of theological anthropology: human nature, sin, and image of God. I attempt to identify plausible and compelling ways to conserve the living intuitions of the biblical tradition by liberating their illuminative power through discourse with contemporary anthropological self-understandings. As one might expect, these three issues are so closely related that one may trace patterns of reciprocal influence throughout their historical development. My goal is not only "reforming" but also "reformative" anthropology, for these themes should not be abstracted from the concrete longings of human creatures for a peaceful relation to divine truth, goodness, and beauty.

I am aiming for a theology of human knowing, acting, and being that articulates the good news about the biblical God whose grace transforms our epistemic, ethical, and ontological anxiety into faith, love, and hope. Elsewhere I have outlined this same matrix of interrelated themes, exploring the implications of developments in the doctrine of God that have emphasized divine Infinity, Trinity, and Futurity for a constructive articulation of the Christian intuition that we are called to share in the knowledge, suffering, and glory of Jesus Christ.[1] I have also argued that these developments, which are connected to the theological (re)turn to relationality, open up conceptual space for un-

---

1. See my "Sharing in the Divine Nature: Transformation, *Koinōnia* and the Doctrine of God," in *On Being Christian . . . and Human,* ed. Todd Speidell (Eugene, Ore.: Wipf and Stock, 2002), 87-127.

derstanding the soteriological themes of personal and political transformation through sharing in sacramental, baptized, and eucharistic community.[2] My efforts in part III of this book are also related to these developments, but my goal is more explicitly programmatic: to clarify the late modern challenges to and the reconstructive opportunities for reforming theological anthropology after the turn to relationality in philosophy and science.

One of the tasks of theological anthropology is to mark the continuity and difference between human creatures and the rest of creation. The term "creatures" already indicates the major theological point about continuity: humans are wholly embedded in creation, and no special part of humanity, not even the mind, escapes this creaturely continuity. A major part (and sometimes the whole) of the Christian answer to the question of human uniqueness has always had to do with knowing. The observation that the intensity and complexity of our knowing makes us different is important for other disciplines besides theology; even the biological designation of our species is *homo sapiens*. Neurobiologists explore the relation between the human brain and consciousness, psychologists and sociologists explore the structural dynamics of human knowing, and philosophers argue about how to justify claims to knowledge. Theology is interested in these questions, but always in the context of its broader inquiry into the ultimate origin, condition, and goal of human knowing itself.

That we do not know what lies beyond the boundaries of our knowing leads to an anxiety about the nature of our boundedness and the mystery beyond it. We long for a secure relation to truth, to get a "hold" on things. Yet we cannot get our minds around all of reality, and this inability evokes both fear and fascination — what we might call "epistemic anxiety." The assertion that persons naturally desire to know does not mean that all are rigorous students, nor that all seek knowledge for altruistic reasons, but simply that personhood is characterized by a yearning to render things intelligible. This desire to know is inherently ambiguous because it operates under the shadow of not-knowing. This shadow hangs over all our longing for truth, even

2. See my book (with Steve Sandage) *The Faces of Forgiveness: Searching for Wholeness and Salvation* (Grand Rapids: Baker Academic, 2003), especially chap. 5.

though we may vacillate between confident exploration and painful frustration as we seek to acquire knowledge. Epistemic anxiety permeates human knowing as the self becomes aware that it is unable to secure all objects of reason in the power of its finite consciousness. This worry is intensified by the longing to be known by other persons, in whom we are confronted by an inherent mystery that we find both alluring and terrifying. Our passionate longing for truth is always threatened by an even greater terror — the fear of a future in which we will neither know nor be known. On the other hand, this longing is also characterized by an even greater fascination — the desire for a future in which our knowing and being known will be infinitely secure in an eternal fellowship of intimate faithfulness.

In the first part of this chapter, I outline the factors that have led many theologians to formulate the doctrine of human nature (and human knowing) by using the terminology of substance dualism and faculty psychology. I briefly trace the influence of Plato and Aristotle on Christian anthropology from the patristic period through the Reformation. In the second part, I show how the turn to relationality created challenges to these traditional formulations, and at the same time provided opportunities for reforming anthropology in dialogue with contemporary culture. This reformation will involve retrieving a more holistic, community-oriented understanding of humanity. One of the desiderata of this reformative task is to maintain the Christian intuition that we will continue to know and be known by God "after death." As we will see, resistance to doctrinal reformation is due in this case not so much to exegetical consensus (which supports holism), but to an underlying commitment to outdated philosophical and scientific assumptions that have privileged particular readings of the relevant biblical texts.

Substance Dualism and Faculty Psychology

Definitions of human nature in Western theology have often been guided by two questions. First, how are the "substance" of the body and the "substance" of the soul so related in an individual human being that together they constitute one's personal identity? Second, how do the "faculties" (or powers) of the soul work together among themselves

165

to control the body? It was commonly assumed that the soul is a substance that is composed of (or has) faculties — distinct powers or capacities through which it knows, acts, or feels. The most popular taxonomies of these faculties focused on the "intellect" and the "will." These powers of the soul were not considered to be inherently linked to the substance of the body, although they somehow operated upon it. As the influence of the human body on thinking and acting became more evident in modern science, a third faculty (or set of faculties) was emphasized — variously called the appetites, passions, feelings, or emotions. Due in large part to the philosophical turn to relationality, substance dualism and the faculty psychology are no longer plausible options in contemporary anthropological science. In the web of theological anthropological belief, however, these ancient and early modern models of human nature have become so deeply embedded that many Christians believe they are essential to the biblical gospel.

Body and Soul

As we saw in chapter one, this language about "substances" may be traced to the Greek philosophers Plato and Aristotle.[3] Plato was an anthropological dualist, arguing for a strong dichotomy between the immortal soul and the mortal body. This anthropology was rooted in his broader metaphysical dualism that distinguished between the eternal realm of Forms (or Ideas) and the temporal realm. Substances are either immaterial or material; the uniqueness of humans is their double composition. The individual person is a "soul" substance that dwells in a "body" substance. For Plato the material body is the prison of the immaterial soul, which strives to be free from the body and return to the realm of the Forms, from which it has fallen. This model clearly allowed for (and even encouraged) the separation of the soul and body. Plato's metaphysics suggested that there is an eternal Form (or Idea) of "humanity," a universal substance from which all human souls derive their being. Aristotle reconceived the concept of "form" as inherently

---

3. In what follows, I am less concerned with the current debates over the original intentions of Plato and Aristotle than with the way in which their ideas in fact were commonly interpreted and influenced the formulation of theological anthropology.

linked to "matter," as that to which matter (as potency) strives to actualize.[4] For him, the universal substance "human" exists, but only *in* particular human individuals. As the "moderate realists" of medieval Scholasticism would put it, universals exist *in re* but not *ante rem*.[5] In Aristotelian anthropology, the soul is the form of the body, and so the two cannot be separated so easily. Humans are living beings that have logos *(zōon logon echōn)*. This model of the individual as a psychosomatic unity lends itself more readily to a holist answer to the question: How many substances constitute a human being?

Christian theology wrestled with these two options as it aimed to make sense both of the unity of embodied conscious experience and of the biblical assertion that bodily death is not the end of conscious life with God. Augustine adopted a Neoplatonic anthropology in which the soul may easily be separated from the body to help him defend belief in the resurrection of the soul and an "intermediate" state after death. For him a human being is primarily the substance of the soul, which dwells in and uses the body as its instrument. The soul is "a certain substance, sharing in reason and suited to the task of ruling the body."[6] For Augustine the substance of the soul is so privileged over the substance of the body that he sometimes appears to view the for-

---

4. This view is sometimes called hylomorphism, because it asserts that we always find *hylē* (matter) and *morphē* (form) together. The anthropological debate between Platonists and Aristotelians was over the ontological status of that which is referred to by a general categorical term (such as "human"), i.e., their underlying theories of "universals." The term "universal" refers to general words that can be predicated of several things, and the question is, as Porphyry put it in his commentary on Aristotle's *Categories:* what is the referent of genera and species?

5. Plato's view is usually called "realism," indicating a belief in the real existence of universals independent of particular things. "Nominalism" is the view that universals are not real at all, merely the sound of the voice, i.e., only "names" *(nomina)*. Few held the extreme form of this view, and many who were called nominalists (e.g., William of Ockham) may have been closer to what is now called the conceptualist position. "Conceptualists" also hold that universals exist, but only as concepts. Generally, this view tends to separate thought from objects, and to denigrate knowledge that attempts to go beyond experienced particulars. Ockham's *via moderna* attacked all forms of moderate realism *(via antiqua)*, especially that of Thomas Aquinas and Duns Scotus. He placed a wedge between form and matter, insisting that matter is actual in its own right. Because Aristotelian concepts were crucial for the *preambulae fidei* of Thomas, Ockham's attack was seen as an attempt to destroy the possibility of a separate natural theology.

6. *On the Greatness of the Soul* 13.22.

mer as the essence of the individual.[7] Both substances are intrinsically good (as created by God), and we must regard the human being as the combination of both substances, at least prior to death.[8]

This Augustinian emphasis carried over into Boethius's definition of the human person as an individual substance of a rational nature.[9] Notice that rationality or "knowing" is the key modifier that marks off the distinctiveness of human creatures. Boethius's phrase, which became the most influential anthropological definition in Western theology, was taken up and defended as the classic view by Thomas Aquinas (*SumTh*, I.29.1). However, Thomas held a view of substances that was closer to Aristotle's and so he usually spoke of a psychosomatic unity of soul and body. Nevertheless, he still posited two substances: the human being is composed of a spiritual and of a corporeal substance. For Thomas too this dualism was important for the belief in life after death; human bodies dissolve at death (like the beasts), but not human souls, for they are incorruptible intellectual substances (*SumTh*, I.75.6). This illustrates a key intuition in the Christian tradition that somehow human knowing (that which distinguishes humans from other terrestrial creatures) is connected to "life after death." This leaves open the question of the best way to account for and illuminate that connection.

The tension between Platonic and Aristotelian anthropological models carried over into Reformation theology. For the early Christian tradition, the question about the substances of the soul and body in human being was answered alongside the question about the substances of the divine and human in Jesus Christ. If the christological heresy of Eutyches was fusing the natures of Christ, we might speak of a Eutychean anthropology in which the distinction between body and soul is completely lost. If the heresy of Nestorius's followers was a separation of the divine and human natures in Christ, we might speak of a correlative anthropology in which the body and soul are merely con-

7. For example, he sometimes seems to view the soul as synonymous with the self: "I, that is, my soul . . ." *On the Doctrines of the Church* 1.27.

8. *City of God* 19.3.

9. "Naturae rationabilis individua substantia" (*Contra Eutychen*, book 3). This definition continues to exert influence in some philosophical circles. See the call for its vindication in the epilogue of M. L. O'Hara, *Substances and Things: Aristotle's Doctrine of Physical Substance in Recent Essays*, ed. O'Hara (Washington, D.C.: University of America Press, 1982), 264ff.

joined but not inherently linked. We see here the heretical extremes of the schools of Alexandria and Antioch. Both schools wanted to hold on to a distinction in unity, and tried to do this in the context of "substance" metaphysics.

Broadly speaking, Calvin tended toward Platonic dualism, which makes sense in light of his preference for the patristic Christology of the Antiochenes, who had emphasized the *distinction* between the two natures of Christ. Calvin followed Plato explicitly by speaking of the soul as an "immortal substance," noting that he was the only philosopher who got it right. Claiming to have shown from Scripture that "the soul is an incorporeal substance," he followed Augustine by describing the soul as ruling the body, in which it "dwells . . . as in a house" (*Inst.* I.15.6). Luther seemed less concerned with the discussion of natures and substances, preferring to make the justification-relation between God and humanity his main anthropological category.[10] Nevertheless, his Alexandrian leanings in Christology (stressing the union of the two natures) naturally led him to emphasize a real *union* of body and soul in anthropology. Both Reformers still spoke of the two substances of body and soul (with its faculties), but they were more focused than many of their predecessors on the relation of the whole person to God. As we will see in chapter ten, this holistic intuition was obscured by the Protestant Scholastic return to Aristotelian substance/accident categories.

Intellect, Will, Affection

The constellation of issues that surround "faculty psychology" may be traced to the same Hellenistic sources.[11] In the *Republic* Plato had subdivided the soul into three parts: the "rational" aspect *(logistikon)*, the

---

10. See Martin Seils, "Luther's Significance for Contemporary Theological Anthropology," in *Luther's Ecumenical Significance,* ed. P. Manns and H. Meyer (Philadelphia: Fortress, 1984), 183-202.

11. A full treatment of this influence would also need to include the impact of the Stoic theory of assent, illuminationist metaphors for knowing, and the various theories of the faculties as they emerged in Western philosophy. For an introduction see Charles H. Kahn, "Discovering the Will: From Aristotle to Augustine," in *The Question of "Eclecticism": Studies in Later Greek Philosophy,* ed. J. M. Dillon and A. A. Long (Berkeley: University of California Press, 1988), 234-59.

"spirited" aspect *(thymikon)*, and the "appetitive" aspect *(epithymētikon)*. In the *Phaedrus* he described reason as the chief faculty, like a charioteer who tries to control the appetites and passions so that it can direct the soul upward. Neoplatonic philosophers revised and refined the model, struggling to explain how psychic activity as the work of an immaterial substance could influence a material body. This tripartite structuring of the soul with its privileging of the faculty of reason was taken up by Augustine in his presentation of Christian anthropology. Augustine described the relational unity of the faculties of memory, understanding, and will and argued that these three are an image of the Trinity because they are one essentially, but three relatively.[12] They are equally substantial with one another, and together (in their unity) they constitute the one substance of the human mind. Augustine believed that the faculty of the intellect (understanding) rules the others. How this faculty can be consubstantial with the others, and the mind as a whole, and at the same time rule the other faculties, creates a conceptual muddle that Augustine never solved, and which continues to plague some streams of Western theological anthropology.

Aristotle divided the soul differently than had Plato, speaking instead of a vegetable (nutritive) soul, an animal (sensitive) soul, and a human (rational) soul.[13] Plants have the first kind of "soul," animals have the first and the second, but humans have all three. Thomas Aquinas appropriated this model and developed a more hierarchical account of the faculties. In the human being the rational soul is the highest and itself has three faculties: the will, the passive intellect, and the active intellect. The animal soul has the faculties of locomotion, exterior and interior senses, and sensory appetite. The vegetable soul has the faculties of growth, nutrition, and reproduction (*SumTh*, I.2.22; I.2.28). At least two questions are driving Thomas here. First, given his anthropological model, how can the soul (which is immaterial) use its powers to act in the material realm?[14] His answer, which is more expan-

---

12. *On the Trinity* 10.11. In an earlier part of this book (9.3-5), Augustine had offered another analogy. The mind, the mind's knowing itself, and the mind's loving itself are three things (substances), but somehow also only one essence: "these three are one."

13. *On the Soul* 2 (413b11-13).

14. Anthony Kenny observes the importance of "causality" in Thomas's view of the relation between soul and body; see "Body, Soul, and Intellect in Aquinas," in *From Soul to Self*, ed. M. James C. Crabbe (London: Routledge, 1999), 46-47.

sive in other works,[15] requires the formation of an ontological category of types of matter that can act without a corporeal organ because they are not immersed in matter, and do not exist through their composition with matter, but are themselves that through which the composite exists. The human soul is the prime example of this invented ontological category. Thomas's solution, insofar as it works at all, presupposes medieval Aristotelian anthropological science.

Thomas also treated the ordering of the faculties of the soul (*SumTh*, I.77.4) and explicitly claimed that the intellect is the highest power (I.82.3). The intellect understands the good and so precedes the will, which is moved by it. However, Thomas also acknowledged in the next article (I.82.4) that the will moves the intellect (and in fact moves all the powers of the soul), because it is the agency of movement and alteration, impelling the intellect to understand. He immediately noticed in his replies to Objections 2 and 3 that he was in danger of an infinite regress, in which the search for the ultimate faculty would move indefinitely back and forth between the will and the intellect. Thus he asserted that we must stop at the intellect.[16] The tension resurfaced later, when he again affirmed the mutual movement of intellect and will, but emphasized that the will moves itself. Thomas's inability to answer the question adequately led to the ongoing debates between "intellectualism" and "voluntarism" that dominated anthropology and theology in later medieval scholasticism and beyond.[17]

Platonic and Aristotelian tendencies overlap in early Christian theology and are intertwined with other doctrinal concerns, especially

15. E.g., see his *On the Unity of the Intellect Against the Averroists,* trans. B. H. Zedler (Milwaukee: Marquette, 1968), chap. 1.

16. The same potential regress recurs in Thomas's treatment of salvation, when he asks whether the believer is determined to the object of faith primarily by the will or the intellect (*SumTh* II.II.2.1-3).

17. "From at least the time of St. Thomas onward, explanations of free choice were cast in terms of the operations of these [two] faculties [intellect and will] severally and upon one another. All of the major competing positions of the middle and late seventeenth century were cast in these terms" (Michael Murray, "Intellect, Will, and Freedom: Leibniz and His Precursors," *Leibniz Society Review* 6 [1996]: 25-59). Murray traces the two dominant schools that had arisen by the end of the sixteenth century, voluntarism (led by Jesuits, whose champions are Suarez and Molina) and intellectualism, a position "held primarily amongst Dominicans and attributed by its critics to a number of sixteenth-century figures, including Bañez, Bellarmine, and Cajetan" (32).

Christology. In his sixth-century debate with followers of Nestorius and Eutyches, Leontius of Byzantium argued that we can speak of the unity of the soul and body in one person, as we do of the unity of the two natures of Christ in one person (see chapter seven above). In both cases the integrity of the two different natures is maintained within a single subsistence *(hypostasis)*. Leontius accepted the Aristotelian dictum that there is no nature without hypostasis *(ouk esti physis anypostatos)* nor body without form *(sōma aschēmatiston);* but in his view of the composition of the soul he was a card-carrying Neoplatonist: the soul (which is a rational essence) has three immaterial qualities *(poiotēs asōmatos)* or faculties, viz., the appetitive, spirited, and cognitive. As with the Greek author Leontius, the Latin-speaking Boethius of the same century also attempted to clarify the question about the number of substances that compose the individual by connecting it to controversies about the two natures of Christ. In fact, his treatise on the topic bears essentially the same title: *Contra Eutychen et Nestorium.*[18]

My task is not to trace the historical development of these ideas,[19] but to make the following point: the way in which human uniqueness was discussed in large streams of the Christian tradition was shaped by the philosophical debate over (1) the quality and quantity of substances that constitute human individuals and (2) the number and hierarchical ordering of the faculties of the soul. This was also true during the Reformation. Calvin tentatively affirmed that there are three cognitive faculties (understanding, reason, fantasy) and three appetitive faculties (the will, the capacity for anger, and the capacity to desire inordinately); but then, rather than allowing the "minutiae of Aristotle" to delay him, he posited simply "that the human soul consists of two faculties, understanding and will" *(Inst.* I.15.7).[20] Luther did not deny the

---

18. In *Boethius: The Theological Tractates,* trans. H. F. Steward and E. K. Rand (Cambridge: Harvard University Press, 1962). See especially book 3 for his attempted clarification of Latin and Greek terms.

19. For this see Grillmeier, *Christ in Christian Tradition,* trans. O. C. Dean (Louisville, Ky.: Westminster John Knox, 1996) and J. N. D. Kelly, *Early Christian Doctrines* (San Francisco: Harper & Row, 1978). The semantic ranges of the Greek terms *ousia, hypostasis,* and *prosōpon* and the Latin terms *substantia, subsistentia,* and *persona* were modified considerably and transformed through their mutual translation in the centuries from Nicea to the early Middle Ages.

20. We find in Calvin assertions that support intellectualism (at least for the origi-

existence of the faculty of the "will" nor did he define it carefully; his concern was to reject any natural freedom of this faculty to move toward God without grace. Although he was equally pessimistic about the faculty of the intellect, Luther did maintain that reason continues to have the ruling position in the soul after the fall of Adam.[21] Both of these early Reformers were less interested in critiquing the underlying presuppositions of sixteenth-century anthropology than they were in underlining the dependence of persons on divine grace for being brought into a right relationship with God.

As early modern science gained a deeper understanding of the body and its impact on human thinking and willing, the faculties of the passions (or "affections") came to be emphasized.[22] The tension that resulted from the earlier division between intellect and will was intensified when the affections were rigorously stirred into the mix. Susan James shows how the "passions" had to be linked to both the body and the soul in early modernity, because they affected both. She notes that in spite of their differences, Hobbes and Spinoza were led to reject dualism as they became aware that "the powers posited by Aristotelian philosophers, along with centuries of dispute about their relation to the soul itself, had come to be regarded as obsolete. There were to be no more digestive powers to digest or sensory powers to sense, and no more mysterious messages passed between them."[23]

---

nal created human nature) and assertions that support voluntarism (more common in discussions of fallen and redeemed human nature). On the one hand, the understanding governs the direction of the will (*Inst.* I.15.7) and God made the will "completely amenable" to reason's guidance (I.15.8). On the other hand, Calvin argues that Adam's fall was due to the will, not the intellect, and later describes the will as the "chief seat" of the whole person (II.2.27).

21. See LW, 51:374; 34:137. For other quotes and analysis, see Paul Althaus, *The Theology of Martin Luther,* trans. R. Schultz (Philadelphia: Fortress, 1966), 64-71.

22. Classical theology had emphasized the two faculties of intellect and will, rendering the affections or emotions subsidiary. This is due at least in part to the belief that the latter are rooted in the body, and so are at best part of the "animal" soul (Thomas) or at worst the source of sinful dispositions over which intellect and will are called to rule (Augustine). For a history of the development of the modern concept of passions, see Roger Smith, *The Norton History of the Human Sciences* (New York: Norton, 1997), especially chaps. 4 and 8.

23. Susan James, *Passion and Action: The Emotions in Seventeenth-Century Philosophy* (Oxford: Clarendon, 1997), 87.

The work of the early-seventeenth-century philosopher René Descartes, who was deeply interested in the science of human anatomy and the practical problem of suffering, had placed substance dualism at the heart of Western anthropological reflection. His infamous distinction between "thinking thing" *(res cogitans)* and "extended thing" *(res extensa)* was in part motivated by his theological belief in life after death. He insisted: "I am truly distinct from my body, and can exist without it."[24] His deepening of the dichotomy between mind (soul) and body in the context of the rise of modern theories of causation led to an intensification of the problem of their interaction. If all movement is the result of the action of material bodies on one another, how can an immaterial substance (the soul) move the human body? Descartes's choice of the tiny pineal gland as the connecting point was not convincing, because no matter how small the organ, the mechanism of interaction could not be explained.

Later in Romanticism, this interest in the "passions" led to a challenge of the Enlightenment delight in the power of human reason to control nature and everything bodily. We can see the impact of this new emphasis in Schleiermacher's desire to derive his dogmatic reflections from the pious self-consciousness, which is a modification not of knowing or doing, but of "feeling" (see chapter five above). By the end of the nineteenth century, we find the empirically oriented William James making the viscera primary, reversing the traditional view so that now the bodily manifestations of emotions drive the mind's noetic and volitional activities, rather than vice versa.[25] Twentieth-century behaviorism, with its reduction of all human acting (including knowing) to bodily mechanisms, was dialectically defined by its negation of the "soul" side of Cartesian dualism. The problems with dualism have been the subject of extensive analysis and debate,[26] but most contemporary philosophical and scientific discussions have moved beyond the focus on substances and abstract faculties to explore more holistic and dynamic models of human nature.

24. *Meditations on First Philosophy*, VI.

25. For an outline and analysis of the emergence of the idea of "emotions" and its relation to theology, see Thomas Dixon, "Theology, Anti-Theology, and Atheology: From Christian Passions to Secular Emotions," *Modern Theology* 15 (1999): 297-330.

26. See, e.g., Karl Popper and John C. Eccles, *The Self and Its Brain* (London: Routledge, 1977), 177ff.

Challenges and Opportunities

Most scholars are aware of the challenges to traditional formulations of theological anthropology that rely on substance dualism and faculty psychology, and there is no need to provide an exhaustive review of this well-worn territory. My goal is simply to point out that the turn to relationality not only lies behind most of these challenges but also is in part responsible for opening up new opportunities for reconstructing anthropological doctrine in late modernity. Clarifying the underlying philosophical and theological assumptions that shape these formulations is an important first step for reforming anthropology. In the case of substance dualism and faculty psychology, the challenges (and opportunities) derive from biblical exegetical research, from discoveries in science, and from philosophical reflection.

Biblical Scholarship

In the last two centuries, biblical scholars have increasingly moved toward a consensus that both the Hebrew Bible and the New Testament provide a holistic model of the human person. The literature in this field has been well summarized elsewhere, and for our purposes a brief review will suffice.[27] Hans Walter Wolff has shown that a variety of Hebrew anthropological terms refer to the whole person as he or she attends to the other, the self, or God.[28] The word *nephesh*, which is variously translated as "throat" or "neck" (Prov. 16:24; 27:7; metaphorically "desire"), "soul" (Jer. 4:31; 2 Sam. 5:8; sometimes implying "feeling"), or "life" (Prov. 7:23; Lev. 24:17-18), refers to the whole person as

27. See, e.g., Joel B. Green, "'Bodies — That Is, Human Lives': A Re-Examination of Human Nature in the Bible," in *Whatever Happened to the Soul? Scientific and Theological Portraits of Human Nature,* ed. Warren S. Brown, et al. (Minneapolis: Fortress, 1998), 149-73. The general consensus is that the biblical view of the human person is holistic, not dichotomistic as in Greek and some Hindu thought. This is not a simplistic opposition between Hebrew "monism" and Greek "dualism," but a recognition that there is in fact a difference. Cf. Colin Gunton, "Trinity, Ontology and Anthropology," in *Persons: Divine and Human,* ed. C. Schwöbel and C. Gunton (Edinburgh: T&T Clark, 1991), 47-61.

28. For what follows see chaps. 2-5 of Wolff's *Anthropology of the Old Testament,* trans. Margaret Kohl (Philadelphia: Fortress, 1974), 10-58.

175

she or he is depicted as a living, desiring person.[29] *Basar,* usually translated "flesh," typically refers to the whole person under the aspect of embodiedness. However, it can also apply to the person in kinship relation (Gen. 37:27), and to the overall weakness of the person in dependence on God (Job 34:14-15). The term *leb* ("heart") is a key term for describing the human self.[30] It typically refers to the center or unity of the self (Ps. 27:8; Prov. 3:5). Often *leb* points to the intellectual (Prov. 15:14; 1 Sam. 25:37; Job 12:3) or ethical operation of the self (Exod. 35:21; Deut. 10:16; Job 34:10; Prov. 24:30, 32; 1 Kgs. 11:3, 4) in relation to the community or to God.[31] The term *ruach* depicts a person as "empowered." This is most often translated as "breath" or "spirit" when applied to humans, whether they are willing (Ezra 1:5; Ps. 51:10), feeling (Jgs. 8:3; Job 15:13), or simply existing in relation to God (Isa. 42:5).[32] Here again the whole person is empowered by the Spirit that gives life and orients persons toward worshipfully recognizing their dependence on God.

The same holism is evident in the New Testament, and scholars are increasingly interpreting terms such as "spirit," "soul," "heart," and even "body" as referring to the whole person under a particular aspect of his or her being in relation. Jesus does not develop an explicit anthropology, but he addresses whole persons and calls them to a new relation to God that transforms all of their embodied conscious life. The extent to which Paul's anthropology was shaped by both Greek and Hebrew understandings of humanity has been the subject of much debate in New Testament scholarship. It is often observed that Paul uses the terms "spirit" *(pneuma)* and "soul" *(psychē)* in a way that is closer to the

29. Animals too have "souls" (Gen. 2:19), but the human *nephesh* is qualitatively different. It is given directly by God through the divine breath (Gen. 2:7), indicating a special relation to God.

30. According to Wolff, this is "the most important word in the vocabulary of Old Testament anthropology" (*Anthropology,* 40). Kallistos Ware has helpfully traced this important integrating symbol in the early Greek fathers: "The Soul in Greek Christianity," in *From Soul to Self,* ed. Crabbe, 56-59.

31. Animals also have hearts (Job 41:24; 2 Sam 17:10; Hos. 7:11), and we find 26 references to the "heart" of God (e.g., 1 Sam. 2:35; Job 7:17; Hos. 11:8-9).

32. When applied to God, *ruach* refers to the empowering vitality of God's Spirit that enlivens human breath (spirit). See Wolff, *Anthropology,* 34-35, with reference to Job 34:14-15; Ps. 104:29-30; Exod. 15:8. However, having *ruach* does not determine the difference between the human and the nonhuman; animals too have "spirit" (Eccl. 3:18-21).

Hebraic model.[33] Like the Hebrew term *ruach,* for Paul *pneuma* describes the vital principle that animates the person (empowering what we call feeling, thinking, and willing), but in a way that emphasizes human dependence on God for life. In the Gospel of John, *pneuma* describes the whole person as he or she is called to honor and worship God "in spirit" (4:23-24).

Udo Schnelle demonstrates how the terms *kardia, psychē, nous,* and *ho esō anthrōpos* also all refer to the center of the whole human self. "As the 'innermost' organ the heart [*kardia*] defines the whole person."[34] The person in relation to Christ "believes" in her or his heart (2 Cor. 3:14-16), and the Spirit of the Son is sent into her or his heart (Gal. 4:6). Feelings and emotions are also ascribed to the heart (2 Cor. 2:4; 7:3). The term *psychē* also refers to the life of the person in its entirety (Rom. 2:9; 13:1). The Pauline blessing of 1 Thess. 5:23 ("may your spirit and soul and body . . .") is not a trichotomous Hellenistic anthropology, but a way of "emphasizing that the sanctifying work of God concerns the whole person."[35] Paul exhorts the Romans to be transformed "by the renewing of your minds" (12:2), but the *nous* that is being renewed registers the activity of the whole person as he or she discerns God's call. Although Paul adopts the distinction between the "outer person" *(exō anthrōpos)* and the "inner person" *(esō anthrōpos)* from Greek philosophy, his appropriation does not necessitate substance dualism but simply offers a consideration of "the one existence of believers from different perspectives."[36]

Much of the debate about dualism in New Testament scholarship is over the meaning of the term *sōma* (body). Since the mid-twentieth century, most scholars have acknowledged Rudolf Bultmann's general point that Paul uses this term in a way that represents the whole person as embodied: "*Man, his person as a whole,* can be denoted by *soma. . . . Man is called soma in respect to his being able to make himself the object of his own action or to experience himself as the subject to whom something hap-*

33. James D. G. Dunn, *The Theology of Paul the Apostle* (Grand Rapids: Eerdmans, 1998), 76. See also the treatment in N. T. Wright, *The New Testament and the People of God* (Minneapolis: Fortress, 1992), 252-56.

34. Udo Schnelle, *The Human Condition: Anthropology in the Teachings of Jesus, Paul, and John,* trans. O. C. Dean Jr. (Minneapolis: Fortress, 1996), 103.

35. Ibid., 104.

36. Ibid., 107.

pens."[37] In his analysis of the term *sōma* as used throughout I Corinthians, E. Earle Ellis argues that "it is because Paul regards the body as the person and the person as the physical body that he insists on the resurrection of the body, placing it at the parousia of Christ in which personal redemption is coupled to and is a part of the redemption-by-transfiguration of the whole physical cosmos."[38] This is true for other New Testament texts as well (e.g., Rom 8:19-23). Anthony Thiselton argues that the author of Hebrews does not think of *sōma* as one component of human nature over against the soul, but uses the term for an explicit theological purpose: to refer to the relationality of the whole person as called into a temporal movement toward salvation as he or she relates to others and God.[39]

Although Paul makes the distinction (paradigmatically in Rom. 8) between living according to the "flesh" *(sarx)* and according to the "spirit" *(pneuma),* this language does not necessarily imply substance dualism. The "spiritual" person is one whose whole self is oriented to the Spirit; the "fleshly" person is one whose whole self is oriented toward fulfilling the passion of worldly desire (cf. Rom. 8:16; 1 Cor. 2:10-11; 6:17). Overall, then, Scripture depicts the human person as a dynamic unity, which it considers from various perspectives using terms such as "soul," "body," "flesh," and "mind." Distinguishing these dimensions of human relationality is important, but the Bible is concerned with the salvation of the whole person in community in relation to God.

---

37. Rudolf Bultmann, *Theology of the New Testament,* trans. Kendrick Grobel, 2 vols. (New York: Scribner's, 1951-55), 1:195. Cf. J. A. T. Robinson, *The Body: A Study in Pauline Theology,* Studies in Biblical Theology 1/5 (London: SCM, 1952). Robert Gundry is critical of Bultmann and others in his *Sōma in Biblical Theology,* Society for New Testament Studies Monograph Series 29 (Cambridge: Cambridge University Press, 1976), arguing for an "anthropological duality" that avoids dualism. Gundry recognizes that while *sōma* does not *mean* "whole person," it may *represent* the whole person (47, 80). For a discussion of these and other scholars on this topic, see Dunn, *Theology of Paul,* 56, 61.

38. Ellis, *Christ and the Future in New Testament History* (Leiden: Brill, 2000), 177.

39. Thiselton, "Human Being, Relationality and Time in Hebrews, I Corinthians and the Western Tradition," *Ex Auditu* 13 (1997): 76-95 at 77.

Discoveries in Neurobiology

One of the major factors in the rapid decline of the use of both substance dualism and faculty psychology as plausible explanatory models has been scientific research in the field of neurobiology. An accidental dynamite explosion that shot a four-foot iron rod through the skull of a railroad worker named Phineas Gage in 1848 has become a symbolic turning point in the demise of ancient and early modern anthropological models and in the rise of neuroscience. Amazingly, Gage's physical health was not seriously damaged by the projectile, but his personality was significantly altered. This phenomenon led to detailed studies about what parts of the brain affect what kinds of attitudes and cognitive activities.[40] The rise and relatively rapid debunking of phrenology in the nineteenth century was the dying gasp of "faculty" psychology.[41] In the twentieth century more technologically advanced ways of studying the brain developed and with these also came more easily verifiable scientific hypotheses. The activities once ascribed to the "soul" and its "faculties" are now accounted for by consciousness as an emergence of patterns of neuronal functioning in the human brain, which in turn are connected to chemical interactions throughout the body. These give rise to "feeling," which cannot be separated from "thinking." Conversely, how we think affects how we feel and act. The work of neurologist Antonio Damasio provides a clear statement and explanation of this research and its implications.[42]

In the light of contemporary neuroscience a hard dichotomy between soul and body and a classification of separate faculties of the soul are no longer tenable.[43] Nancey Murphy shows how these findings

40. It was commonly held in ancient times that our "thoughts" are connected to our hearts (which we feel pumping within us) and not to the gray stuff in our skulls (which was considered a coolant of some kind).

41. Phrenology is the study of bumps or curves on the skull and their alleged relation to what is going on in the mind. See Richard L. Gregory, "Phrenology," in *The Oxford Companion to the Mind*, ed. Gregory (Oxford: Oxford University Press, 1987), 618.

42. See, e.g., his *Descartes' Error: Emotion, Reason, and the Human Brain* (New York: Avon, 1994); and *The Feeling of What Happens: Body and Emotion in the Making of Consciousness* (New York: Harcourt and Brace, 1999).

43. On the basis of her work on the human brain using various imaging techniques, Susan Greenfield questions the idea of the "soul" having a seat within the brain. She of-

affect theological anthropology, using Thomas Aquinas as her example. What he called the faculties of the soul can now be explained through neuroscience. The operations he ascribed to the passive intellect are located (through MRI and PET scans) in the medial temporal lobe of the brain. The operations of the active intellect, which involve the use of language, derive from the semantic capacities that are located in a complex of regions in the brain, including Wernicke's area and Broca's area.[44] Even in the most intense religious experience of contemplatives, imaging techniques have shown that during deep meditation very particular patterns of neural functioning are operative.[45]

What were once called the "faculties" of the soul are now described as registers of the behavior of the whole person. Today personality as a whole is seen as the basis for understanding the parts. The whole person registers itself in particular behaviors. This more psychodynamic approach shapes much of contemporary psychology. These sciences still allow for a weak sense of duality, i.e., a distinction between biological and mental events, but not for dual*ism,* in the sense of two separate substances. The whole embodied person is involved in knowing, but we may still recognize a plurality of dynamic patterns as registers of the whole. Instead of a discrete power of an immaterial soul, human knowing is understood as an emergent and complex differentiated relational unity: for example, psychologists speak of "multiple intelligences" and paleobiologists of "cognitive fluidity."[46] The demise of substance dualism and faculty psychology in theology, however, has not been simply a reaction to current science. The problems with these models were already evident when theologians were formulating doctrine in dialogue

fers the suggestion that "consciousness is spatially multiple, yet effectively single at any one time. It is an emergent property of non-specialized groups of neurons (brain cells) that are continuously variable with respect to an epicentre" ("Soul, Brain and Mind," in *From Soul to Self,* ed. Crabbe, 112).

44. Murphy, "Darwin, Social Theory, and the Sociology of Scientific Knowledge," *Zygon* 34, no. 4 (1999): 596. See also the constructive proposals of James B. Ashbrook and Carol Rausch Albright, *The Humanizing Brain* (Cleveland: Pilgrim, 1997).

45. See Eugene d'Aquili and Andrew Newberg, *The Mystical Mind: Probing the Biology of Religious Experience* (Minneapolis: Fortress, 1999); idem, "The Neuropsychological Basis of Religions, or Why God Won't Go Away," *Zygon* 33, no. 2 (1998): 187-202.

46. Cf., respectively, Howard Gardner, *Frames of Mind* (New York: Basic Books, 1985); Steven Mithen, *The Prehistory of the Mind: The Cognitive Origins of Art, Religion and Science* (London: Thames & Hudson, 1996).

with fourth-century science. More recent objections have arisen not only from renewed analysis of the biblical texts (above), but also from philosophical analysis of the radically relational nature of human knowing.

Philosophical Reflection

Today most philosophers no longer describe human nature with the categories of substance ontology, as in ancient philosophy, nor in terms of autonomous subjectivity, as in early modern philosophy. In both of these models, the "self" is dualistically separated from its "knowing." The human subject is defined prior to and over against the objects of its knowledge. In late modernity, however, we find a new emphasis on the self as always and already immersed in the dynamic processes of knowing and being known in community.[47] The hard dichotomy between subject and object is rejected. The self and its knowing-in-relation are mutually implicated. To conclude from this, as some radical deconstructionists do, that no substantial "self" exists at all follows only if we completely divorce relation from substance. If being is essentially relational, however, we may still speak of the "self" as substantial and real — precisely because of the intensity of its self-relationality. As Calvin Schrag points out, the rejection of old anthropological models does not mean a jettisoning of every sense of self. One may argue instead for "a praxis-oriented self, defined by its communicative practices, oriented toward an understanding of itself in its discourse, its action, its being with others, and its experience of transcendence."[48]

Much of the contemporary discussion about human nature in the philosophy of mind orbits around the problem of "consciousness." More and more philosophers and scientists are acknowledging that consciousness is an essential aspect of the universe, which must be in-

---

47. It is important to note that this was not wholly new; already in ancient Greece some philosophers emphasized the becoming of human knowing, the role of reflexivity, and (to speak anachronistically) the "historicity" of the self. Hierocles spoke of "the self's attachment to self," Plutarch of "the self weaving a biography," and Epictetus of "the self moulding an inviolable self." For analysis, see Richard Sorabji, "Soul and Self in Ancient Philosophy," in Crabbe, ed., *From Soul to Self*, 8-32.

48. Schrag, *The Self after Postmodernity* (New Haven: Yale University Press, 1997), 9.

cluded in any theory.[49] At the same time, we find a growing consensus that human consciousness (or mind) cannot be explained either by completely reducing it to brain functions (monism)[50] or by separating it substantially from the body (dualism). The former cannot account for subjectivity, and the latter cannot elucidate the interaction between body and mind. An increasing number of "naturalists," who by definition eschew dualism, maintain the failure of reductionism.[51] On the other side, more and more dualists are admitting the insolubility of the problems on their end, appealing either to religious mystery or to inherent epistemic limitations.[52] Many of the current constructive

49. It appears that consciousness (as an essential feature of human experience) is built into the quantum reality of the universe; see Menas Kafatos and Robert Nadeau, *The Conscious Universe: Part and Whole in Modern Physical Theory* (New York: Springer, 1990).

50. Reductionism has been keenly criticized by Mary Midgley, who notes that this view usually brings with it determinism and, she argues, fatalism. Such a view is due to the fact that reductionists "are still thinking of consciousness as a separate, supernatural entity . . . rather than as a normal activity, an emergent capacity acquired by social creatures during the regular course of evolution" ("Consciousness, Fatalism and Science," in *The Human Person in Science and Theology*, ed. N. H. Gregersen, et al. [Edinburgh: T&T Clark, 2000], 27).

51. David J. Chalmers argues that consciousness simply cannot be explained by current physics, so we must seek to discover new fundamental laws that include the experience of self-consciousness (*The Conscious Mind: In Search of a Fundamental Theory* [New York: Oxford University Press, 1996]. Joseph Levine is less optimistic, suggesting that we are far from identifying the conceptual resources for resolving the antinomy of consciousness. As a materialist, he argues that mind must be reducible to physical phenomena, but believes that the explanatory gap between brain functions and conscious experience cannot be crossed. See his *Purple Haze: The Puzzle of Consciousness* (New York: Oxford University Press, 2001). Nicholas Humphrey claims that we will never explain consciousness because of what he calls "biological Gödel sentences," i.e., self-referential systems will always have true statements that cannot be proven from the bottom up, from analysis of lower systems (*A History of the Mind: Evolution and the Birth of Consciousness* [New York: Simon and Schuster, 1992], 208). Well-known reductionists include Richard Dawkins, E. O. Wilson, Daniel Dennett, Patricia Churchland, and Francis Crick. But this is not the dominant group. For a survey of the current issues in the field of the philosophy of the mind, see John Heil, *Philosophy of Mind: A Contemporary Introduction* (London: Routledge, 1998).

52. David Ray Griffin provides a summary account of these admissions in *Religion and Scientific Naturalism: Overcoming the Conflicts* (Albany: SUNY Press, 2000), chap. 6.

53. David Ray Griffin, *Unsnarling the World-Knot: Consciousness, Freedom, and the Mind-Body Problem* (Berkeley: University of California Press, 1998).

proposals for dealing with the traditional brain/mind problem involve more rigorous reflection on the dynamic relationality itself rather than trying to conceptualize the combination of two substances. For example, David Ray Griffin speaks not of mental and physical substances but of rudimentary spatiotemporal sentient units as events.[53] These developments have emerged partly in response to centuries of failed attempts to make philosophical sense of the idea of an immaterial substance being somehow linked to and impacting a material substance.

Another philosophical problem with faculty psychology is that it is hard to avoid determinism once one asks which "faculty" controls the others. If none of the faculties has at least marginal control, then human behavior *ex hypothesi* would either be impossible or inexplicable. Does the intellect first move the will or vice versa? Thomas Aquinas was aware of the problem of an infinite regress, but his attempts to halt it make him susceptible to the charge of determinism. Michael Murray explains the problem: "for Aquinas, the will, like any other faculty, must have its powers reduced from potency to act by some entity distinct from itself, since there can be no such thing as a created self-moving power. But if this is the case, must not Aquinas admit that the will must be moved, even in this 'first instance,' by something external to it?"[54] Whatever this external something is, it would determine the knowing or acting, making it difficult to pin responsibility on the soul. Thomas's dependence on faculty psychology led to this form of the dilemma. Neo-Thomists like Bernard Lonergan for the most part abandoned the categories of the will and intellect, preferring the intentionality analysis of phenomenology.[55] The important point here is that under the influence of the turn to relationality, and particularly due to contributions from liberation and feminist thought, human knowing is no longer understood as wholly self-determined nor as undetermined, but rather as condi-

54. Murray, "Intellect, Will, and Freedom," 30-31.
55. Cf. Lonergan, *Method in Theology* (Toronto: University of Toronto Press, 1971). In his monumental exposition of the dynamics of human knowing in *Insight: A Study of Human Understanding* (New York: Harper & Row, 1978), Lonergan avoids these categories for nearly 700 pages; they appear on pp. 698ff. but are not central to his analysis. Anthony Kelly takes Lonergan's lead but more explicitly moves beyond Aristotelian faculty psychology; cf. *The Trinity of Love* (Wilmington, Del.: Glazier, 1989), 150-51, 172.

tioned and mediated by the embodied communal relations of the knower.[56]

Theologians who still cling to anthropological dualism appear to be motivated primarily by the desire to maintain belief in the survival of the person after death.[57] For example, John Cooper argues that the most obvious cost of abandoning traditional dualistic anthropology is that "the beliefs virtually all ordinary Christians have about the afterlife must also be jettisoned. If souls are not the sort of thing which can be broken loose from bodies, then we do not actually exist between death and resurrection, either with Christ or somewhere else, either consciously or unconsciously."[58] Cooper admits that Scripture offers a holistic model of the human person but insists, based primarily on his reading of Paul's anticipation of being "with Christ" after bodily death (Phil. 1:20-23), that we must at least argue for a holistic dualism.[59] This kind of desperate defense of dualism presupposes that the latter is the only option besides monism; notice that both answers assume that the right question is: How many substances constitute an individual human being? Instead of accepting this question, which is rooted in the substance metaphysics discussed in chapter one, perhaps we may find some other way of imagining our being "with Christ" that does not demand substance dualism.

56. See, e.g., James McClendon's treatment of embodiment in black American Christianity, *Ethics: Systematic Theology*, vol. 1 (Nashville: Abingdon, 1986); and Mary Field Belenky, et al., *Women's Ways of Knowing: The Development of Self, Voice, and Mind* (New York: Basic Books, 1986).

57. See, e.g., Gary Habermas and J. P. Moreland, *Beyond Death: Exploring the Evidence for Immortality* (Wheaton, Ill.: Crossway, 1998), 35. This drive is so powerful that it can lead to a facile dismissal of science. See J. P. Moreland and Scott B. Rae, *Body & Soul: Human Nature and the Crisis in Ethics* (Downers Grove, Ill.: InterVarsity Press, 2000), where the authors argue that "science provides little evidence at all for settling the issue" (170).

58. *Body, Soul, and Life Everlasting: Biblical Anthropology and the Monism-Dualism Debate*, updated ed. (Grand Rapids: Eerdmans, 2000), 3. It turns out that the only other cost he mentions is "the loss of another plank in the platform of traditional Christian belief, pried loose and tossed into the shredder of modern scholarship."

59. Cooper, *Body, Soul, and Life Everlasting*, 153. A more moderate account is offered by Robert K. Jewett, *Who We Are: Our Dignity as Human — A Neo-Evangelical Theology* (Grand Rapids: Eerdmans, 1996), 35-46. Nevertheless, Jewett still defends both anthropological (body/soul) and cosmological (material/immaterial) dualism.

We find a similar resistance among some theologians to reforming "faculty" psychological constructs in theological anthropology. They appear to be unaware of the scientific and philosophical reflection that had led to the obsolescence of this model already in the nineteenth century. Dewey Hoitenga Jr. criticizes the inconsistencies in Calvin's teaching on the mutual relationship between will and intellect, and attempts to correct it with the help of so-called Reformed epistemology.[60] The corrective, however, still presupposes the early modern idea of the "will" as a faculty of the soul. Rejecting what he calls a modern functionalist prejudice, Hoitenga prefers the "commonsense" view "that for every noetic or volitional function of a human being there is a faculty of the soul that possesses that function, by which it produces the noetic or volitional state in question, just as for every bodily function there is a gland, organ, or structure of some kind that functions to produce it — for example, the heart, which circulates the blood."[61] It should be noted, first, that this view emerged only in Western cultures with male-oriented conceptions of the *power* of the soul. This is not the "commonsense" view of human knowing in most cultures. Second, and more importantly, in the late sixteenth and early seventeenth centuries when these anthropological terms became fossilized in Protestant theology, it was also "common sense" to think that the sun revolved around the earth. Today, not only in cosmology but also in psychology, we know better. Faculty psychology is in part responsible for much of the befuddlement that has plagued many formulations of the doctrines of salvation and human freedom,[62] and as we will see in the next two chapters it has also led to difficulties in the doctrines of sin and the image of God.

After the turn to relationality in philosophy and science, theology has a new opportunity to retrieve the holistic anthropology of the biblical tradition. Most theologians, scientists, and philosophers engaged in the burgeoning dialogue between theology and science have moved beyond substance metaphysics. Several proposals in this literature attempt to conserve the intuition of life after bodily death without the

60. *John Calvin and the Will: A Critique and Corrective* (Grand Rapids: Baker, 1997).
61. Ibid., 16.
62. Paul R. Hinlicky hints at this in "Theological Anthropology: Toward Integrating *Theosis* and Justification by Faith," *Journal of Ecumenical Studies* 34, no. 1 (1997): 38-73.

trappings of outmoded scientific anthropology.[63] After all, the biblical material does not demand the existence of an immortal soul separate from a mortal body. On the contrary, in 2 Corinthians 5:4 Paul announces that his desire is "not to be unclothed but to be further clothed, so that what is mortal may be swallowed up by life." In 1 Corinthians 15:53 he expresses his anticipation that the perishable body will "put on" imperishability. Here we have the idea of a further intensification and integration of our creaturely life in relation to God. The biblical emphasis is on the resurrection of the whole person, who is called into a community that will share in the glory of the crucified and resurrected Christ. If we understand Philippians 1:23 in light of the rest of the biblical witness, we can see that it does not demand substance dualism but simply expresses the anticipation of being "with Christ" after the structural dissolution of the biological organism we call a "body." The Pauline theme of being "with Christ" is taken up again in Colossians, where we hear that "you *have been* raised with Christ" (3:1) and that "you have died, and your life *is* hid with Christ in God" (3:3). The early believers were *already* with Christ although they still anticipated a further eschatological intensification of that "withness" when they will appear with him in glory (3:4).

The longing for eternal life is indeed connected to human knowing, but the Christian intuition that we will know and be known by God in eternity does not require the idea that we will be "unclothed" and split into different substances. The Johannine literature commonly links eternal life to knowing God. "And this is eternal life, that they know you, the only true God, and Jesus Christ whom you have sent" (John 17:3). In his first epistle, John admits that "what we will be has not yet been revealed," although we shall be "like him" (1 John 3:2). But this is not a blind wishing for eternal life that is only in the future, for through the Spirit we already abide "in him" and he "in us." For Christians, the epistemic anxiety that plagues our longing for truth is

---

63. See, e.g., Arthur Peacocke, *Paths from Science toward God* (New York: Oxford University Press, 2001); Keith Ward, *Religion and Human Nature* (New York: Oxford University Press, 1998); Ted Peters, "Resurrection of the Very Embodied Soul," in *The Neurosciences and the Person: Scientific Perspectives on Divine Action,* ed. R. J. Russell et al. (Berkeley: Center for Theology and the Natural Sciences, 1999), 305-26; and Alan Padgett, "The Body in Resurrection: Science and Scripture on the 'Spiritual Body' (I Cor 15:35-38)," *Word & World* 22, no. 2 (Spring 2002): 155-63.

relieved by our being "in him who is true, in his Son Jesus Christ" (1 John 5:20). This is possible by the Spirit who "is the truth" (5:6). The one who "has the Son has life" (5:12) by which we "know him who is true. . . . He is the true God and eternal life" (5:20). This is not merely a cognitive assent, but a knowing as we are known. Paul rejoices that the Galatians "have come to know God," but immediately clarifies himself: "or rather to be known by God" (4:9). "Knowledge puffs up," Paul observes, but "anyone who loves God is known by him" (1 Cor. 8:3). Moreover, our knowing of God is not static or "finished" — Paul recognizes that now he knows "in part" but he anticipates knowing fully, "even as I have been fully known" (1 Cor. 13:12).

Rather than appealing at the end of an argument to the mystery of the Infinite God in order to fill a conceptual gap in our knowledge, theological anthropology should demonstrate the appeal of the mysterious Infinity of the trinitarian God as an explanation of the existential gap in our knowing. This mystery is not merely one of the many "objects" of our reason, an "idea" grasped by the faculty of the intellect. It is the presence of the Infinite God who grasps us and knows us more deeply than we know ourselves. This being-known is the mystery made known in the intimate mutual knowing of the Father and the Son (Matt. 11:27), a communion into which we have access by the power of the Spirit (Eph. 2:18). Here we have the opportunity to move beyond an emphasis on the "rational" nature of the "individual" in our theological discussions of human nature. Such emphases have led us to downplay the importance of our physicality and sociality. Late modern philosophical reflection has challenged us to account for the embodied and communal nature of human knowing. Facing the ambiguity of our knowing as persons is an important step in moving beyond the early modernist demand for certitude, and recognizing the illuminative power of the idea of the truly Infinite God in whom we live and move and have our knowing.

Our task is to retrieve the resources of the biblical tradition as we articulate the Christian claim that the mystery of God made known in Christ answers the human longing to know and be known in intimate communion. The revival of trinitarian doctrine in the last few decades can help us forge a theology of human knowing that focuses on our participation in the Son's knowledge of the Father by the power of the Spirit. The hard distinction between substance and accidents that

187

flourished in the patristic and early modern periods led to an inner/outer anthropological dichotomy and a spirit/matter cosmological dichotomy. Under these constraints theologians were pressured to accept soul/body dualism in order to salvage the Christian idea of salvation after death. However, if the origin, condition, and goal of salvation is essentially relational (the eternal knowing and being-known of the Father, Son, and Holy Spirit), and if the eternal life into which humans are called involves an intensification of creaturely sharing in this knowledge, then we ought not allow Christian soteriology to be constrained by the substance-oriented categories of Aristotelian or Cartesian philosophy. Christians are finding their personal identity (are being saved) as they know themselves and others in relation to God — as they are drawn into a more intense sharing *(koinōnia)* in the eternal communal knowing and being known that is the divine life.[64]

Our personal response to this presence affects not only our knowing, but also our acting and being — all of which are shaped by our sinning against God and neighbors and our imaging of God vis-à-vis our neighbors. We turn now to explore the possibilities for reforming these doctrines in late modernity.

64. See chapter four above. I have spelled out the idea of intensification and its soteriological implications in more detail in *The Faces of Forgiveness,* chap. 5.

Relationality and the Doctrine of Sin

In addition to examining human knowing, theological anthropology also has the task of understanding and explaining human *acting*. My purpose in what follows is to pursue a theology of human acting, which once again requires a critical appropriation of the biblical tradition and engagement with contemporary culture. This chapter treats the same issues that are usually explored under the heading "the doctrine of sin," but I am explicitly trying to shift the focus to the broader question of the dynamics of human agency. In Protestant theology the doctrine of sin has sometimes taken on a life of its own, swelling into an isolated hamartiology that dominates other doctrines.[1] Too often it is abstracted from Christology and soteriology, which are then driven by it. It may well be that some of the formulations of the doctrine no longer serve to uphold the key Christian intuition that human agency is wholly dependent on divine grace for a right relation to goodness. Perhaps the best way to conserve the tradition will be to liberate its illuminative power in dialogue with late modern culture. This will

---

1. For example, Augustus Strong's treatment of the doctrine of sin takes three times more space that his treatment of the Trinity and one and one-half times more space than his treatment of "Soteriology, or the Doctrine of Salvation through the Work of Christ and of the Holy Spirit." Cf. his *Systematic Theology,* 3 vols. (Philadelphia: Judson, 1907). Even G. C. Berkouwer's volume on *Sin,* trans. Philip C. Holtrop (Grand Rapids: Eerdmans, 1971), is noticeably thicker than any of the other volumes in his *Studies in Dogmatics,* including *The Person of Christ* and *Faith and Justification.* I am not suggesting that understanding "sin" is not important, but merely that we may well wonder whether our focus on it is in part due to ways of formulating the question that are intrinsically problematic.

mean accepting the task of reforming theological anthropology after the turn to relationality in philosophy and science.

Sinning must be understood in the context of its relation to the general human longing for goodness. In both the Hebrew Bible and the New Testament, the problem of human sinning is inherently linked to its resolution in God's provision of salvation. A passion for righteousness characterized the Israelite religion, and the Torah was the guide to upright living. In the New Testament, Jesus engages and interprets the Jewish law, proclaiming that it is fulfilled in the commandments to love God and neighbor. Paul interacts with the ethical dialogue of his culture, especially Stoic philosophy,[2] but claims that the good life is possible only by sharing in the righteousness of Christ and the love of the Spirit. In each case the problem of human evil is linked with an idea of the good. Even nontheological anthropological theories try to explain why humans act in ways that are self-alienating and other-abusing rather than in ways that promote love and goodness.[3] Such nontheological "hamartiologies" often produce a nontheological "soteriology," which may involve better intellectual training, therapy, a social contract, or the revolution of the proletariat. Specific questions about which things a particular moral agent should desire, or about how to determine the goodness of things, are dependent on a prior and more basic question: What is the ultimate origin, condition, and goal of human agency?

Human acting, like human knowing, reflects both a continuity and

---

2. For the similarities and differences see Troels Engberg-Pedersen, *Paul and the Stoics* (Louisville: Westminster John Knox, 2000).

3. We may point, for example, to psychological explanations of human misery as rooted in the suppression of the intellect (Spinoza) or the repression of sexuality (Freud) and to sociological explanations of cultural agony as having originated in prehistoric times when happy naked savages piled up more wheat than necessary (Rousseau), leading to a primal accumulation (Marx) that led to the unequal distribution of capital. More recently biologists like Richard Dawkins and E. O. Wilson have argued that human acting may be explained as nothing more than the functioning of "selfish" genes trying to survive. This reductionistic approach has difficulty explaining not only the indefatigable human drive for transcendence, but also the emergence of altruistic behavior (however rare) that does not help genes survive. For theological responses to biological reductionism, see Philip Hefner, *The Human Factor: Evolution, Culture, and Religion* (Minneapolis: Fortress, 1993); and Holmes Rolston III, *Genes, Genesis and God* (Cambridge: Cambridge University Press, 1999).

a discontinuity with other creatures. Other animals desire what is good in the sense that they act in ways that attempt to secure their survival. The intensity of human desire, however, leads to a self-related agency unparalleled among the other animals. If humans have sometimes been called "moral" animals, this does not mean that they are naturally good, but that their identity as agents is characterized by an ambiguous orientation toward desiring and doing what is right. To be a person is to long for goodness, to desire to secure one's relation to objects that are loved. Here we find a nexus of interrelated concepts: we act intentionally because we love objects that we judge to be in some sense good. Desire for a particular good leads us to act. Our intentional activity moves us toward a perceived good, an object of desire. The emerging agent is embedded in a dynamic trajectory in which one finds oneself loving and longing to be loved. What I will call "ethical anxiety" emerges as a result of this ambiguous relation to goodness and the objects of love.[4]

In some streams of Western theology, questions about human agency have been formulated in the following ways: Is the substance of human nature tainted with sin? Is an individual guilty for having been born with a sinful nature or is one responsible only for those actual sins that are the result of one's intellectual or volitional powers? These hamartiological questions presuppose the substance metaphysics and faculty psychology that we examined in chapter eight, and they are directly related to the problems in the doctrine of the image of God that we will identify in chapter ten. To understand the rationale behind these questions it is necessary to trace their historical development from Augustine, whose influence on Western theology can hardly be overestimated. After this brief summary, the second part of this chapter examines the challenges (and opportunities) that have been opened up by the theological (re)turn to relationality.

The Western Theory of Inherited Sin

Before we explore the factors that led to the development of this formulation and trace its legacy, it is important to recognize that we are deal-

---

4. Cf. my book (with Steven Sandage) *The Faces of Forgiveness: Searching for Wholeness and Salvation* (Grand Rapids: Baker Academic, 2003), chap. 5.

ing with a *theory* about *inherited* sin that is *Western*. First, the idea that each individual is born into the race with guilt already accruing to one's person is not found in either Judaism[5] or the Eastern church.[6] This suggests that the implication of such a theory from biblical texts is not automatic or necessary. Second, Augustine's doctrinal proposal was, like the work of other creative theologians, a theoretical model to synthesize the biblical data and his own empirical experience of the failure of human agency. He engaged particular interlocutors who came with their own explicit philosophical and scientific concerns. As we will see, Augustine himself was open to the ongoing process of reconstructing doctrine in light of such concerns. Third, we must distinguish between "inherited" and "original" sin. Much of the debate is confused by mistaking these as synonyms. Original sin can be taken broadly to refer to the claim that all persons find themselves already and always bound

---

5. For the lack of such a doctrine see, e.g., Sybil Sheridan, "Judaism" in *Human Nature and Destiny*, ed. J. Holm (London: Pinter, 1994), 125-26; and Anthony J. Tambasco, *A Theology of Atonement and Paul's Vision of Christianity* (Collegeville, Minn.: Liturgical Press, 1991), 39ff. Genesis itself does not emphasize a relation of causality between the acts of Adam and Eve and their descendants. Later in the Jewish tradition, a more explicit connection was made ("O Adam. . . . For though it was you who sinned, the fall was not yours alone but ours also who are your descendants," 4 Ezra 7:118), but it does not appear that the first parents cause later sins or pass on guilt ("Adam is, therefore, not the cause, save only of his own soul, but each one of us has been the Adam of his own soul," 2 Bar. 54:15-19). In the Christian canon of the Old Testament, Adam and Eve are not mentioned outside Genesis.

6. John Meyendorff demonstrates that the Eastern church did not follow the Augustinian view of inherited sin (*Byzantine Theology: Historical Trends and Doctrinal Themes* [New York: Fordham University Press, 1974], 145). In a three-part series of articles, David Weaver offers an exhaustive treatment of this issue in Eastern Orthodox theology. He concludes that it is inaccurate to apply the term *originale peccatum* to the Greek-speaking theologians, since it represents a Western concept. "The most critical point of departure is the absence among the Greeks of any notion of inherited culpability — i.e., inherited guilt, which was the central point of the Latin doctrine and which made humanity's inheritance from Adam truly sin, unequivocally a sin of nature, which rendered the individual hateful to God and condemned him to eternal damnation prior to any independent, willful act." For the East, we may have inherited mortality from Adam, but not guilt. Cf. Weaver, "From Paul to Augustine: Romans 5:12 in Early Christian Exegesis," *SVTQ* 27, no. 3 (1983): 187 (part I). For extensive quotes from Greek fathers repudiating the Latin theory, see Weaver, "The Exegesis of Romans 5:12 Among the Greek Fathers and Its Implications for the Doctrine of Original Sin: The 5th-12th Centuries," *SVTQ* 29, no. 2 (1985): 133-59 (part II); 29, no. 3 (1985): 231-57 (part III).

by sin. It is original, radical, and basic to our agential relations. The theory of inherited sin (and guilt), as that which results from the fall of our first parents from paradise, is one attempt to explain this reality.

The Augustinian Synthesis

Augustine did not simply invent the doctrine of inherited sin; he pulled together strands from previous theologians and articulated his intuitions through exegetical and philosophical debate with those whom he saw as endangering the health of the church. Nevertheless, his theory was a creative synthesis, which diverged in several ways from earlier Christian formulations. Most theologians in the first centuries of the church, in line with the New Testament itself, expressed much less interest in Adam than in Jesus Christ. The experience of redemption through the Spirit of the One who raised Jesus from the dead had transformed and gripped their imaginations, so that peripheral issues were left to the side, or subsumed within reflections on their Savior.[7]

The second-century theologian Irenaeus of Lyons focused on the similarities and differences between the first Adam and Eve (who failed to obey God) and the second Adam, that is, Christ, and Mary (who succeeded). Unlike Augustine, however, Irenaeus did not see the world created as "perfect." Humans were created imperfect (unfinished), but "good" because of their orientation toward becoming perfect.[8] The two

7. In this important period, during which Christianity grew so quickly, Henri Rondet, S.J., observes that when the early theologians dealt with sinful humanity, they did "not dream of throwing into special relief the sin of Adam, nor our solidarity with him; still less does one think of commenting on the primitive state of man" (*Original Sin: The Patristic and Theological Background,* trans. Cajetan Finegan, O.P. [New York: Alba House, 1972], 27). The main point of the gospel is the salvation made available through Jesus Christ. Atonement is described without reference to original sin in the *Letter of Barnabas,* and the language of a "fall" is absent from the theology of salvation in the writings of Ignatius of Antioch. In their dialogue with pagan philosophers, the Apologists were more likely to speculate on origins, but it is more common for them to focus on Satan as the source of evil rather than the first parents. In *Dialogue with Trypho* Justin Martyr makes only a few allusions to Adam and Eve; the idea of inherited sin as a doctrine had not yet arisen.

8. See the analysis in Douglas Farrow, "St. Irenaeus of Lyons: The Church and the World," *Pro Ecclesia* 4 (1995): 333-55.

most obvious precursors for the idea of "inherited" sin are Tertullian and Origen, both of whom worried quite a lot about sex. The traducian idea that the soul may inherit unclean substances from its parents through procreation may be found in the former,[9] while the latter tended to interpret the transmission of sin as a defilement that is passed on through "impure" blood.[10] Like the other Cappadocians in the fourth century, Gregory of Nazianzus emphasized Christ and redemption rather than the first sin of the first parents.[11] Several of Augustine's emphases are clearly evident in his teacher Ambrose, who spoke of all humanity as "in Adam" when he was cast out of paradise.[12] Ambrose affirmed the idea of hereditary sin and its being washed away at baptism,[13] but he did not develop a theory of inherited guilt.

Why and how, then, did Augustine develop such a theory? A combination of at least three interrelated factors shaped his formulation: his controversies with the Pelagians, on the one hand, and the Manichees on the other, and a desire to defend his understanding of infant baptism in the face of these challenges.[14] It is not clear how widely established pedobaptism had become in the rest of Christendom, but it was obviously important in Augustine's context. He believed that all baptism is for the remission of sins, but he could not imagine that an infant could have committed any actual sins. Given the fact that the church baptizes infants, something must be remitted. Why does the infant need to be

---

9. Tertullian *Treatise on the Soul*, chap. 40; see ANF 3:220.

10. See, e.g., his *Homilies on Leviticus* 12.4; and *Homilies on Luke* 14.5-6.

11. *Oration* 38.4; NPNF[2] 7:345-46. For discussion of other Cappadocians, see Rondet, *Original Sin*, 100ff.

12. *On the Decease of His Brother Satyrus* 2.6; NPNF[2] 10:175.

13. *On the Mysteries*, chap. 6; NPNF[2] 10:321.

14. These were not the only factors, but an examination of them will suffice to help us understand those aspects of his formulation that were most influential and stand now in most need of reconstruction. For analysis of Augustine's desire to suppress the Donatist schism as a major factor driving his search for a new expression of the doctrine of sin, see Peter Iver Kaufman, "Augustine, Evil and Donatism: Sin and Sanctity Before the Pelagian Controversy," TS 51 (1990): 115-26. Several scholars have described the tension between fighting the Pelagians on the one side and the Gnostics on the other. See, e.g., Robert R. Williams, "Sin and Evil," in *Christian Theology: An Introduction to Its Traditions and Tasks*, ed. Peter C. Hodgson and Robert H. King (Philadelphia: Fortress, 1985), 194-221; Steven J. Duffy, "Our Hearts of Darkness: Original Sin Revisited," TS 49 (1988): 597-622.

washed? Augustine answered: because the substance of its soul has inherited from Adam both the blemish *(vitium)* that had weakened human nature through his rebellion, and the legal penalty *(reatus)* accrued because of his guilt. The weakness is concupiscence (inordinate desire) and the penalty for the guilt is eternal punishment. Both of these are passed on to the infant from the parents. Baptism takes away the penalty but the faulty nature remains (which explains later sinning). Unbaptized infants are implicated by inherited sin as "guilty and as children of wrath, even if they die in infancy," thus condemned to eternal punishment.[15] This hardly seems fair, as Augustine himself realized. Understanding the rationale for his proposal requires a sense of his broader context. He was developing this theory over against two types of opponents. On the one side, he was concerned about the anthropological optimism of the Pelagians, and wanted to insist that humans (including infants) are wholly bad. On the other side, he was worried about the metaphysical pessimism of the Manichees, and wanted to hold on to the goodness of God's creation, including humanity.[16] How could he resolve both problems at the same time?

Pelagius was a British monk and theologian who was passionate about urging fellow Christians toward virtuous living, and most of his writings were aimed at motivating believers to pursue righteousness. He found it difficult, however, to motivate people to do something that they believed was by definition impossible for human beings to do, that is, to avoid sin. Pelagius argued that infants are born like Adam and Eve before the fall, and because of this they could avoid sin *(posse non peccare),* just as the first parents could have. He claimed that we have actual instances of biblical characters (like Enoch) who in fact did avoid sin. Such persons represent the ideal toward which Christians should strive. The human "will," argued Pelagius, is indeterminate or neutral. Humans are not born with a tendency toward virtue or vice; rather, sin is essentially "voluntary" and emerges freely as an act of the will. Therefore, the divinely created human will is capable of choosing goodness.

---

15. Augustine, "On the Merits and Remission of Sins, and on the Baptism of Infants" 2.4; NPNF[1] 5:45.

16. Augustine himself pairs these two heresies and responds to them together in book 2 of "Against Two Letters of the Pelagians," NPNF[1] 5:391-401.

Augustine saw this as a weakening of the Christian intuition that humans are wholly dependent on grace for their relation to goodness. He believed that Pelagius's teaching opened the door to the possibility that righteousness could be achieved by human effort alone through the power of its natural virtue. Such a view could only feed our pride, and so lead more deeply into sin. Augustine insisted that the very substance of all newly born human souls is corrupted by Adam's sin and guilt, which they have inherited. This also corrupts the faculties of each soul, such as intellect and will, which after Adam are now wholly turned away from righteousness. For this reason it is not possible for the infant to avoid sin *(non posse non peccare)*. The human creature and all of its agential functions are essentially sinful and corrupt.

This brings us to the second front of Augustine's theological battle, the fight against the Manichees over the origin of evil. Earlier in his life he had been attracted to the teachings of Mani, whose Gnostic philosophy asserted a radical metaphysical dualism: light and darkness are two cosmological "beings" that are eternally in conflict. Matter is linked to darkness and evil, while Spirit is linked to light and goodness. The Manichean religious struggle was for an escape from the passions of the material world through spiritual knowledge *(gnōsis)*. Mani had taught that Adam and Eve were the creatures of demons, who imprisoned some of the divine light in their bodies. Gnostic salvation is the release of this light from the dense bodies of material darkness. As a Christian, however, Augustine wanted to defend the goodness of God's finite and material creation. To do so, he painted a glowing picture of paradise in the garden of Eden, and the glory and beauty of Adam and Eve.

After turning away from his youthful enthusiasm for Manicheanism and to Christianity, Augustine wanted to uphold the biblical intuition that God created all things and that creation was "good." So he argued that the first parents in their original estate had been created by God as perfect and righteous, unperturbed by the desires of the flesh. In his "literal" interpretation of Genesis,[17] he poured enormous energy

---

17. The term "literal" has to be understood in context, for he did not take it literally quite in the way a contemporary six-day creationist might, but rather "nonallegorically." For example, he did not take the six days literally, for God created instantaneously. See *The Literal Meaning of Genesis* (trans. John H. Taylor, 2 vols., Ancient Christian Writers [New York: Newman, 1982]), book 4, chap. 34; book 5, chap. 23. He did not take God

into depicting their holiness and immortality. If "inherited guilt" was
the missile against the Pelagians, "original righteousness" was aimed at
the Manichees. For Augustine, evil and sin arose not from the nature of
material finitude itself, but from the first misuse of the faculty of the
will (and the intellect). When Adam and Eve listened to the temptation
of the serpent, their rebellion led to the loss of righteousness and immortality. This affected not only their own souls, but the souls of all
their progeny, who were *in* the loins of Adam and so "fell" with him
from paradise.

Following Augustine

Much of the Christian West followed Augustine by repeating his theory
of inherited sin, although with considerable variations on the theme.
Anselm had accepted the idea of the transmission of sin from Adam,
which was linked to his satisfaction theory of atonement.[18] The
christological and soteriological implications of this view, which require an immaculate conception of Mary to avoid the transmission of
sin to Jesus, may easily be traced through the canons of Orange,
Thomas Aquinas and the other medieval theologians, the Council of
Trent, and into the post–Vatican II era.[19] In Roman Catholicism the
doctrine remains official teaching, although it has received increasingly critical scrutiny since the early twentieth century. For example, in
response to genre criticism and scientific objections, Hans Urs von
Balthasar faced squarely the mythical elements in the Genesis text, and
tried to move beyond "hereditary guilt."[20] In the last few decades Catholic scholars who are engaged in the science and religion dialogue have

---

"walking" in the garden literally (book 11, chap. 33). However, he spends five chapters
worrying about how a single spring could water the whole earth (Gen. 2:6), offering several speculative options.

18. See his *Cur Deus Homo*. Cf. Anselm, "The Virginal Conception and Original Sin,"
in *A Scholastic Miscellany: Anselm to Ockham*, ed. and trans. Eugene R. Fairweather (Philadelphia: Westminster, 1956), 197-98.

19. See Rondet, *Original Sin*; G. Vandervelde, *Original Sin: Two Major Trends in Contemporary Roman Catholic Reinterpretation* (Amsterdam: Rodopi, 1975).

20. Hans Urs von Balthasar, *A Theological Anthropology* (New York: Sheed and Ward,
1967).

increasingly called for moving beyond the Augustinian formulation.[21] For my purposes here, however, I limit myself to a brief history of the Protestant tradition.

Like Augustine, John Calvin wanted to emphasize that sin is substantial, real, and radically pervasive. Human nature is not just formally weak; it is materially depraved. As Calvin explains,

> the natural depravity which we bring from our mother's womb, though it bring not forth immediately its own fruits, is yet sin before God, and deserves his vengeance: and this is that sin which they call original. For as Adam at his creation had received for us as well as for himself the gifts of God's favor, so by falling away from the Lord, he in himself corrupted, vitiated, depraved, and ruined our nature; for having been divested of God's likeness, he could not have generated seed but what was like himself.[22]

The well-known Reformed insistence on "total depravity" was oriented against the idea that sin was merely a formal privation, which the Reformed took to be the Catholic position.[23]

For Martin Luther too original sin is more than just a "privation" of all the faculties of the soul; it is "the readiness to do evil, the repugnance for good, the distaste for light and wisdom, the love of error and darkness, the avoidance of and supreme contempt for good works, the unrestrained drive for evil."[24] In the seventeenth century, followers of both Luther and Calvin developed the idea that there is nevertheless a "remnant" or "relic" of goodness that was not affected by the fall of Adam and Eve. I will carefully examine the problems surrounding this development in chapter ten when I deal with human *being* in relation to

21. See, e.g., Denis Edwards, *The God of Evolution: A Trinitarian Theology* (New York: Paulist, 1999).

22. Calvin, *Commentaries on the Epistle of Paul the Apostle to the Romans,* trans. and ed. John Owen (reprint Grand Rapids: Baker, 1984), 200-201. Calvin was working with a better translation than had Augustine, and so did not need to accept the Augustinian idea of all humans as substantially "in Adam."

23. The position against which they focused their attack was that of Duns Scotus, who emphasized the "formal" element of sin, the lack of original righteousness, but resisted identifying the "material" natural faculty of the soul (concupiscence) with sin.

24. Luther, *Lectures on Romans,* ed. and trans. Wilhelm Pauck, LCC 15 (Philadelphia: Westminster, 1961), 167.

the image of God, but my primary concern here is with the Protestant explanation of sinful human *acting.*

For exegetical and scientific reasons I explore below, the idea of Adam's "natural" headship (which presupposes that all humans were physically "in Adam") had by the mid-seventeenth century lost its plausibility. The primary warrant for holding on to the doctrine was that Augustine had proposed it. As we will see below, objections had already been raised in the late patristic period, and not only by Pelagians. Most of the Protestant Scholastics saw the untenability of the idea of "hereditary" sin, but they needed a theory to accomplish the same task, viz., linking our sin to the sin of Adam. The idea of Adam's "federal" headship was one dominant and influential such theory. In the federal theology of seventeenth-century Dutch theologian Johannes Cocceius the human race is related to God on a covenantal basis. Sinners are linked to Adam covenantally (rather than seminally), while believers are bound by the covenant of Christ. Adam and Christ were each sovereignly appointed by divine governance to be the head and therefore representative for each of their families. If the federal head binds himself in covenant, each member of his "family" is also bound.

Federal theology argued that when Adam sinned he legally and lawfully bound all of his descendants to the state of sin, depravity, and guilt. Christians escape this bondage through a new covenant. This view became popular in Geneva through the work of Francis Turretin, and was transmitted to American theology through the writings of Charles Hodge in the nineteenth century. Moving from natural to federal headship, however, required the legal idea of a universal *imputatio* of the sin of Adam to the rest of humanity, and as Barth has noted, it is not clear what the biblical basis is for this idea (*CD,* IV/1, 511). Like the natural headship theory, it still traces the responsibility for sinful agency ultimately to God, who places all humans under a covenantal "head."[25] This left unresolved the problem of evil and the sense of injustice in God's imputing to us the penalty for the legal transgression of someone else.[26]

25. For the importance of the original state of Adam in the debate between "covenant" theologians during this period, see Mark W. Karlberg, "The Original State of Adam: Tensions within Reformed Theology," *EvQ* 87, no. 4 (1987): 291-309.

26. Like a representative government where all citizens are bound to the laws enacted by their legally elected representatives, the federal headship of Adam is a kind of representation. But we did not vote for Adam.

The greatest apologist of the doctrine in the eighteenth century was Jonathan Edwards, although even he was wary of the idea of "inheriting" sin. In *The Great Christian Doctrine of Original Sin Defended*,[27] Edwards's goal was to offer rational arguments for the doctrine against its Enlightenment critics. A key element for Edwards was his view of reason as the highest faculty of the human soul, which ought to govern the other faculties. On the one hand, he did not want the doctrine to imply contempt for "the noble faculties and capacities of man's nature."[28] On the other hand, natural (unredeemed) reason was depraved, which meant that the minds of his (unredeemed) opponents would not be able to understand his rational arguments because they were tainted by sin. This did not endear him to his critics.[29] Edwards was not always internally consistent in his argumentation,[30] and his view still seemed to trace evil and sin to God (since *ex hypothesi* God ordained the fall).[31]

The lack of a satisfactory resolution led to several attempts at reconstruction by American Presbyterian theologians. In the nineteenth century the denomination was split on this issue. The "New School" argued that the sin of Adam was imputed "mediately," while the "Old School" held on to the doctrine of the "immediate" imputation of Adam's sin and guilt to each individual.[32] Later in the century, under

27. Edited by Clyde A. Holbrook (reprint New Haven: Yale University Press, 1970).

28. Ibid., 423.

29. See Clyde A. Holbrook, "Jonathan Edwards Addresses Some 'Modern Critics' of Original Sin," *Journal of Religion* 63, no. 3 (1983): 211-30.

30. Although he offers him as an example of "faith seeking understanding," Paul Helm points to the inconsistencies in Edwards's attempts to salvage the doctrine; see his *Faith and Understanding* (Grand Rapids: Eerdmans, 1997), chap. 17. Edwards argues in *Freedom of the Will* (1754) that all human actions are caused by human volitions. Yet in *Original Sin* (1758) he supported the justice of God's imputing guilt to us from Adam by appropriating Locke's metaphysical account of identity through time, making God the causal agent. As Helm notes, it is difficult to see how both can be true.

31. C. Samuel Storms, who admires and follows Edwards most of the way in his analysis of the doctrine, argues that Edwards's view simply fails as a theodicy, for it cannot "exonerate God from being the author of evil" (*Tragedy in Eden: Original Sin in the Theology of Jonathan Edwards* [Lanham, Md.: University Press of America, 1985], 258). For a discussion of the Unitarian challenge to native depravity, as well as the emergence of the "New Haven" school at Yale, which emphasized the free will of humans even after the fall, see H. Shelton Smith, *Changing Conceptions of Original Sin: A Study in American Theology since 1750* (New York: Charles Scribner's Sons, 1955), chaps. 4-6.

32. The former was represented by Henry B. Smith and Albert Barnes, and the latter

the influence of William G. T. Shedd, Samuel J. Baird, and James Thornwell, there arose the "Realistic School," so called because it resisted the "federal" explanation of the link between Adam and each individual, arguing instead that the connection is natural and "real."[33] This school emphasized that the idea of a "federal" connection appears nowhere in Scripture, and seems to be determined by seventeenth-century assumptions about jurisprudence rather than exegesis.

Later the "Agnostic School" led by Robert W. Landis and Robert L. Dabney pointed out the conceptual problems with both the "federal" and the "natural" ways of connecting us to Adam. They insisted that we simply do not know how we are connected, but we do know by faith both that somehow we are made guilty through our relation to Adam and that God is just. In the twentieth century the Westminster Seminary theologian John Murray argued for a position that rejected the term "federal" and denied the mode of connection offered by the realistic school. Unlike the agnostics, however, he proffered an explanation: depravity is conceived as the "evil disposition" that is "implicated" by the solidarity with Adam as each member of the race begins existence as a distinct individual.[34]

Challenges and Opportunities

The doctrine of sin has become one the most problematic issues for contemporary theology. The challenges to the Western theory of inherited sin came to a head in the Enlightenment, and exegetical, scientific,

---

especially by Charles Hodge and the Princeton School. See the overview and analysis by George P. Hutchinson, *The Problem of Original Sin in American Presbyterian Theology* (Nutley, N.J.: Presbyterian & Reformed, 1972).

33. See the chapter on "Anthropology" in Shedd's *Dogmatic Theology*, 2d ed., vol. 3 (reprint Nashville: Nelson, 1980), 249-77. He dislikes the so-called modern theology that has arisen since the death of Jonathan Edwards and strives to return to the Augustinian/Calvinist positions.

34. John Murray, *The Imputation of Adam's Sin* (Grand Rapids: Eerdmans, 1959), especially chap. 4. In his discussion of all these positions, Hutchinson notes that we still do not have an explanation for how the legal and natural spheres are linked (the same charge against Augustine by his contemporaries), nor how we can consider God to be "just" if individuals are considered guilty for something they did not do (*Problem of Original Sin*, 112-16).

and philosophical considerations in late modernity have continued to undermine traditional formulations. Here again we have a new opportunity for Christian theology to take up its task of clarifying the conditions of human misery in light of the relation of socially embedded persons to the trinitarian God revealed in Jesus Christ by the power of the Holy Spirit.

Exegetical Considerations

Augustine's detractors have pointed to the exegetical inadequacy of his interpretation of Genesis. Today scholarly consensus holds that the Augustinian idea of a "fall" from a state of original perfection is not present in Genesis.[35] Since the discovery of the Babylonian creation story *Enuma Elish* in the nineteenth century, it has been recognized that the Genesis texts must be understood in light of the Israelite experience of YHWH in the context of other ancient religions. Bruce Waltke insists that the genre of Genesis is neither straightforward history nor science, and complains that the American theological discussion has been hindered by "adherence to the epistemic principle that valid scientific theories must be consistent with a woodenly literal reading of Genesis."[36] The early chapters of Genesis are theological documents that serve specific theological purposes. Claus Westermann argues that one of the main theological points of the early Genesis narratives from the expulsion from Eden to the dispersion at Babel is "to show that man created by God is defective man."[37] The ancient Hebrew stories do

35. This exegetical concern was forcefully treated by N. P. Williams in *The Ideas of the Fall and Original Sin* (London: Longmans, 1927). For a summary of recent literature, see W. Sibley Towner, "Interpretations and Reinterpretations of the Fall," in *Modern Biblical Scholarship*, ed. Francis A. Eigo, O.S.A. (Villanova, Pa.: Villanova University Press, 1984), 53-85.

36. Bruce Waltke, "The Literary Genre of Genesis, Chapter One," *Crux* 27, no. 4 (1991): 9. Similarly, Tremper Longman III bemoans the hermeneutical naiveté in the evangelical debate, arguing that "Genesis 1 did not intend to teach about the mode of creation . . . [we must] acknowledge [that] evangelicalism and its doctrine of inerrancy was birthed in a modern furnace that insists on scientific precision" ("Reading the Bible Postmodernly," *Mars Hill Review* 12 [Fall 1998]: 29).

37. Claus Westermann, *Creation*, trans. John J. Scullion (Philadelphia: Fortress, 1974), 26; cf. 89; cf. also Walter Brueggemann, *Genesis* (Atlanta: John Knox, 1982), 41.

not share Augustine's concern to present humanity as originally righteous, nor his dualistic categories of "mortal" and "immortal" as he used them in the debate with the Manichees.

That the two creation stories in their redacted form were not understood as a journalistic chronology should be evident from the obvious differences between them as they lie side by side. For example, in the first story (1:1–2:4a) the plants and animals were created before humankind *('adam)*, male and female, while in the second story (2:4b–3:24) the particular man named "Adam" is created before the plants and animals, and Eve comes after them all. Besides these contextual and genre issues, a careful examination of the content and structure of the second creation story (which features the garden of Eden) shows that it will not bear Augustine's interpretation. The text states that only *after* Adam and Eve ate from the forbidden tree did they "become like one of us, knowing good and evil" (3:22). How then can we speak of the first parents as choosing between good and evil *before* they had eaten from the tree that would bring them "knowledge of good and evil"? How could they be responsible for this choice if their eyes were "opened" (3:7) to this knowledge only after they ate from the tree? Further, the text does not confirm Augustine's depiction of the first couple as immortal; on the contrary, they were removed from the garden so that they could not eat from the tree of life and "live forever" (3:22-23).

Augustine's theory was propped up on two pillars: (1) a particular interpretation of a Latin mistranslation of Romans 5:12ff., and (2) the traducian view of the origin of souls. He treats the Romans passage throughout his writings, using it to demonstrate that all humanity was "in Adam."[38] It is well known that Augustine had little expertise in Greek and was using a translation that improperly rendered the Greek phrase *eph' hō* (in 5:12) with the Latin *in quo*. The latter implied the idea of being *in* Adam, while the Greek phrase has to do with causality: not "in [Adam] all sinned," but "because all sinned." Only on the presupposition that all infants were "in Adam" (and so present at the rebellion in the garden) could Augustine argue that they accrued the guilt of Adam at the same time. On this hypothesis, infants are born guilty, not innocent or neutral. This is because they were "in Adam" when he sinned;

38. See, e.g., *City of God* 13.14; *On the Merits and Remission of Sins* 1.10; *On Nature and Grace* 48; *Literal Meaning of Genesis* 10.16.

humanity as a whole sinned and is now *massa damnata*. This exegesis has come under severe criticism, primarily because of its basis in a faulty translation. This fact has long been recognized by critical scholarship, and even conservative exegetes have admitted the failure of Augustine's appeal to Romans for support.[39] The theory founded on this exegesis, however, has been remarkably resilient in the West.

It is important to emphasize that Augustine's exegetical deductions were by no means universally accepted even by patristic theologians. Objections to the idea of "inheriting" sin were not invented in the modern period. For example, Cyril of Alexandria in his commentary on the epistle to the Romans explicitly denies the idea that the rest of the human race transgressed with Adam. How could this be, he observes, since later humans did not yet exist?[40] He accepts the claim that we have incurred a penalty equivalent to Adam's, but this is because we "copied" *(mimētai)* his sin,[41] not because we were there in Eden. Jaroslav Pelikan has pointed to fragments of Theodore of Mopsuestia's *Against the Defenders of Original Sin* which argue clearly that "it is only *nature* which can be inherited, not sin."[42] Romans 5 is dealt with in more detail in the extant passages of Theodoret of Cyrus's *Interpretation of the Letter to the*

---

39. Henri Blocher concludes that in Rom. 5:12ff. Paul is not talking about "inherited" sin. A better reading, truer to the text, would be to recognize that "the notion of inherited sin is not really in view here. Paul is talking about the universal nature of sin in that it affects all peoples" (Blocher, *Original Sin: Illuminating the Riddle* [Grand Rapids: Eerdmans, 1997], 81). One major journal of conservative American theology carried an article that makes the same point, and argues further that reading inherited sin into the text would appear to entail universal salvation; see Mark Rapinchuk, "Universal Sin and Salvation in Romans 5:12-21," *Journal of the Evangelical Theological Society* 42, no. 3 (1999): 427-41, especially 433. Douglas Moo argues that Paul is just not clear on how we are related to Adam, and we should be content with an affirmation of solidarity without being able to explain it (*The Epistle to the Romans* [Grand Rapids: Eerdmans, 1996], 328n61). In "Original Sin: A Study in Evangelical Theology," David Parker even concludes that "original sin" is not the most accurate phrase to employ. "Happily, it may be set on one side without any fear of either compromising biblical teaching about sin or undermining soteriology. . . . To discard the terminology would be no loss for it is not biblical in any case, and what we have to do is maintain the 'anti-Pelagian motif' not its 'formulation in a doctrine of Original Sin' as such" (*EvQ* 61, no. 1 [1989]: 69).

40. *In Epistolam ad Romanos; PG* 74, 788D-789B.

41. *PG* 74, 784C.

42. Jaroslav Pelikan, *The Emergence of the Catholic Tradition: 100-600* (Chicago: University of Chicago Press, 1971), 285.

Romans. He states explicitly that it is not from the sin of Adam but from the personal sin of each person that death comes to reign over each life.[43] In Theodoret's dialogue *Eranistes,* he notes that "although the race had not participated in the famous transgression, yet it committed other sins, and for this cause incurred death."[44] Many patristic theologians believed that mortality was inherited from Adam, but the idea that sin was inherited is less popular than commonly supposed. St. John Chrysostom, for example, argues that it is reasonable to accept the claim that later humans received their mortal nature from Adam, but it does not follow from this that Adam's disobedience *made* them sinners. "For at this rate a man of this sort will not even deserve punishment, if, that is, it was not from his own self that he became a sinner."[45]

An examination of the broader context of the enigmatic Romans 5:12ff. passage, upon which Augustine built his theory of inherited sin, suggests that Paul's primary intention is not to tell his readers about a first parent and the beginning of mortality, but to point them to the abundance of grace and righteousness and life for those who share in the victory of Christ over sin. By sharing in Jesus' death, we may consider ourselves "dead to sin and alive to God in Christ Jesus" (Rom. 6:3-11). We have been baptized "into his death." We have been "united with him in a death like his." But what kind of "death" does Paul have in view in this context? Elsewhere in the Pauline literature, readers are told that they "were dead" (Eph. 2:1, 5; Col. 2:13) because of their sins. We are dealing here with a theological view of "death" that is bigger than the dissolution of our current organic embodiment. Romans 5:14 says that "death exercised dominion from Adam to Moses," but we know that physical death did not stop with Moses. Paul is making a threefold comparison of Adam, Jesus, and Moses. The fullness of life and righteousness does not come through controlling the passions of the flesh (represented by Adam) or obeying the law (represented by Moses). It is through Jesus Christ that we now have both righteousness and life (5:21). The truest thing to say about sinning is that (along with death) its power to bind us has been overcome by God's gracious forgiveness manifested in the history of Jesus Christ and the outpouring of the divine Spirit.

43. PG, 82, 100AB.
44. PG 83, 248; NPNF, Second Series, 3:224.
45. PG 60, 477; NPNF, First Series, 11:403.

Scientific Considerations

Beside his exegesis of Genesis and Romans, the other pillar supporting Augustine's theory of inherited sin was a scientific anthropological theory called "traducianism." This view asserts that the substance of the soul is passed on *(traduce)* through procreation. Its strongest competitor was "creationism," the theory that each soul is a new creation by God and implanted in the womb at or soon after conception. Augustine needed traducianism to secure the idea that the substance of sin may be inherited from the first parents. Julian of Eclanum (a vocal follower of Pelagius) knew Greek quite well and so understandably would have been surprised by Augustine's appeal to Romans 5:12. Julian focused his attack, however, on the inherent link between Augustine's theory of inherited sin and traducianism, implying the inadequacy of the former because of its reliance on the latter. Ironically, the majority of theologians during the following centuries would follow the Pelagians on this one, affirming creationism rather than traducianism, which had already lost its plausibility in the fifth century. In medieval theology creationism of souls was almost universally accepted, from Hugh of St. Victor to Thomas Aquinas.[46] Augustine had acknowledged that creationism would make more sense in light of his broader philosophical and scientific views but to accept it would have undermined his entire theory. Why? Because asserting that God creates souls every day that are defiled with sin and guilt and places them in embryos would mean affirming precisely what the doctrine of inherited sin was developed to avoid: tracing the creation of sin and evil to God.[47]

It is important to note Augustine's own attitude toward the rela-

46. Scientific objections to Augustine's theory have increased since Julian's concerns with his traducianism. One may point simply to the discovery of mitochondrial DNA and other developments in genetics, along with the broader concerns with the idea of a separate "soul" discussed above in chapter eight. Today a few theologians still presuppose traducianism, apparently unaware of its roots in fifth-century biology and its rejection by the majority of the Christian tradition. For example, Gordon Lewis and Bruce Demarest preface their adoption of Augustine's view with the undefended dependent clause: "Granting the unity of the race and a traducian origin of the soul . . ." (*Integrative Theology*, 3 vols. [Grand Rapids: Zondervan, 1996], 2:221).

47. See the analysis in Rondet, *Original Sin*, 138-39.

206

tion of theology, science, and Scripture. In his exposition of Genesis, he acknowledges the possibility of a scientific discovery that would challenge his understanding of the nature of light (celestial and supercelestial). "If reason should prove that this [new] opinion is unquestionably true," he would return to the text for a new attempt at interpretation.[48] Augustine wisely accepted his own fallibility and the need to continue dialogue with science and philosophy. He describes a phenomenon that is only too familiar in twenty-first-century American theology:

> It is a disgraceful and dangerous thing for an infidel to hear a Christian, presumably giving the meaning of Holy Scripture, talking nonsense on these [scientific] topics; and we should take all means to prevent such an embarrassing situation, in which people show up vast ignorance in a Christian and laugh it to scorn. . . . If they find a Christian mistaken in a field which they themselves know well and hear him maintaining his foolish opinions about our [Augustine's] books, how are they going to believe those books in matters concerning the resurrection of the dead, the hope of eternal life, and the kingdom of heaven, when they think their pages are full of falsehoods on facts which they themselves have learnt from experience and the light of reason?[49]

Reforming theological anthropology will require that we follow Augustine not by repeating exactly what he said, but by doing what he did: articulating the illuminative power of the gospel by engaging contemporary scientific and philosophical understandings of human agency.

The general theory of evolution, which has dominated biological science since the nineteenth century, renders Augustine's theory even less plausible. Many Christians perceive evolutionary science itself as essentially an enemy of the faith, and so expend considerable energy attempting to deny its explanatory power. A similar resistance was evident in the sixteenth and seventeenth centuries in response to Galileo's theories in cosmological science. In both cases (and many others) these efforts to defend the faith often fail to distinguish between "the faith" and a particular philosophically shaped interpretation of our experience of the biblical God. In these few pages I do not expect to change

48. *Literal Meaning of Genesis* 1.19.
49. Ibid., p. 43.

many minds, nor is this my primary task here. Nevertheless, it is incumbent on me to refer to the relevant challenges,[50] and to remind readers of my efforts in previous chapters to show that every theological theory operates within some scientific framework and that the individual interdisciplinarian's way of holding on to these relations is crucial. The idea of a first couple coming into existence in a state of perfection sometime in the last ten thousand years simply cannot be reconciled with evolutionary science.[51] The sciences of embryology and genetics demonstrate the continuity of human organisms with the rest of organic life as it has emerged and become more complex over millions and millions (not merely thousands) of years. Analysis of the mitochondrial deoxyribonucleic acid of contemporary *homo sapiens* indicates that human populations never consisted of fewer than several thousand individuals.[52] Paleological evidence shows that death and suffering were in the world long before the emergence of human beings. Augustine's reading of the first part of Genesis also runs afoul of other contemporary sciences, including geology[53] and astronomy.[54]

50. For an introduction to the issues see J. Wentzel van Huyssteen, *Duet or Duel? Theology and Science in a Postmodern World* (Harrisburg: Trinity Press International, 1998); Kenneth Miller, *Finding Darwin's God: A Scientist's Search for Common Ground Between God and Evolution* (New York: HarperCollins, 1999); Loyal Rue, *Everybody's Story: Wising Up to the Epic of Evolution* (Albany: SUNY Press, 2000).

51. See, e.g., Jerry Korsmeyer, *Evolution & Eden* (New York: Paulist, 1998); Arthur Peacocke, *Theology for a Scientific Age: Being and Becoming — Natural, Divine, and Human* (Minneapolis: Fortress, 1993); Dennis Minns, O.P., "Traditional Doctrine and the Antique World-View: Two Case Studies, the Virgin Birth and Original Sin," in *The Task of Theology Today*, ed. Victor Pfitzner and Hilary Regan (Grand Rapids: Eerdmans, 1998), 160.

52. Francis Ayala, "Human Nature: One Evolutionist's View" in *Whatever Happened to the Soul?* ed. Warren S. Brown, et al. (Minneapolis: Fortress, 1998), 35-36. For a comprehensive analysis of the scientific problems with the transmission of a sinful nature from a first pair, see Patricia A. Williams, *Doing Without Adam and Eve: Sociobiology and Original Sin* (Minneapolis: Fortress, 2001).

53. See the problems with accepting the story of a universal flood as literal science in the treatment by Davis A. Young, *The Biblical Flood: A Case Study of the Church's Response to Extrabiblical Evidence* (Grand Rapids: Eerdmans, 1995).

54. For example, if the cosmos is only a few thousand years old, how do we explain the light that we see from distant galaxies, which has been traveling for billions of years? Arguing for a young earth entails that the Creator is in some sense deceptive, making it appear that the universe is very old. For an assessment of the strange speculations to

The good news is that today many Christian scholars are creatively engaging twenty-first-century science as they articulate theological interpretations of the human condition,[55] just as Augustine engaged fifth-century science. As theologian Keith Ward points out, if humanity became "a dominant species by being more efficient at replicating, obtaining scarce energy supplies, and eliminating competitors in the struggle for life, then it is perfectly understandable that they should have strong drives to sexuality, possessiveness, and aggression."[56] Recognizing the illuminative power of these sciences does not excuse human behavior but it does render intelligible the biological conditions that have led to this behavior. Such a recognition still leaves open the theological question about how this behavior may be overcome so that humans can live together in peace. One can accept the illuminative force of evolutionary hypotheses without denying the heart of the doctrine of original sin, which is that each and every person is bound by relations to self, others, and God that inhibit the goodness of loving fellowship, and that only by divine grace may humans share in the righteousness of God.

Perhaps some of the antagonism among Christians toward these findings is based not primarily on biblical interpretation or on review of the scientific evidence, but on a deeper resistance to the philosophical turn to relationality that has led to a new understanding of nature and humanity. Evolutionary theory is and always will remain in flux; this is the nature of science. However, the basic assertion that humans

which young-earth creationists are driven, and the social and cultural factors that have shaped their anxiety about science, see Ronald Numbers, *The Creationists* (Berkeley: University of California Press, 1993); idem, *Darwin Comes to America* (Cambridge: Harvard University Press, 1998).

55. See, e.g., Fraser Watts, "The Multifaceted Nature of Human Personhood: Psychological and Theological Perspectives," in *The Human Person in Science and Theology*, ed. Niels H. Gregersen, et al. (Grand Rapids: Eerdmans, 2000), 53; Holmes Rolston III, *Genes, Genesis and God* (New York: Cambridge University Press, 1999), 300-301; Arthur Peacocke, "Biology and a Theology of Evolution," *Zygon* 34, no. 4 (1999): 695-712; John Haught, *God After Darwin* (Boulder, Colo.: Westview, 2000); Ian Barbour, "Neuroscience, Artificial Intelligence, and Human Nature: Theological and Philosophical Reflections," *Zygon* 34, no. 3 (1999): 364-65; Nicholas Lash, "Production and Prospect: Reflections on Christian Hope and Original Sin," in *Evolution and Creation*, ed. E. McMullin (Notre Dame: University of Notre Dame Press, 1985), 273-89.

56. Ward, *Religion and Human Nature* (Oxford: Clarendon, 1998), 163.

are inherently related to the historical development of the whole cosmos is an insight that may be embraced by Christian theological anthropology (cf. Rom. 8:19-23).

Philosophical Considerations

In the first part of this chapter, I observed several attempts to salvage the Augustianian link between humanity and Adam, but each of them is still susceptible to the same philosophical objections that attached to his original formulation of "inherited" sin. Their failure is most obvious precisely in relation to the task for which they were developed: explaining the origin of sin in a way that defends God from the charge of causing evil.[57] In the Augustinian theory, the prelapsarian Adam and Eve are portrayed as morally and intellectually perfect, immune to suffering and death because of their intimate fellowship with God. If this was the case, then how do we make sense of a fall from this paradise? Stephen J. Duffy summarizes the dilemma:

> Did God withdraw His presence, thus making Himself responsible for the original sin? Or is the sin sheer human rebellion, thus making the gifted and protected original pair completely irrational? A dilemma faces us. Either sin is impossible because of the gift of original righteousness or it is inescapable because of a tragic flaw inherent in humankind which renders temptation and sin ineluctable.[58]

If God created the first parents perfectly righteous and set them in a paradise that provided all their needs, it is incomprehensible that they would choose evil. A perfectly good will would (by definition) will the good. In Augustine's theory they did indeed "fall" from this paradise, and this implies that God created their wills with an inherent capacity to choose evil.

---

57. Ernst Cassirer has shown how the rejection of the classical doctrine in the Enlightenment was closely tied to problems in theodicy (*The Philosophy of the Enlightenment*, trans. Fritz C. A. Koelln and James P. Pettegrove [Boston: Beacon, 1951], 137ff.).

58. Stephen J. Duffy, "Our Hearts of Darkness: Original Sin Revisited," *TS* 49, no. 4 (1988): 608.

Augustine could not escape the dilemma: "If the first man was created wise, why was he misled? And if he was created foolish, how can God not be the cause of vice, since folly is the greatest of the vices?"[59] Although Augustine sometimes argues that the first evil will is simply incomprehensible,[60] at other times he supplements this appeal to mystery. For example, he attempts to protect the goodness of God's creation by interpreting the serpent in the garden as Satan (the fallen angel Lucifer) and suggests that his temptation is the origin of evil. This simply pushes the objection back one step, and would still require an explanation of the origin of the evil choice of a glorious angel of light who lived in the immediate presence of absolute divine goodness. Even if a satisfactory theory of the mechanism that connects the sin of the first parents (or Satan) to the rest of us was constructed, Augustine would still be faced *ex hypothesi* with the problem that God is the one who predestined the connection between that sinful act and our own. Augustine never offered a satisfactory response to this objection, and the idea that the problem of the origin of sin is inherently and even appropriately inscrutable has registered its effect on Reformed theology.[61] Perhaps scru-

59. T. D. J. Chappell, "Explaining the Inexplicable: Augustine on the Fall," *JAAR* 62, no. 3 (1994): 873.

60. Cf. Robert F. Brown, "The First Evil Will Must Be Incomprehensible: A Critique of Augustine," *JAAR* 46, no. 3 (1978): 315-29, who faults the bishop of Hippo for backing down from his original insistence that no explanation of this mystery should be explored.

61. For example, G. C. Berkouwer spends over a chapter at the beginning of his monumental book on *Sin*, trans. Philip C. Holtrop (Grand Rapids: Eerdmans, 1971), emphasizing the inscrutability of sin and its inherent irrationality. Unlike other riddles, "the riddle of sin . . . lies on an entirely different plane. It can never permit a greater or deeper insight into the nature and origin of sin. . . . We deny that anything, including faith, can shed a particle of light on the enigmatic character of sin" (131). The question *Unde peccatum?* is not an innocent one. When we ask it, we are "already engaged in the power and murkiness of sin" (23). This is true, of course, but applies to *all* our theological questions; it is not clear why we should give up our attempts to explain the conditions that give rise to our sinful questioning. Cornelius Plantinga Jr. describes sin as "culpable shalom-breaking," but acknowledges this is a criteriological rather than an ontological definition of sin (*Not the Way It's Supposed to Be: A Breviary of Sin* [Grand Rapids: Eerdmans, 1995]). Plantinga limits himself to a comment in a footnote that sin is "the power in human beings that . . . lies paradoxically behind our neglects and inattentions as well as behind our assaults and trespasses" (13). The whence of that paradoxical power, which is the driving question of "original" sin, he does not address.

211

tinizing the assumptions behind its apparent inscrutability may open up conceptual space for moving beyond this impasse.

Another philosophical problem that has surfaced throughout this exposition is the perceived ethical injustice at the core of the theory. As Pascal commented: "nothing is more shocking to our reason than to say that the sin of the first man has implicated in its guilt men so far from the original sin that they seem incapable of sharing it. This flow of guilt does not seem merely impossible to us but indeed most unjust."[62] We consider it unethical to discriminate against or penalize persons simply due to their racial (or biological) background. We recoil at the idea of punishing people for the actions of their ancient ancestors. We typically think of an individual as "guilty" in relation to his or her own actions, not in relation to the particular transgressions of his or her parents.[63] It seems strange to say that an infant is guilty, even before birth, and so deserves punishment. Such punishment would seem unethical whether it was simply for being a corrupted soul or for committing actual sins that could not possibly have been avoided. As Reinhold Niebuhr put it: "Here is the absurdity in a nutshell. Original sin, which is by definition [in the traditional formulation] an inherited corruption, or at least an inevitable one, is nevertheless not to be regarded as belonging to [man's] essential nature and therefore not outside the realm of his responsibility."[64] Further, Paul Ricoeur has pointed out that Augustine's formulation inappropriately mixes the categories of jurisprudence (punishable crime) and biology (natural generation).[65] Once this mixture is dissolved, however, the theory evaporates. On top of all this, Augustine's theory presupposes not only faculty psychology but also the Greek "substance" metaphysics we examined in chapters one and eight.

The collapse of ancient and early modern substance dualism and the demise of faculty psychology are good news for theology, and provide

---

62. Pensées 354, quoted in Susan James, Passion and Action: The Emotions in Seventeenth-Century Philosophy (New York: Oxford University Press, 1997), 239.

63. Even if an heir has to settle a debt, we do not consider him or her guilty of the ancestor's monetary mismanagement or theft.

64. Niebuhr, The Nature and Destiny of Man, 2 vols. (New York: Scribners, 1941-43), 1:242.

65. Ricoeur, "Original Sin: A Study in Meaning," in The Conflict of Interpretations, ed. D. Ihde (Evanston, Ill.: Northwestern University Press, 1974), 269-86.

us with new opportunities to reclaim the intrinsically relational insights of Christian faith. Resources for the task of reformation may be found in several late modern trends in anthropology and philosophy. For example, "narrative theology," which stresses the inescapable implicatedness of the self in the ongoing story of the community, demonstrates the impact of the philosophical challenge to the classical anthropology that focused on individuals and substances.[66] Charles Taylor has argued that the self exists in the space of constitutive concerns that "touch on the nature of the good that I orient myself by and on the way I am placed in relation to it."[67] Criticizing the early modern idea of a person as a neutral or "punctual" self, he suggests that moral subjectivity is a structured self-relation that is not established by the self. Our agency as persons emerges within a narratival becoming in which we discover ourselves as already emplotted in a historical context and in a community that mediates criteria for good behavior.

Late modern reflection on the concrete historical and communal nature of human existence is another important dialogue partner for theological anthropology. Here we have the opportunity to conserve the intuition that persons are essentially bound in sinful relational structures (to self, others, and God) while moving beyond the traditional emphasis on the abstract substance of individuals. It is becoming more and more common for theologians to see the limits of substance metaphysics and to stress instead the dynamic structures of human acting and sinning.[68] Alistair McFadyen argues for the continued illuminative power of the core idea of "original" sin (separated from the idea of inheritance) as clarifying our experience of finding

66. See Stanley Hauerwas and L. Gregory Jones, eds., *Why Narrative? Readings in Narrative Theology* (Grand Rapids: Eerdmans, 1989); Alasdair MacIntyre, *Whose Justice? Which Rationality?* (Notre Dame: University of Notre Dame Press, 1988); this is also related to the "rhetorical turn" in anthropology and literary theory, in which the self is construed as embedded in dialogic acts, through which it is "presenced" to both itself and the other. See, e.g., Robert S. Perinbanayagam, *The Presence of Self* (New York: Rowman & Littlefield, 2000); and M. M. Bakhtin, *The Dialogic Imagination* (Austin: University of Texas Press, 1981).

67. Charles Taylor, *Sources of the Self: The Making of Modern Identity* (Cambridge: Harvard University Press, 1989), 50.

68. See, e.g., Josef Pieper, *The Concept of Sin*, trans. Edward T. Oakes (South Bend, Ind.: St. Augustine's Press, 2001).

ourselves "bound" to sin.[69] Edward Farley identifies three retrievable features of the classical view that are not affected by the challenges I have outlined above: these are "the differentiation of sin from suffering and tragic finitude, the view of sin as distortion of (human) reality, and theocentrism."[70] Christof Gestrich is among those theologians who question the validity of the very distinction between "original" and "actual" sins, and wonder whether it was an early theological mistake.[71] At any rate, it is clear that the distinction itself relies on the substance/accident categories examined above that have now been problematized by the turn to relationality. To claim today that sin really has to do with our essence as persons requires that we speak of personhood in relational and not merely substantial terms.

The insight that responsibility, agency, and sinning inherently have to do with community and sociality has been especially evident in feminist and liberation theology. Marjorie Suchocki shows how much the doctrine of sin has been shaped by male-oriented interests and power, and develops an understanding of original sin as rebellion against creation. Focusing on the violence of human sinning that is "inherited" socially through our solidarity with others, she upholds the traditional intuition that only by the grace of God are forgiveness and transformation possible.[72] From liberation and Asian theology we have learned that sin is not only about individual guilt — it is also about oppression and shame in community. Redemption from sin involves not merely an abstract legal decree, but concrete transformation and healing of the pain and bitterness that destroy our ability to move toward each other in acts of love.[73] As noted at the beginning of this chapter, what we call

69. McFadyen, *Bound to Sin: Abuse, Holocaust and the Christian Doctrine of Sin* (New York: Cambridge University Press, 2000).

70. *Good and Evil: Interpreting a Human Condition* (Minneapolis: Fortress, 1990), 124ff.

71. *The Return of Splendor in the World,* trans. Daniel Bloesch (Grand Rapids: Eerdmans, 1997), 236-45.

72. Suchocki, *The Fall to Violence: Original Sin in Relational Theology* (New York: Continuum, 1994).

73. For a classic treatment, see Gustavo Gutiérrez, *A Theology of Liberation* (Maryknoll, N.Y.: Orbis, 1988). For an Asian perspective, see Andrew Sun Park, *The Wounded Heart of God: The Asian Concept of Han and the Christian Doctrine of Sin* (Nashville: Abingdon, 1993). See also Donald Capps, *The Depleted Self: Sin in a Narcissistic Age* (Minneapolis: Fortress, 1993); and C. Norman Kraus, *Jesus Christ Our Lord* (Scottsdale, Pa.: Herald, 1987), chap. twelve.

"sinning" has to do with the inability of human activity to establish or maintain a relation to the good it seeks. We desire objects that we hope will bring happiness, and we act in order to secure them. But our acting is overshadowed by an ambiguous relation to goodness, an ambiguity that is intensified as we come to recognize over time that our acting will never be able to secure our relation to those objects that we love.

Ethical anxiety arises as we attempt to determine which objects we should pursue. However, ethics is not merely about the propriety of particular desires, but also about who we are becoming as agents. When we sense that we cannot fulfill our ethical obligations, this threatens our very identity as responsible agents. When we act in ways that fall short of the glorious goodness of God (Rom. 3:23), we call this sinning. Persons are formed through their historical, dynamic grasping for goodness, and are miserable because of their separation from it. Guilt emerges in relation to this failure of our agency, as we act in ways that depend on our own power to love and secure what we perceive as good. If sinning is understood primarily as that which blocks our relation to the source of goodness, then salvation from sin is not merely pardoning, but also reconciliation in relation to the good *(sub ratione boni)*. A theology of human acting explores the nature of the ultimate source that secures this relation, and tries to render intelligible the failure of finite human agents to secure the love and good they seek.

The gospel is that "God is love" (1 John 4:8). The righteousness of God has been revealed through Jesus Christ (Rom. 3:21-22). The divine love has been manifested by the power of the Spirit through the history of Jesus "so that in him we might become the righteousness of God" (2 Cor. 5:21). We cannot fulfill our longing for goodness no matter how deeply we drink from the "goods" of the finite world. By the Spirit of Christ, God's creative coming (in)to the world overcomes our attempts to turn away from divine grace and secure goodness on our own. God's love is manifested in the activity of Jesus Christ, which shows us how we are to share in that love: "We know love by this, that he laid down his life for us — and we ought to lay down our lives for one another" (1 John 3:16). As Christians share in the suffering of Jesus Christ,[74] their

---

74. For analysis of this biblical phrase, see part 2.2 of my "Sharing in the Divine Nature: Transformation, *Koinōnia* and the Doctrine of God," in *On Being Christian . . . and Human,* ed. Todd Speidell (Eugene, Ore.: Wipf and Stock, 2002).

agency is freed to participate in the infinitely vulnerable reconciling love of God. Here too in the doctrine of sin we are confronted with an opportunity to return to the relational roots of the biblical tradition and reflect on human acting in light of the trinitarian God. For Christians, ethical anxiety is alleviated by the atonement effected in the history of Jesus Christ. The whole experience of Christian salvation is structured by the dynamics of the Trinity: "If the Spirit of him who raised Jesus from the dead dwells in you, he who raised Christ from the dead will give life to your mortal bodies also through his Spirit that dwells in you" (Rom. 8:11). The *good* news is that human agency may be transformed as it participates in a righteousness that is not its own, but is infinitely secured by divine love. We are becoming good as we are drawn into fellowship with the trinitarian God who is love — as we are formed into the image of Jesus Christ.

10 Relationality and the Doctrine of *Imago Dei*

I turn finally to a third task of theological anthropology: understanding and explaining the uniqueness of human *being* in light of the biblical claim that our existence as human creatures has to do with imaging God. As observed in chapters eight and nine, the primary reason for resisting the reformulation of theological anthropology may not be biblical interpretation but rather an underlying philosophical commitment to substance dualism and faculty psychology and the scientific hypotheses that were developed under their reign. We have also seen that humans are differentiated from other conscious creatures by the intensification of their knowing and acting, which is precisely what makes personal identity ambiguous and gives rise to sinning.

In human "being"[1] as well, we find a similar ambiguity: the intensity of human striving to determine a place in reality is inherently linked to a fear of nonbeing. Here we are dealing with what might be called "ontological anxiety." Under the threat of perishing, humans hope for a secure existence in the future; we long to belong within an ultimate reality that includes our personal particularity. Facing the uncertainty of the future, we realize that our very being is at stake. Throughout the biblical tradition we find attempts to give an account for the hope within us by linking human being to the concept of the "image of God." This phrase is apt for the purpose because it holds together all at once the intuitions that the nature of humanity must be

---

1. I am using the word "being" here as a gerund; this helps us remember that human being is not a static substance, but a becoming — a dynamic, historically configured movement in search of a secure reality. Like human knowing and acting, human "being" is also experienced as both gift and call.

ultimately understood in terms of its relation to God, that the good-ness of the human creature is tied up with its call to responsible stewarding of its relations of solidarity with other creatures, and that humanity is intrinsically oriented to life with God in the Spirit dis-closed in Jesus Christ, who is the image of God. A theology of human being explores the metaphysical conditions that render intelligible our hoping (whether anxious or peaceful) for ultimate belonging.

The existence of human beings in community is characterized by a desire for harmony, for patterns of reality that will hold personal life together without crushing it — for a metaphysical matrix in which joy and peace flourish. To be a person is to be becoming in openness to a future outside the self, and to hope for being in relation to that future.[2] When hope begins to fade, the being of the person does as well, and when hope is truly gone, personal becoming ends.[3] We may link this hoping to *being* by pointing to the human longing for beauty.[4] Moving beyond questions about which particular things are beautiful, or about how to secure this or that particular thing in a pattern of peaceful exis-tence, we enter the domain of the *religious* by asking: What are the con-ditions that make possible the longing itself?[5] Our passion for a tran-

2. Hope, argues psychologist and philosopher William Lynch, "comes close to be-ing the very heart and center of a human being." Yet it would be unbearable "if hope turned out to be a rigidly and exclusively interior thing" (*Images of Hope: Imagination as Healer of the Hopeless* [Notre Dame: University of Notre Dame Press, 1965], 31).

3. Psychological research has demonstrated the centrality of hope for human health. For a summary of some of these results, see C. R. Snyder, "The Past and Possible Futures of Hope," *Journal of Social and Clinical Psychology* 19, no. 1 (2000): 11-28; idem, "Conceptualizing, Measuring, and Nurturing Hope," *Journal of Counseling and Develop-ment* 73 (1995): 355-60. For a Christian treatment of hope that is sensitive to psychological and existential themes, see Dan Allender, *The Healing Path* (Colorado Springs: Waterbrook, 1999). Hopelessness brings nonbeing. "The by no means arbitrary metaphor that hope is light while anxiety is shadow brings out already the supremacy of hope. . . . Radical hopelessness is in fact lifelessness. It is the death of humanity" (Helmut Thielicke, *Being Human . . . Becoming Human: An Essay in Christian Anthropology,* trans. G. W. Bromiley [Garden City, N.Y.: Doubleday, 1984], 343).

4. Thomas Aquinas noted the connection between the ancient Greek words *kalos* (beauty) and *kaleō* (to call), and appropriated this link for his depiction of God as the one who calls all things into the harmony of the divine purpose. For the importance of this connection in Thomas and others in the theological tradition, see Yandell Woodfin, "The Futurity of Beauty," *TZ* 29 (July-Aug 1973): 256-79.

5. Frederick Ferré notes the "kalogenic" character of the universe, in which the pro-

scendent reality sets us apart from other creatures. Human hope is drawn into existence (being) through the gracious gift of the Aesthetic.[6] Human longing to *be* confronts the idea of God as the Absolute and evokes hope that our being will be secure in the future. Robert Jenson has pointed out the importance of Jonathan Edwards's privileging of "beauty" among the transcendental concepts: "God is truth and goodness because he is beauty."[7] Whether or not we rank them in this way,[8] it may be illuminating to explore the extent to which an emphasis on the ontological import of beauty may help us show the connection between the biblical God and human being in hope.

Initially it may seem strange that the phrase "image of God," which appears only three times in the Hebrew Bible (all in the early chapters of Genesis), has dominated the Christian tradition's depiction of the dignity of the human creature. Why not use "children of God" or some other more popular biblical phrase to emphasize the uniqueness of persons in relation to the divine? Theologians had another reason, besides the paucity of its occurrences, to worry about overusing this phrase; would the claim that human being per se is the "image" of God conflict with the biblical sense of the inappropriateness (and impossibility) of representing the divine with images (Exod. 20:4)? "To whom then will you liken God, or what likeness compare with him?" (Isa.

---

cess of becoming actual gives rise to beauty *(kalos)* or complexity. He observes the need for an "ontological grounding" for this actualizing process, which we could call "god," but he leaves open the question of the nature of this ground *(Being and Value: Toward a Constructive Postmodern Metaphysics* [Albany: SUNY Press, 1996], 340, 367).

6. Here I do not mean merely "pleasure" or "feelings," but the transcendental condition of our longings for beauty. In literary theory George Steiner wants to speak of "real presences" in terms of our experience of hope that accompany aesthetic figurations. "We know about Sunday . . . the lineaments of that Sunday carry the name of hope (there is no word less deconstructible) . . . but ours is the long day's journey of the Saturday . . . the apprehensions and figurations in the play of metaphysical imagining, in the poem and the music, which tell of pain and of hope . . . are always Sabbatarian. They have risen out of an immensity of waiting which is that of man" *(Real Presences* [Chicago: University of Chicago Press, 1989], 232).

7. Jenson, *Systematic Theology*, vol. I, *The Triune God* (New York: Oxford University Press, 1997), 235-36. The transcendental concepts are those "convertible" with being.

8. The worry about determining what is real is mingled with the worry about determining what is intelligible and moral. The longing for the presence of beauty is inextricably linked to the longings for truth and goodness.

40:18; cf. 40:25). At least two factors contributed to the prevalence of the concept in early Christian theology. First, the New Testament applies the phrase to Jesus Christ, the focus of the Christian faith; Jesus *is* the image of God, and the ultimate reality and possibility of human being require sharing in his life. Second, early apologists were engaging the important idea of image *(eikōn)* in Greek thought, aiming to articulate the truth claims of Christianity in a way that illuminated and transformed the philosophical self-understanding of that culture. This remains our task in late modern culture as we struggle to reform theological anthropology after the turn to relationality in philosophy and science.

Classical Interpretations of the Image of God

Classical theologians typically formulated their presentations of the doctrine of the image of God by responding to questions such as: What is the difference between the substance of humanity before the fall *(homo creatus)* and after the fall *(homo peccator)?* To what extent was the power (or virtue) of the intellectual and volitional faculties of the soul lost (or distorted) by the rebellion of the first parents? Setting aside for the moment the issue of biblical warrant for this way of asking the question, let us examine the problems that arise on the hypothesis that the image was "lost." The early tradition, as we will see, believed that the image was connected both to human reason and to human righteousness. When the former (as the substance of the soul/mind) is emphasized, then it appears that the image was not lost, although perhaps distorted; this led to the uncomfortable implication that the restored souls of the saved are more rational than unsaved souls. When "virtue" (as a power or capacity for goodness) is emphasized, then it appears that the image was lost, or again perhaps only distorted; the Apologists found many examples of virtue among their pagan interlocutors. In either case observation of many of those who are "saved" made it difficult to maintain the coherence of this theological theory. Appeal could be made at this point to the idea of a substantial soul that lies beneath the erring faculties of the saints, but this only pushes the problem back one step.

Rationality or Righteousness?

How then can we speak of the image of God as having to do with *both* human reason and human righteousness? One popular approach, which may be traced from Irenaeus through the Protestant Scholastics, is to distinguish between the "image," which is essential to human nature (and could not be lost), and the "likeness" to God, which is merely accidental to human nature (and was lost). Although Irenaeus probably did not intend to separate them, he did introduce a distinction between the terms "image" (Hebrew *tselem*) and "likeness" (Hebrew *dĕmût*) of God in Genesis 1:26.[9] The Greek words that translated these Hebrew terms in the Septuagint (and which also appear in several places in the NT) are *eikōn* and *homoiōsis;* theologians working in the Latin translated them respectively as *imago* and *similitudo*. Unlike much of the Western tradition that followed him, Irenaeus did not believe that the first parents were created "perfect" (i.e., finished). Rather, they were created with an orientation to the Logos; Irenaeus portrayed Adam as an innocent child rather than a mature and righteous adult. His focus was on the *anakephalaiōsis* (recapitulation) of creation in Christ, wherein redemption is not a return to an original order but a gracious transformation beyond the initial conditions of human existence. For Irenaeus, the key issue for Christian anthropology is the relation between the Incarnate One and human being.

Allowing the New Testament witness to the manifestation of the Word of God to shape his interpretation of the Genesis texts, Irenaeus argued that it is Jesus Christ who *is* the image of God; humans are created "after" his likeness. Since the image had not yet been shown, the first parents easily lost the similitude.[10] Human nature, then, is a copy of the original, that is, of the Word who *is* the image of God, as disclosed

9. Gustaf Wingren downplays the importance of the few passages in Irenaeus that make this distinction in his *Man and the Incarnation: A Study in the Biblical Theology of Irenaeus*, trans. Ross Mackenzie (Philadelphia: Muhlenberg, 1959), 16. My interest here is less in the interpretation of Irenaeus than it is in demonstrating the impact of his comments on later theologians, as they interpreted them. Note that this distinction can also be seen in later fathers, including Origen's disciple Didymos the Blind, who argued that being "in the image" belongs to the nature of human being, whereas being "in the likeness" belongs to virtue; *Sur la Genèse* [Sources chrétiennes 233, 151], quoted in K. P. Wesche, "'Mind' and 'Self' in the Christology of Saint Gregory the Theologian: Saint Gregory's Contribution to Christology and Christian Anthropology," *GOTR* 39, no. 1 (1994): 46.

10. *Adv. Haer.* 5.16.2; ANF I:544.

in the Incarnation. Because humans are created in the image of God by the Son *and* the Spirit (the "hands" of God), the Spirit also plays a key role in the fulfillment of God's creative intention for humanity. A person only begins to fulfill her or his destiny to become a copy of Christ the prototype when she or he receives the Spirit.[11] Through participation in the church as the body of Christ, and by the work of the Spirit, human beings are fashioned after the image and likeness of God. Here we can see that Irenaeus's interpretation of the image was eschatological, as indeed was his entire theology. Irenaeus deeply influenced the Eastern Orthodox tradition, which has generally preferred a cosmological model in which all things are from the Father and to the Father (in and through the Son and Spirit). This means that human creatureliness is determined by the goal of *theōsis*, sharing in the life of God.[12]

In Eastern Orthodoxy, the Greek term *eikōn* plays a particularly important role, immediately evident in the role of icons in their worship and spirituality. Here the theological focus is less on individual human substances and more on the broader cosmological implications of the relation between God and humanity in and through Christ. This is closely related to the doctrine of the uncreated "energies"[13] by which the infinite gulf between Creator and creature is graciously bridged. Panayiotis Nellas displays the central role of the theme of the "image of God" played in Orthodox theology: "The energies of God, which support and conserve the created order, and have in relation to the world the aim of guiding it towards its perfection, acquire in man a specific created vehicle, which is the freedom of man, and a specific direction, which is the union of man with the divine Logos. This is the meaning of the expression 'in the image.'"[14] This doctrine is embedded in the

11. The importance of pneumatology for anthropology in Irenaeus's thought is well documented in Douglas Farrow's *Ascension and Ecclesia: On the Significance of the Doctrine of the Ascension for Ecclesiology and Christian Cosmology* (Grand Rapids: Eerdmans, 1999), 59ff.

12. The classical Orthodox treatment is summarized in Vladimir Lossky, *Orthodox Theology: An Introduction* (Crestwood, N.Y.: St. Vladimir's Press, 1978), 51-73; idem, *In the Image and Likeness of God* (Crestwood, N.Y.: St. Vladimir's Press, 1974).

13. For a concise treatment of the doctrine of the uncreated energies in Eastern Orthodoxy from a Western perspective, see Duncan Reid, *Energies of the Spirit: Trinitarian Models in Eastern Orthodox and Western Theology* (Atlanta: Scholar's Press, 1997).

14. Panayiotis Nellas, *Deification in Christ: The Nature of the Human Person* (Crestwood, N.Y.: St. Vladimir's Seminary Press, 1987), 31.

broader Eastern concern with the mystical relation to God, an emphasis that shows the influence of thinkers like Pseudo-Dionysius and Gregory Palamas.

The general consensus of the patristic period was that the "image of God" in Genesis refers to the "rationality" or "spirituality" of the human being, wherein the essence of God (who is Mind or Spirit) is reflected. This doctrinal emphasis in early Christian theology emerged out of an engagement with the anthropological, philosophical, and theological views that shaped their cultural context. The emphasis on reason was already evident in the Jewish philosopher Philo, who explicitly argued that by "image of God" the author of Genesis meant "mind" *(nous)*.[15] Stoic philosophy, which saw human souls or minds as *logoi spermatikoi*, participating in the essential activity of the divine Logos, also registered an effect during this era. Following the Aristotelian categories that define a thing by identifying its genus and species, the human being was typically defined as the *rational* animal, or the "living being having logos" *(zōon logon echōn)*.

Early Christian theology *critically* appropriated Greek philosophy, insisting that aspects of its anthropological vision must be modified in light of trinitarian and christological convictions. For example, Origen argued against the Neoplatonic idea that the human mind emanates from the Logos; on the contrary, the mind or soul is *created*.[16] Similarly Athanasius said that humans are in the image of God because of their orientation to the Logos.[17] The Cappadocians shored up the distinctiveness of Christian anthropology by striving to overcome the tendency in Greek thought to see the human mind as inherently divine or having an essential divine component. In his refutation of Apollinaris's claim that Christ did not assume a human mind, Gregory of Nazianzus insisted that the human mind was created by God with the natural capacity for union with the divine Logos, a capacity that was

15. Philo, *De Opificio Mundi* 23.15 §69, in *Philo,* trans. F. H. Colson and G. H. Whittaker, Loeb Classical Library (London: Heinemann, 1929), 1:55: "it is in respect of the Mind, the sovereign element of the soul, that the word 'image' is used; for after the pattern of a single Mind, even the Mind of the Universe as an Archetype, the mind in each of those who successively came into being was moulded."

16. Origen, *Peri Archōn* 1.3.3 (PG 11:147-48; ANF 4:252); *Contra Celsum* 4.30 (PG 11:1071-74; ANF 4:510).

17. Athanasius, *On the Incarnation of the Word* 3 (PG 25:101B).

fulfilled in the Incarnation.[18] Unfortunately, many early theologians also adopted the misogynistic tendencies of their culture. At least implicitly (and often explicitly), the image of God was more closely connected to males, for they allegedly were better ruled by reason, while females were tied to their embodiedness.[19] The concept of reason does not exhaust the meaning of the image for early theologians, but it is the central material point. In his *Letter to Calosyrius*, Cyril of Alexandria observes that

> the human person alone, of all the living creatures on earth, is rational *(logikos)*, compassionate, with a capacity for all manners of virtue, and a divinely allotted dominion over all the creatures of the earth, after the manner and likeness of God. Therefore, it is on account of the fact that he is a rational *(logikon)* animal, a lover of virtue, and earth's sovereign that the human person is said to have been made in God's image.[20]

Here we see at work the intuition that the image also has to do with the ideas of "virtue" and "dominion." The problem was finding a way to hold all these ideas together in a coherent doctrine of an "image" that has been lost or distorted.

The emphasis on the mind as the image of God was solidified through the influence of Augustine's modified Neoplatonic anthropology, which we have already observed in chapters eight and nine. Augustine's understanding of the image was tied to his claim that the individual human mind or soul exists (like God) as a triunity; the one

---

18. See Gregory of Nazianzus, *Orations* 29 and 30; and especially his first letter to Cledonius (*Ep.* 101) in *Christology of the Later Fathers*, ed. E. R. Hardy, LCC 3 (Philadelphia: Westminster, 1954), 215-24. For discussion and quotations demonstrating that the image of God is the "rational element" of the soul for both Basil and Gregory of Nyssa, see Wesche, *GOTR* 39, no. 1 (1994): 33-61.

19. A new awareness of these patriarchical tendencies has been a major contribution of feminist theology. See especially Kari Elisabeth Børresen, ed., *The Image of God: Gender Models in Judaeo-Christian Tradition* (Minneapolis: Fortress, 1995). For an assessment of misogyny in the Antiochene school, see Frederick G. McLeod, S.J., *The Image of God in the Antiochene Tradition* (Washington, D.C.: Catholic University of America Press, 1999), chap. 6.

20. Quoted in Peter C. Phan, *Grace and the Human Condition* (Wilmington, Del.: Glazier, 1988), 142.

human mind is constituted by memory, understanding, and will. As *one* mind, humans are the image of God.[21] His other well-known analogy for the Trinity is based on distinctions among the mind, the mind's loving of itself, and the mind's knowing of itself. The mind is a substance, says Augustine, just as "knowledge" and "love" are substances, but they are also of the same substance, the same essence (*On the Trinity* 9.4.6-7). Here is the font of the psychological doctrine of the Trinity in the West, with all of its modalist temptations.[22] Augustine's influence is evident in what is perhaps the best-known theological definition of human being, offered by Boethius: a person is an individual substance of a rational nature.[23] Notice here the presupposition of substance ontology, the emphasis on the individual, and the definitive importance of rationality.

In Thomas Aquinas we also hear clear echoes of Augustine; the intellectual nature of a human being imitates God insofar as, like God, it understands and loves itself. The rational aptitude of humans for understanding and loving God consists in the very nature of the human mind (*SumTh* I.93.4). We also find an explicit link between reason and the image of God in Thomas: "only in a rational creature do you find a resemblance to God in the manner of an image. . . . Now what puts the rational creature in a higher class than others is precisely intellect or mind. So it follows that not even in the rational creature will you find God's image except with reference to mind" (*SumTh* I.93.6). As Thomas critically engaged his own culture, he was buoyed by the new enthusi-

---

21. See Augustine, *On the Trinity,* especially 10.11-12. In 14.4.6 he emphasizes that properly speaking the image of God cannot be something transient, so he locates it in the immortality of the intellectual soul. In 14.8 he argues that we must consider the mind as it is in itself, apart from its becoming a "partaker" in God, which implies that the image is something in the soul per se, not inherently the relation of the person to God. Here Augustine's strong distinction between nature and grace leads him to forget the ancient Hebrew intuition that to be a living person is always and already to be granted life in and through and by the *ruach* of God.

22. Here too we find that Augustine's views are shaped by Neoplatonic concepts of "image." For analysis see John Edward Sullivan, O.P., *The Image of God: The Doctrine of St. Augustine and Its Influence* (Dubuque: Priority Press, 1963), 4ff.

23. "Persona est naturae rationalis individua substantia" (*De persona et duabus naturis* 3; PL 64:1343C). Boethius even adopted the Neoplatonic view in which the immortal soul "descends" into the body. Cf. John Magee, *Boethius on Signification and Mind* (Leiden: Brill, 1989), 132, 142; Boethius, *Consolation of Philosophy,* book 5.

asm for the power of human reason that came with the medieval redis-
covery of Aristotelian logic.

The Image-Likeness Distinction

Aristotle's substance-oriented theory of categories (which we examined
in chapter one) provided Thomas with a conceptual tool that would
help him develop an integrative solution to the problems that had
plagued the classical formulation of the doctrine. Following the lead of
John of Damascus,[24] Thomas sharpened the Irenaean distinction between the image and likeness. The "image" of God is our essential nature (rationality), but the "likeness" was a supernatural gift (righteousness). On this side of the fall we can see both that what survived
(reason) is the essence of the human soul, and that the gift of holiness
(likeness) was probationary. This likeness is restored in Christ (*SumTh*
I.93.9). By hardening the dichotomy between the *imago* (as rational
soul) and the *similitudo* (as a supernatural gift of virtue added to human nature), and placing them respectively in the Aristotelian categories of "substance" and "accident," Thomas was able to explain the difference between human beings before and after the fall. The *imago*
survives (even though it carries with it an element of concupiscence),
while the *dona superaddita* are lost. Even a human being estranged from
God is capable of "natural reason," for the ontological determination
of the rational soul cannot be destroyed by human sin.

Martin Luther noted the Scholastic distinction between image and
likeness (along with other distinctions) in his *Lectures on Genesis*, indicating that he did not find it very useful.[25] He argued that both the image
and the likeness have to do with original righteousness, making
Thomas's material conception of the "likeness" subsume the term "image" as well. The "image and likeness" was holiness, which the primal
parents lost with their first sin. For Luther, both the intellect and the will
remained after the fall, but they were impaired. The restoration of the
image and likeness is made possible through the gospel of Christ.[26] Lu-

---

24. *De Fide Orthodoxa* 2.12.
25. *Lectures on Genesis*, trans. George V. Schick, LW, 1:60.
26. Ibid., 64.

ther could appeal here to Augustine, who for the most part did not distinguish sharply between image and likeness. For Augustine, the *one* "spirit" or mind (whose very unity makes it like God) of a human being may either be oriented away from God in sin or oriented toward God as it is being renewed.[27] However, Luther was critical of Augustine's equation of the *imago* with the triunity of memory, understanding, and will in the human mind, for this would imply that Satan too was created in the image of God. For Luther, the image is found in the being of the first man, for Adam "not only knew God and believed He was good, but . . . he also lived a life that was wholly godly; that is, he was without the fear of death or of any other danger, and was content with God's favor."[28]

For the most part, John Calvin followed Augustine by describing the image of God in relation to the mind. Attacking those who understood Christ as the sole image of God (Servetus) and those who claimed the image has to do with the whole person (Osiander), Calvin insisted on the "settled principle" that the image is "spiritual." He allowed that "sparks" of God's glory may have shone even in the physical body of Adam (and, may we assume, Eve?), but "the primary seat of the divine image was in the mind and heart, or in the soul and its powers" (*Inst.* I.15.3). On exegetical grounds, Calvin rejected the hard distinction between *imago* and *similitudo,* implying that it was simply Hebrew parallelism. For Calvin, human self-knowledge cannot be separated from knowledge of God. Therefore only in light of the relation to God can we understand the mystery of humanity, the whole and real human being. Like Irenaeus, Calvin desired to interpret the image primarily in light of Jesus Christ; the reparation of the image will shed light on the original nature of the image (*Inst.* I.15.4). Calvin described the image of God as knowledge, righteousness, and holiness, a triad that clearly emphasizes *conformitas* to God; that is, a new conforming of human beings to the divine that restores what the first parents had lost.

In contrast to Renaissance humanists who believed that under the agonistic structures of human existence lies a grandeur essential to human nature, the early Reformers wanted to say that both the dignity and the misery of human being are part of the real *humanum.* Both sin

---

27. *On the Trinity* 12.7. It is important to remember that the idea of the human "spirit" in Augustine relates to the one human "mind" or "soul."

28. *Lectures on Genesis,* 62-63.

and the image have to do with the whole human person in relation to God. Their radical and revolutionary focus on justification by faith alone opened space for speaking of human being not in abstract metaphysical terms but in historical terms as created and addressed by the Word.[29] Clear articulation of this intuition was inhibited, however, when the seventeenth-century Protestant Scholastics reverted to the medieval categories. Because of their acceptance of the classical way of formulating the question about a "lost" image, they felt compelled to return to Thomas Aquinas's structural solution. In their attempts to treat the problems that surround the distinction between *imago* and *similitudo*, which was part of their Western theological inheritance, these early modern Protestant thinkers did not escape the assumptions of substance metaphysics. Rather, they proposed new types of distinctions, such as the difference between a "broader" sense of the image (that was not lost) and a "narrower" sense of the image (that was lost).[30] However, any distinction of this type made it difficult to hang on to the early Reformer's insight that the image of God has to do with the real and whole human being.

Lutheran Scholastics like Chemnitz stuck closely to the Augsburg Confession, arguing that the image of God was "original righteousness," which included knowledge of God and so was connected to the mind.[31] They could appeal to Luther for the idea of a "remnant," for in reference to Eve he says that "her very nature was pure and full of the knowledge of God to such a degree that by herself she knew the Word of God and understood it. Of this knowledge we have feeble and almost completely obliterated remnants."[32] In his enthusiasm for excluding

29. See, e.g., Martin Seils, "Luther's Significance for Contemporary Theological Anthropology," in *Luther's Ecumenical Significance,* ed. Peter Manns and Harding Meyer (Minneapolis: Fortress, 1984), 183-202.

30. For a survey of the debates on this issue between the Reformed and Lutheran Scholastics, and their shared desire to hold on to the unity of the person in relation to God, see G. C. Berkouwer, *Man: The Image of God,* trans. Dirk W. Jellema (Grand Rapids: Eerdmans, 1962), esp. chap. 6.

31. See "Apology of the Augsburg Confession," in *The Book of Concord: The Confessions of the Evangelical Lutheran Church,* trans. and ed. Theodore G. Tappert (Philadelphia: Muhlenberg, 1959), 102. For the views of Chemnitz and Calovius, see Heinrich Schmid, *The Doctrinal Theology of the Evangelical Lutheran Church,* trans. C. A. Hay and H. E. Jacobs, 3d ed. (1899; reprint Minneapolis: Augsburg, 1961), 226ff.

32. *Lectures on Genesis,* 67.

synergism, Flacius argued that human nature itself is utterly corrupted; after the fall humans are *imago Satanus*. But this could suggest
that humans are now essentially a different kind of creature altogether,
rendering impotent the Creator's original intent. Strigel tried to solve
the problem with the Scholastic categories of substance and accidents;
the "substance" of the image is not lost, but the "accident" of the original righteousness before God is lost. This Thomistic-sounding distinction (which is rooted in Aristotelian metaphysics) became the prevalent
view.[33] For Quenstedt the image of God is the "conformity" of humans
to God's infinite perfections; these gifts and graces granted to the first
parents are the "accidental" image, which was lost in the fall and restored in salvation. Gerhard described the image as righteousness and
holiness, which have been lost at the fall. However, he also suggested
that "remnants" *(reliquiae)* of this original righteousness remain after
the fall, although obscured by sin.

The Reformed Scholastics also spoke of a "relic" of the image of
God that remained after the fall.[34] Most of the image of God was lost,
but the extant relic differentiates humans from animals. Here too an
appeal could be made to Calvin, who had noted that the image was not
totally annihilated, but was almost blotted out — what is left is "fright-
ful deformity" *(Inst.* I.15.4). The Canons of Dort used the language of
remnants, but to protect the doctrine of total depravity it emphasized
that we should not say that there is some part of the human that is untouched by sin; the rebellion of humanity penetrates even the remnants. Polanus broke with Calvin and went back to an exegetical distinction between the terms *imago* and *similitudo,* distinguishing between
the "spiritual substance, incorporeal and immortal," and the "endow-
ments or attributes assigned to the rational creature." While the body
may secondarily or derivatively relate to the image, the consensus was
that the image resides primarily in the soul and its faculties. Bucanus
also reintroduced the Scholastic distinction between substance and accidents. For him, the essence of humanity was the incorporeal soul, but
in addition to this nature Adam was provided with "supernatural

33. For quotations see Schmid, *Doctrinal Theology,* 217-31.
34. For quotations in support of the following, see Heinrich Heppe, *Reformed Dogmatics: Set Out and Illustrated from the Sources,* rev. and ed. E. Bizer, trans. G. T. Thomson
(1861; reprint London: Allen & Unwin, 1950), 220-50.

gifts," including original righteousness. The latter was not the substance of humanity, but an accident of Adam's nature (for only God is righteous by nature). When Adam fell, he did not lose the substance of the image, but God took away the gifts and powers that adorned it. Theologians who recognized that the image is still extant in Genesis 5:1-3 and 9:6-7 tended to reserve the term "image" for human nature per se. For if the image has to do with an original righteousness, and remnants of it remain, then even sinners after the fall still have in their very nature a relic of prelapsarian holiness.[35] But this is precisely what the anti-Pelagian force of the Reformation was intended to preclude. Such a conclusion was particularly problematic for the Reformed, who desired to uphold *total* depravity.

Challenges and Opportunities

The discovery of the Babylonian creation myth *Enuma Elish,* which George Smith made available to biblical scholarship in 1876, shed new light on the genre of the Genesis texts that use the terms "image" and "likeness." The striking similarities between the Babylonian story and the account in Genesis (which both include watery chaos, separation of heaven and earth, prevalence of the number seven, and the phenomenon of light before the creation of the sun and moon) led to the claim that this material similarity was due to a response by Babylonian Jews to the creation myth of their conquerors. The timing of Darwin's *Descent of Man* (1871) certainly complicated the task of responding theologically to the new awareness of Israel's cultural embeddedness.

---

35. In Berkouwer's view the language of "remnants" leads inevitably to this division, so we need to rethink the concept of image in relation to God concretely and holistically as the Reformers did, without the concept of remnant. Berkouwer notes that often the wide/narrow distinction ends with excluding the human "body" from the image. But Scripture simply speaks of "man" in the image, giving no warrant for identifying it with a "part" of humanity. If we think of some remnant of goodness left over from the fall, it leads to the danger of Pelagianism, deemphasizing the effects of sin and of total depravity. Berkouwer emphasizes that it is *in* our whole *humanitas* that we sin against God. We are alienated as sinners, in our humanness, from God and from ourselves.

Functional Interpretations

The emergence of the historical-critical method of biblical scholarship spurred a rethinking of the idea that the image of God in Genesis should be interpreted with primary reference to "reason" or as original "righteousness," and led to a renewed focus on the language of human "dominion" over the earth. When Julius Wellhausen proposed his theory of the four main sources (JEDP) for the Hexateuch in 1878, it was rightly judged to be radical. Nevertheless, within a decade it was the dominant view of European scholarship.[36] Wellhausen argued that the first creation story in Genesis (where we find the terms "image" and "likeness") was from a "priestly" source, which he took to be among the latest of the sources. That the story is not repeated elsewhere in the Hebrew Bible supported his suggestion that it was compiled at the culmination rather than the beginning of Israel's ancient history. Gerhard von Rad's critical appropriation of the documentary hypothesis in the twentieth century illustrates its profound effect on biblical theology. He suggested that the statement about the image is not concerned with explaining its constitution; "its real point is rather in the *purpose* for which the image is given to man."[37] In his commentary on Genesis, von Rad argued that the original audience would have understood that the first human beings were God's sovereign emblem, placed on earth as God's representatives, enforcing God's claim to dominion of the earth.[38] Here we find a fresh awareness of the fact that ancient Israel did not share the Greek ontological emphasis on substances.

Over the centuries, theologians had of course noted the importance of the command to multiply, fill the earth, and rule over the living creatures, and its proximity to the statements about the image and

36. For a brief overview of the impact of the Wellhausenian school on Hebrew Bible scholarship generally, and the interpretation of the "image" particularly, see Gunnlaugur Jónsson, *The Image of God* (Philadelphia: Coronet Books, 1988), 18ff. In the last century and a half the JEDP hypothesis has been significantly modified, but few scholars challenge the consensus that the Pentateuch in its current form was redacted from a variety of sources from different time periods.

37. G. von Rad, *Old Testament Theology*, trans. D. M. G. Stalker, 2 vols. (reprint Louisville: Westminster John Knox, 2001), 1:144. Original German published in 1957-60.

38. G. von Rad, *Genesis*, trans. John H. Marks, Old Testament Library, rev. ed. (Philadelphia: Westminster, 1972), 57ff.

likeness of God. After Wellhausen, however, most Hebrew Bible scholars came to the view, which is still the consensus, that the primary meaning of the "image and likeness" language in Genesis refers to a task or function given to humanity, namely "dominion" over the earth. This functional interpretation of the phrase was given further impetus by James Barr's *Semantics of Biblical Language*,[39] in which he argued that we must understand the terms "image" and "likeness" in the broader context of the Priestly documents. Barr concludes that the whole phrase, "created in our image, after our likeness," points to the *function* of humans as God's ruling representatives; the parallelism of the concepts in the original context could not bear the traditional exegetical interpretation that distinguished them.[40] Calvin's intuition about the parallelism is here confirmed. Most importantly, however, the exegetical basis for the Scholastic distinction is further undercut. Hans Walter Wolff summarizes the consensus that the original meaning of the text was that precisely in the function as ruler do we find the human being as God's image and likeness.[41]

As the functional aspect of the image and likeness of God came to dominate the interpretation of Genesis, it became easier for systematic theologians to acknowledge that the text does *not* teach that the image or likeness was lost. The worry about its having been "lost" is surprising, since both times that the phrase "image of God" is used after the exit from Eden, the text clearly implies that the image and likeness are still present. There is no hint even of distortion of that image. The phrase appears a second time in Genesis 5:1-3: "When God created humankind, he made him in the likeness of God. Male and female he created them, and he blessed them and named them 'Humankind' when they were cre-

39. Oxford: Oxford University Press, 1961.

40. Barr argues that the parallelism is a literary device wherein "likeness" clarifies the meaning of "image" and this explains why later in the text one may be used without the other ("The Image of God in the Book of Genesis — A Study of Terminology," *Bulletin of the John Rylands Library* 51 [1968]: 11-26).

41. Hans Walter Wolff, *Anthropology of the Old Testament*, trans. Margaret Kohl (Philadelphia: Fortress, 1974), 160. This also had antecedents in other ancient cultures, including Egypt in the 13th century B.C.E., whose pharaoh was the image of god (Re). As ruler the pharaoh mediated the peoples' relation to the divine. The use of the term in Dan. 3 also suggests the influence of the Babylonian idea of a statue as an image of a ruler whose dominion covers the sphere in which the statue is placed although the ruler is absent.

ated. When Adam had lived one hundred thirty years, he became the father of a son in his likeness, according to his image, and named him Seth." The point of the text depends on that fact that the image and likeness remain; Seth's being in the image and likeness of Adam is connected to the latter's being created in the likeness of God. A third and final use of the phrase occurs during the blessing of Noah after the flood (Gen. 9:6-7): "Whoever sheds the blood of a human, by a human shall that person's blood be shed; for in his own image God made humankind. And you, be fruitful and multiply, abound on the earth and multiply in it." The prohibition against murder presupposes that humans continue to be "in" the image of God. The text does not speak of "remnants," or of a loss or distortion of the image, any more than it speaks of a "fall" or of "inherited" sin. It may also come as a shock to note that these texts say nothing about rationality or righteousness!

Existential Interpretations

These developments provided conceptual space for exploring the possibility that the ideal of creaturely imaging of God is related not to the past but to the transhistorical "present." What I here call an "existential" interpretation of the image is closely associated with twentieth-century neo-orthodox theology and what is sometimes called the "relational" model of *imago Dei*. Engaging existentialist philosophy brought a depth and profundity to theological analysis of the human condition, as theologians began applying the biblical language directly to current human existence rather than focusing on the first parents in paradise.

Emil Brunner explicitly affirmed the value of existentialist and personalist philosophy, which he believed was made possible by the biblical intuitions of thinkers like S. Kierkegaard, M. Buber, and F. Ebner.[42] Brunner argued that the "relic" doctrine was "the point at which, at the time of the Enlightenment, the whole Reformation front was pierced and crumpled up. This, too, is the point at which we must

---

42. Brunner, *Man in Revolt,* trans. Olive Wyon (Philadelphia: Westminster, 1939), 546. A key element in avoiding the problems of the traditional answers is to recognize that the image of God is not a "self-existing substance" but a "relation" of responsibility; see idem, *The Christian Doctrine of Creation and Redemption,* trans. Olive Wyon (Philadelphia: Westminster, 1952), 59.

start our work afresh."[43] Brunner himself tried to overcome the problems of the Scholastic separation of image and likeness and the consequent "relic" doctrine by distinguishing between a formal element of the image, which is "responsible existence," and a material element of the image, which is "responsibility from love, in love, for love," disclosed only in Jesus Christ.[44] Although he acknowledged that for scientific reasons it is no longer possible to affirm an "Adam in Paradise,"[45] it was for the sake of Christian doctrine itself that he believed we must abandon the historical form of the doctrine.[46] The image is not something in the past, but confronts us as the core and ground of our own existence.

In his well-known 1934 response to Brunner *(Nein!)*, Karl Barth rejected the idea of a natural or formal human capacity for responding to the Word of God. Barth argued that the fact that we are humans, rather than cats, tortoises, or lumps of lead, is unimportant and uninteresting; what matters is the wholly new creation of hearers of the Word, which is a miracle.[47] Barth translates Genesis 1:26 as: "let us make man in our original, according to our prototype" (*CD*, III/1, 197). What is this original? For Barth, it is "the relationship and differentiation between the I and the Thou in God Himself" (III/1, 198). By focusing on this relation, Barth can say that the image of God is not lost (III/2, 324). It cannot be lost because it is not something humans "have"; rather, it is upheld by God's grace. Although Barth still used the language of "lost" and "fall," he did not explicitly engage the question of a historical Adam in paradise. He spoke of the Genesis texts not as myth but as "saga." In *Credo*, Barth responded to the question whether the serpent in paradise really spoke by suggesting that we should interest ourselves instead in what the serpent said.[48] Brunner called this a clever evasion of a problem that ought not to be evaded.[49]

43. *Man in Revolt*, 96.

44. Ibid., 97-99.

45. Brunner, *Creation and Redemption*, 49ff.

46. *Man in Revolt*, 88.

47. See the reprint of key sections of the article "No! Answer to Emil Brunner," in *Karl Barth: Theologian of Freedom*, ed. Clifford Green (Minneapolis: Fortress, 1991), 151-67.

48. *Credo*, trans. S. Strathearn McNab (London: Hodder & Stoughton, 1936), 190.

49. *Man in Revolt*, 88n1. For additional analysis of Barth's anthropology, see my chapters six and seven above.

In twentieth-century American theology, we find several examples of existentialist interpretations of the image of God. Reinhold Niebuhr emphasized that "rationality" is not enough to capture the dignity of humanity. Humans are driven to something beyond reason; this self-transcendence, this existential longing for a God who transcends the world, sets human beings apart from other creatures.[50] He rejected literalistic interpretations of the Adam and Eve story and the idea of perfection "before the Fall," but still spoke of an "original righteousness" that, on the analogy of "health," is present in the consciousness of the self "in a moment of the self which transcends history, though not outside of the self which is in history."[51] Paul Tillich also rejected a literal fall, and so the idea of "losing" the image of God; if the story is taken as a myth, however, he believed that Genesis "can guide our description of transition from essential to *existential* being."[52] In the latter part of the twentieth century, however, concerns were increasingly raised that existentialist interpretations were not sufficient and that a more careful assessment of the biblical material was necessary.

Eschatological Interpretations

The recent emphasis on interpreting the image of God primarily in relation to the future is tied to the broader renewal of eschatological reflection in the twentieth century. In part these developments have emerged as a result of an increased exegetical focus on the message of Jesus Christ about the coming kingdom of God. Perhaps the ideal relation of human beings to God is located neither in the past nor in a transhistorical present, but in the future. Here the turn to Futurity in the doctrine of God refers not simply to the abstract temporal mode of time we call "future," but to the absolute future of God's reign of peace that has arrived and is arriving and will ultimately arrive through the presence of the Spirit of Christ.

Although a general eschatological interpretation of the "image of

50. Niebuhr, *The Nature and Destiny of Man*, 2 vols. (New York: Scribner, 1941-43), 1:161-65.

51. Ibid., 279.

52. Tillich, *Systematic Theology*, vol. 2, *Existence and The Christ* (Chicago: University of Chicago Press, 1957), 31; emphasis added.

God" can be traced to Greek-speaking patristic theologians, as illustrated in the review of thinkers like Irenaeus and Athanasius above, it received new stimulus and significant alteration during the Enlightenment. J. G. Herder's influential *On the Origin of Language* (1772) argued against an original state of perfection, and proposed instead that the *imago Dei* should be conceived as a *disposition* toward a final state. Unlike other animals, humans are born with very little instinct to help them survive, but God gave them the image (which Herder roughly equated with "religion") in its place. This teleological focus implies that the image is not yet actualized, but exists as a predisposition to the operation of providence that draws us toward the final state of being in God's image. In Schleiermacher's *Christian Faith* (1831), he argued that the "original perfection" of humans does not refer to the state of our first parents, but to the feeling of absolute dependence that is an inner impulse, the *predisposition* to God-consciousness. Schleiermacher had an aversion to "special doctrines concerning the first men," and for him the focus of the doctrine is Christ, who as the Redeemer marks the turning point, the completion of the creation of human nature.[53] Many other nineteenth-century theologians identified human uniqueness in terms of a moral or ethical destiny. The idea that being created in God's image means that humans are oriented toward a moral goal ordained by God may be found in theologians as diverse as Edward Irving[54] and Ernst Troeltsch.[55]

The best-known contemporary proponents of an eschatological interpretation are Wolfhart Pannenberg and Jürgen Moltmann, and not surprisingly both have been deeply immersed in dialogue with the Eastern Orthodox tradition. Pannenberg connects human nature and the *imago Dei* through the idea of "exocentricity," which is intrinsic to the nature of human persons, but intrinsic precisely as a natural dynamic that points human being toward a destiny that has not yet been reached. He links Luther's idea that Christians are *extra se in Christo,*

---

53. Schleiermacher, *CF,* §60. See chapter five above.

54. See Graham McFarlane, *Christ and the Spirit: The Doctrine of the Incarnation According to Edward Irving* (Carlisle: Paternoster, 1996), 98ff.

55. "The doctrine that man was made in the Image of God does not mean the loss of an original condition, but a goal to be reached through historical development" (Troeltsch, *Glaubenslehre,* ed. Gertrud von le Fort [1925; reprint Aalen: Scientia, 1981], 295; quoted in Brunner, *Man in Revolt,* 87).

"outside themselves in Christ," to the thesis of late modern philosophical anthropology that although persons are naturally egocentric, they organize their lives by reaching out to that which is outside themselves. In volume 2 of his *Systematic Theology*, Pannenberg argues that this dynamic structure of personal human existence (exocentricity) is the creaturely condition for being formed into the image of the Son (exocentric destiny).[56] For Pannenberg, the fact that personal exocentricity always reaches out toward the future leads him to give an "eschatological turn" to "the fellowship with God that Jewish wisdom viewed as the deeper meaning of the divine image and likeness of Adam before the fall. It [this fellowship] is reinterpreted as our final destiny, which is manifested already in Jesus Christ and in which believers share already through the power of the Spirit, who is already effecting the eschatological reality of the new man in them."[57]

Similarly, Moltmann argues in *God in Creation* that "the true likeness to God is to be found, not at the beginning of God's history with mankind, but at its end," and that this likeness appears as "a historical process with an eschatological termination; it is not a static condition."[58] For Moltmann, all human beings are designated as *imago Dei*, but believers are those who respond to the messianic calling and become *imitatio Christi*; yet they still look forward to the eschatological consummation in which as glorified human beings they will become *Gloria Dei*, the glory of God.[59] Although this glory is future for us, we already share in it by grace as we are drawn into union with God through spiritual life in Christ. Whether or not we agree with the details of these particular proposals, the value of this eschatological hermeneutic is the way it opens up a trajectory that may help us in the task of reforming the doctrine of the image of God after the turn to relationality, in which the dynamics of temporality have played such an important role.

An eschatological interpretation does not exclude the other interpretations but may incorporate and integrate them. The functional interpretation may be subsumed within a more general presentation of

56. *ST*, 2:230. See chapter six above.

57. *ST*, 2:220.

58. Moltmann, *God in Creation: A New Theology of Creation and the Spirit of God*, trans. Margaret Kohl (San Francisco: Harper & Row, 1985), 225, 227.

59. Ibid., 228.

the call of human creatures in relation to the whole cosmos.[60] Not only human being, but indeed all creaturely being, the whole universe, is "subjected in hope" (Rom. 8:20). In Colossians 1 the claim that Jesus Christ is the image of God implies that all things were created in him and through him and for him. Further, through him God was pleased to reconcile to himself "all things, whether on earth or in heaven" (v. 20). If we are called to be like Jesus, then our "rule" of the earth will take the form of servanthood, not oppressive domination over the creation of which we are an integral part.

An eschatological interpretation also accounts for the essential elements of the traditional Western emphases on rationality and righteousness, and may even more adequately uphold their key intuitions. Human rationality involves the organization of parts in light of wholes, which includes an anticipation of ideal future wholes. Persons are indeed rational creatures who grasp for intelligibility, and this longing is ultimately oriented toward knowing and being known by the eternal God. Righteousness too is intrinsic to our call to image God, for we long to share in the goodness of the trinitarian life. However, holiness is not a substance or natural capacity lost in the past, but the goal to which we are called. As the presence of the promised Holy Spirit, this telos breaks into and constitutes our present experience of being transformed into the likeness of Christ so that we may "become the righteousness of God" (2 Cor. 5:21).

---

60. Building on concerns raised in feminist, liberation, and ecological theological literature, many recent appropriations of the "functional" interpretation have attempted to rescue the idea from a patriarchical vision of "dominance" that has sometimes appeared to support the rapacious control of the earth, leading to our environmental crisis. For example, Douglas John Hall takes the dominion of Jesus as "Lord" as our model; here dominion is not primarily described as mastery or ownership, but as stewardship or as sacrificial service to others for whom one is responsible. See Hall, *Imaging God: Dominion as Stewardship* (Grand Rapids: Eerdmans, 1986). For Michael Welker the mandate of dominion should be reconceived as the "obligation to hierarchically ordered partnership with animals and to dominion through caretaking." See Welker, *Creation and Reality* (Minneapolis: Fortress, 1999), 70. Other ecologically sensitive interpretations include Jan-Olav Henriksen, "Body, Nature and Norm: An Essay Exploring Ways of Understanding the Integrity of Creation," *Irish Theological Quarterly* 62 (1996): 308-23; Gregory R. Peterson, "The Evolution of Consciousness and the Theology of Nature," *Zygon* 34, no. 2 (1999): 283-305; Peter Scott, "Imaging God: Creatureliness and Technology," *New Blackfriars* 29 (1998): 260-74.

This hermeneutical trajectory may also claim a stronger biblical warrant than many of its predecessors; after the late modern turn to relationality, it is easier to understand and hold together the varied scriptural passages on the topic. The early chapters of Genesis do not say that humans *are* the image of God, only that they are created after, or according to, or oriented toward it. Although the phrase "image and likeness of God" does not appear again in the Christian canon of the Old Testament, we do find in the wisdom literature of ancient Israel that Wisdom is materially linked to the idea of the image of God. The Wisdom of Solomon states that "because of her pureness she [Wisdom] pervades and penetrates all things" and describes Wisdom as "a breath of the power of God, and a pure emanation of the glory of the Almighty . . . she is a reflection of eternal light, a spotless mirror of the working of God, and an image of his goodness" (7:25-26). Proverbs 8:30 depicts Wisdom as present with Yahweh at creation as a "master worker." In the New Testament the attributes of divine Wisdom are applied to Jesus, most notably in the Colossian hymn (1:15ff.). For the author of Hebrews too, Jesus Christ "is the reflection of God's glory and the exact imprint of God's very being *(charaktēr tēs hypostaseōs autou),"* who sustains (or bears along) all things (Heb. 1:3).

For the New Testament authors, then, the concepts of the image and likeness of God refer directly to Jesus Christ,[61] and our sharing in the glory of the divine image is possible only by our becoming like him and in him. Colossians 1:15 equates the image with Jesus: "He is the image of the invisible God." Similarly, in 2 Corinthians 4:4 the good news is "the gospel of the glory of Christ, who is the image of God." Paul and the other New Testament authors are not looking backward at Adam

61. There are two cases in the New Testament that apply the concepts of image and likeness without explicit reference to Christ. James 3:9 speaks of the tongue as cursing "those who are made in the likeness of God." The Greek *kath' homoiōsin theou* is susceptible of the same "eschatological" interpretation given to Gen. 1:26, viz., humans are created with reference to or oriented toward sharing in the divine glory (see below). 1 Corinthians 11:7 calls "man" the image and glory of God, while woman is the glory of man. It is commonly held that the use of these terms in the context of this Corinthian letter is not intended to make an anthropological point but an ecclesiastical one; see Philip Edgcumbe Hughes, *The True Image: The Origin and Destiny of Man in Christ* (Grand Rapids: Eerdmans, 1989), 15-23; cf. Kari Elisabeth Børresen, "God's Image: Is Woman Excluded? Medieval Interpretation of Gen. 1:27 and I Cor. 11:7," in *Image of God*, ed. Børresen, 210-35.

and Eve, but forward to what lies ahead. With the resurrection of Jesus Christ, who is the *eschatos Adam* (1 Cor. 15:45), the future reality of human being in its proper relation to God is revealed. The believer's relation to the image of God is future: "we will also bear the image of the man of heaven" (1 Cor 15:49); and Christ "will transform" our humble body so "that it may be conformed to the body of his glory" (Phil. 3:21). John says we "will be like him, for we will see him as he is" (1 John 3:2). However, we *already* experience this arriving future now as we are "conformed to the image of his Son" (Rom. 8:29). The new self is being "created according to the likeness of God in true righteousness and holiness" (Eph. 4:24). The new is already breaking in as the self "is being renewed in knowledge according to the image of its creator," and this renewal is through Christ who "is all and in all" (Col. 3:10-11). This "being conformed" to the image of Jesus Christ is mediated by the active presence of the Holy Spirit, who dwells in and among believers and in whom they also dwell, as we saw in chapter four.

The turn to relationality offers us an opportunity to refigure one of the most important emphases in classical Reformed theological anthropology — the relation of human being to the glory of God.[62] The chief end of humanity is indeed to glorify God and enjoy God forever. Early modern Reformed theology was right to focus on the glory of God. Yet we may still ask whether the Bible describes a God whose highest goal is glorifying himself as a single self-conscious Subject. The lack of attention to the robust trinitarian personal relations in the Augustinian and early modern Protestant models of God led to a picture of an infinitely intelligent and powerful Subject who is intent on self-glorification. This does not account for the radical claim of the New Testament authors that God must be understood essentially as three persons in relation, even when we are speaking of the divine glory. As John's Gospel makes clear, the glory of God is not about the self-glorification of an autonomous divine Individual but about the mutual glorification of the three persons of the Trinity. The mission of the

---

62. I describe this in more detail, and with special attention to the biblical idea of sharing in the glory of Jesus Christ, in section 2.3 of my "Sharing in the Divine Nature: Transformation, *Koinōnia* and the Doctrine of God," in *On Being Christian . . . and Human,* ed. Todd Speidell (Eugene, Ore.: Wipf and Stock, 2002).

Son is to glorify the Father, but the Father also glorifies the Son (12:16; 16:14; 17:1, 22-24, etc.). The Father raised Jesus from the dead and "gave him glory" (1 Pet. 1:21). Christ was raised by the power of the Spirit, the "Spirit of glory" (4:14) through whom we "glorify God" (4:16) as Christ did, and so partake *(koinōnia)* in the "glory that is to be revealed" (5:1).

As noted above, it is by the power of the Spirit that we are already being transformed "into the same image from one degree of glory to another" (2 Cor. 3:18). The Christian dynamically receives salvation as life in hope, as a proleptic participation *(koinōnia)* in divine glory. Imaging God has to do with sharing in the mutual divine glorifying, which for us occurs only though union with the Son in the Spirit, that is, through spiritual intensification of filial identification. Here the revival of trinitarian doctrine should be incorporated into the renewal of eschatological reflection. The essence of human creatureliness is disclosed by its end — being formed by the Spirit into the image of Jesus Christ. The *imago Dei* as the goal of personal and communal being, the telos of humanity, was revealed in the resurrection of the incarnate Word and the outpouring of the Spirit at Pentecost. Humans are created "in" the image and "after" the likeness of God because their very being as persons is oriented toward sharing in the wisdom of the One whose Spirit raised Christ from the dead (Rom. 8:11). Our imaging of God vis-à-vis our neighbors means precisely that (like Christ) we do not seek our own glory but lay down our lives (our ontological security) for the other in love. We are able to "suffer with him" (Rom. 8:17a) in this way only when we stop trying to establish our own ontological security (glory) and instead receive our identity in relation to divine grace "in order that we may also be glorified with him" (8:17b). In this way we also share in the Son's glorification of the Father as we rely wholly on the Spirit of life in and through whom we are empowered to call others into the glory of divine fellowship.

The presence of the God of peace "calls into existence the things that do not exist" (Rom. 4:17, *kalountos ta mē onta hōs onta*). Our ontological anxiety is dissolved as we focus wholly on the risen Lord, whose *parousia* (presence) is both already experienced through the indwelling Holy Spirit (as its "pledge," Eph. 1:14) and still anticipated as a consummation in which God will be "all in all" (1 Cor. 15:28). Jesus' message centered on the coming presence of the kingdom of God, and the early church was consumed by a passion for participating in the reconciling

241

activity of the One who is "making all things new" (Rev. 21:5). All of their attention was on the future that breaks into the present, on the promising presence of the One who is coming so that they may be glorified with him along with all of creation (Rom. 8:10-25). What is most true about human nature is not its primordial past but its eschatological future, an arriving determination that addresses us and calls us to spiritual union with God in Christ. Instead of looking to the past for the proper relation between God and humanity, the Christian may look to a future fellowship with God, a *koinōnia* in and through the Spirit of Jesus Christ whose *parousia* is already bringing the kingdom of divine peace nearer to us than we are to ourselves. The eternal future of God's glory has been manifested in the face of Jesus Christ, and the Christian community receives that future through life in the divine Spirit, whose charismatic presence evokes joy and thanksgiving as we share in the glorious reign of the peace of God, who graciously transforms all of our knowing, acting, and being.

Bibliography

Albrecht, C. "Schleiermachers Theorie der Frommigkeit: Ihr wissenschaftlicher Ort und ihr systematischer Gehalt in den Reden, in der Glaubenslehre und in der Dialektik." In H. Fischer et al. (eds.), *Schleiermacher-Archiv*, vol. 15. Berlin: Walter de Gruyter, 1994.

Allender, Dan. *The Healing Path*. Colorado Springs, CO: Waterbrook Press, 1999.

Althaus, Paul. *The Theology of Martin Luther*. Trans. by R. Schultz. Philadelphia, PA: Fortress Press, 1966.

Anselm, St. "The Virginal Conception and Original Sin." In Eugene R. Fairweather (ed.), *A Scholastic Miscellany: Anselm to Ockham*, pp. 184-200. Philadelphia, Pa.: Westminster Press, 1956.

Anz, W. "Schleiermacher und Kierkegaard: Übereinstimmung und Differenz." *Zeitschrift für Theologie und Kirche* 82/4 (1985): 409-29.

Aristotle. *The Complete Works of Aristotle*, 2 vols. Ed. by Jonathan Barnes. Princeton, NJ: Princeton University Press, 1984.

Ashbrook, James B., and Carol R. Albright. *The Humanizing Brain*. Cleveland, OH: Pilgrim Press, 1997.

Ayala, Francis. "Human Nature: One Evolutionist's View." In Brown et al. (eds.), *Whatever Happened to the Soul?*, pp. 31-48. Minneapolis: Fortress Press, 1998.

Bakhtin, M. M. *The Dialogic Imagination*. Ed. by M. Holquist. Trans. by C. Emerson and M. Holquist. Austin: University of Texas Press, 1981.

Barbour, Ian. "Neuroscience, Artificial Intelligence, and Human Nature: Theological and Philosophical Reflections." *Zygon* 34/3 (Sept. 1999): 361-98.

————. *Religion in an Age of Science*. San Francisco: HarperCollins, 1990.

Barr, James. "The Image of God in the Book of Genesis — A Study of Terminology." *Bulletin of the John Rylands Library* 51 (1968): 11-26.

————. *The Semantics of Biblical Language*. Oxford: Oxford University Press, 1961.

Barth, Karl. *Church Dogmatics*, 4 vols. Trans. by G. W. Bromiley and T. F. Torrance. Edinburgh: T&T Clark, 1936-69.

―――. *Credo.* Trans. by S. Strathearn McNab. London: Hodder & Stoughton, 1936.

―――. *Göttingen Dogmatics,* vol. I. Trans. by G. W. Bromiley. Grand Rapids: Eerdmans, 1991.

―――. *The Humanity of God.* Trans. by J. N. Thomas. Richmond, VA: John Knox Press, 1960.

―――. "No! Answer to Emil Brunner." In Clifford Green (ed.), *Karl Barth: Theologian of Freedom,* pp. 151-67. Minneapolis: Fortress Press, 1991.

―――. "Philosophy and Theology." In H. Martin Rumscheidt (ed.), *The Way of Theology in Karl Barth: Essays and Comments,* pp. 79-95. Allison Park, PA: Pickwick, 1986.

―――. *Protestant Theology in the Nineteenth Century.* New edition. Grand Rapids: Eerdmans, 2002.

Becker, Dieter. *Karl Barth und Martin Buber: Denker in dialogischer Nachbarschaft? Zur Bedeutung Martin Bubers für die Anthropologie Karl Barths.* Göttingen: Vandenhoeck & Ruprecht, 1982.

Belenky, Mary Field, et al. *Women's Ways of Knowing: The Development of Self, Voice and Mind.* New York: Basic Books, 1986.

Berkouwer, G. C. *Man: The Image of God.* Trans. by Dirk W. Jellema. Grand Rapids: Eerdmans, 1962.

―――. *Sin.* Trans. by Philip C. Holtrop. Grand Rapids: Eerdmans, 1971.

―――. *The Triumph of Grace in the Theology of Karl Barth.* Trans. by Harry R. Boer. Grand Rapids: Eerdmans, 1956.

Blair, Christine. "Understanding Adult Learners: Challenges for Theological Education." *Theological Education* 34/1 (Autumn 1997): 11-24.

Blocher, Henri. *Original Sin: Illuminating the Riddle.* Grand Rapids: Eerdmans, 1997.

Braaten, Carl E., and Robert W. Jenson, eds. *Union with Christ: The New Finnish Interpretation of Luther.* Grand Rapids: Eerdmans, 1998.

Bracken, Joseph A., S.J. and Marjorie Hewitt Suchocki (eds.). *Trinity in Process: A Relational Theology of God.* New York: Continuum, 1997.

Boethius. *The Consolation of Philosophy.* Trans. by P. G. Walsh. Oxford: Oxford University Press, 2000.

―――. *The Theological Tractates.* Trans. by H. F. Steward and E. K. Rand. Cambridge, MA: Harvard University Press, 1962.

The Book of Concord: The Confessions of the Evangelical Lutheran Church. Trans. and edited by Theodore G. Tappert. Philadelphia: Muhlenberg, 1959.

Børresen, Kari Elisabeth (ed.). *The Image of God: Gender Models in Judaeo-Christian Tradition.* Minneapolis: Fortress Press, 1995.

Brookfield, Stephen. *Understanding and Facilitating Adult Learning.* San Francisco: Jossey-Bass, 1988.

Brown, Delwin. *The Boundaries of Our Habitations: Tradition and Theological Construction.* Albany: State University of New York Press, 1994.

Brown, Harold. *Rationality.* New York: Routledge, 1990.

Brown, Robert F. "The First Evil Will Must Be Incomprehensible: A Critique of Augustine." *Journal of the American Academy of Religion* 46/3 (Sept. 1978): 315-29.

Brueggemann, Walter. *Genesis.* Atlanta: John Knox Press, 1982.

Brunner, Emil. *The Christian Doctrine of Creation and Redemption.* Trans. by Olive Wyon. Philadelphia: Westminster Press, 1952.

————. *Man in Revolt.* Trans. by Olive Wyon. Philadelphia: Westminster Press, 1939.

————. "The New Barth: Observations on Karl Barth's Doctrine of Man." *Scottish Journal of Theology* 4/2 (1951): 123-35.

Buckley, Michael, S.J. *At the Origins of Modern Atheism.* New Haven, CT: Yale University Press, 1987.

Bultmann, Rudolf. *Theology of the New Testament.* Trans. by Kendrick Grobel. New York: Scribner's, 1965.

Burtt, E. A. *Metaphysical Foundations of Modern Science.* Atlantic Highlands, NJ: Humanities Press, 1932.

Butkus, Russell A. "Linking Social Analysis with Curriculum Development: Insights from Paulo Freire." *Religious Education* 84 (Fall 1989): 568-83.

Calvin, John. *Commentaries on the Epistle of Paul the Apostle to the Romans.* Trans. and edited by John Owen. Grand Rapids: Baker, 1984.

————. *Institutes of the Christian Religion.* Edited by John T. McNeill and trans. by Ford Lewis Battles. Philadelphia: Westminster Press, 1960.

Campbell, Cynthia. "*Imago Trinitatis:* An Appraisal of Karl Barth's Doctrine of the *Imago Dei* in Light of His Doctrine of the Trinity." Diss., Southern Methodist University. Ann Arbor: University of Michigan Press, 1981.

Capps, Donald. *The Depleted Self: Sin in a Narcissistic Age.* Minneapolis: Fortress Press, 1993.

Cassirer, Ernst. *The Philosophy of the Enlightenment.* Trans. by Fritz C. A. Koelln and James P. Pettegrove. Boston: Beacon Press, 1951.

Chalmers, David J. *The Conscious Mind: In Search of a Fundamental Theory.* Oxford: Oxford University Press, 1996.

Chappell, T. D. J. "Explaining the Inexplicable: Augustine on the Fall." *Journal of the American Academy of Religion* 62/3 (Fall 1994): 869-84.

Charry, Ellen. *By the Renewing of Your Minds: The Pastoral Function of Christian Doctrine.* Oxford: Oxford University Press, 1998.

Clayton, Philip. *The Problem of God in Modern Thought.* Grand Rapids: Eerdmans, 2000.

Cooper, John W. *Body, Soul, and Life Everlasting: Biblical Anthropology and the Monism-Dualism Debate.* Grand Rapids: Eerdmans, 2000.

Come, Arnold. *Kierkegaard as Humanist.* London: McGill-Queens' University Press, 1995.

————. *Kierkegaard as Theologian.* London: McGill-Queens' University Press, 1997.

245

Crouter, R. "Hegel and Schleiermacher at Berlin: A Many-sided Debate." *Journal of the American Academy of Religion* 48 (1980): 19-43.

Daley, Brian, S.J., "The Origenism of Leontius of Byzantium." *Journal of Theological Studies* 27 (1976): 333-69.

———. "A Richer Union: Leontius of Byzantium and the Relationship of Human and Divine in Christ." In E. Livingstone (ed.), *Studia Patristica,* vol. 24 (1993): 239-65.

d'Aquili, Eugene, and Andrew Newberg, *The Mystical Mind: Probing the Biology of Religious Experience.* Minneapolis: Fortress Press, 1999.

———. "The Neuropsychological Basis of Religions, or Why God Won't Go Away." *Zygon* 33/2 (June 1998): 187-202.

Damasio, Antonio. *Descartes' Error: Emotion, Reason, and the Human Brain.* New York: Avon, 1994.

———. *The Feeling of What Happens: Body and Emotion in the Making of Consciousness.* New York: Harcourt and Brace, 1999.

Dembrowski, H. "Schleiermacher und Hegel: ein Gegensatz." In H. Betz (ed.), *Neues Testament und christliche Existenz,* pp. 115-41. Tübingen: J. C. B. Mohr, 1973.

Derrida, Jacques. *The Gift of Death.* Trans. by David Wills. Chicago: University of Chicago Press, 1995.

Descartes, René. *Meditationes de prima philosophia/ Meditations on First Philosophy.* A bilingual edition. Edited and trans. by George Heffernan. Notre Dame, IN: University of Notre Dame Press, 1990.

Dieckmann, Elisabeth. *Personalität Gottes — Personalität des Menschen: Ihre Deutung im theologischen Denken Wolfhart Pannenbergs.* Altenberge: Oros, 1995.

Dixon, Thomas. "Theology, Anti-Theology and Atheology: From Christian Passions to Secular Emotions." *Modern Theology* 15 (1999): 297-330.

Duffy, Steven J. "Our Hearts of Darkness: Original Sin Revisited." *Theological Studies* 49 (1988): 597-622.

Dunn, James D. G. *The Theology of Paul the Apostle.* Grand Rapids: Eerdmans, 1998.

Edwards, Denis. *The God of Evolution: A Trinitarian Theology.* New York: Paulist Press, 1999.

Edwards, Jonathan. *Original Sin.* Edited by Clyde A. Holbrook. New Haven, CT: Yale University Press, 1970.

Einstein, Albert. *Ideas and Opinions.* New York: Bonanza, 1954.

———. *Relativity: The Special and General Theory.* New York: Crown, 1961.

Ellis, E. Earle. *Christ and the Future in New Testament History.* Leiden: Brill, 2000.

Engberg-Pedersen, Troels. *Paul and the Stoics.* Louisville: Westminster John Knox, 2000.

Evans, David. *Leontius of Byzantium: An Origenist Christology.* Washington, DC: Dumbarton Oaks, 1970.

Farley, Edward. *Good and Evil: Interpreting a Human Condition.* Minneapolis: Fortress Press, 1990.

Farrow, Douglas. *Ascension and Ecclesia: On the Significance of the Doctrine of the Ascension for Ecclesiology and Christian Cosmology.* Grand Rapids: Eerdmans, 1999.

————. "St. Irenaeus of Lyons: The Church and the World." *Pro Ecclesia* 4 (1995): 333-55.

Ferguson, Everett. "God's Infinity and Man's Mutability: Perpetual Progress according to Gregory of Nyssa." *The Greek Orthodox Theological Review* 18/2 (1973): 59-78.

Ferré, Frederick. *Being and Value: Toward a Constructive Postmodern Metaphysics.* Albany, NY: State University of New York Press, 1996.

Fiorenza, Elisabeth Schüssler. "Theological Education: Biblical Studies." In Don Browning et al. (eds.), *The Education of the Practical Theologian,* pp. 1-19. Atlanta: Scholars Press, 1989.

Ford, Lewis S. *Transforming Process Theism.* Albany, NY: State University of New York Press, 2000.

Freire, Paulo. *Pedagogy of the Oppressed.* Trans. by Myra Bergman Ramos. New York: Continuum, 1985.

————. *The Politics of Education — Culture, Power and Liberation.* Trans. by Donaldo Macedo. South Hadley, MA: Bergin & Garvey, 1985.

Frykberg, Elizabeth. "Karl Barth's Theological Anthropology: An Analogical Critique regarding Gender Relations." *Studies in Reformed Theology and History* 1/3 (1993).

Gardner, Howard. *Frames of Mind.* New York: Basic Books, 1985.

Gestrich, Christof. *The Return of Splendor in the World.* Trans. by Daniel Bloesch. Grand Rapids: Eerdmans, 1997.

Green, Joel B. "Bodies — That Is, Human Lives": A Re-Examination of Human Nature in the Bible." In Warren S. Brown et al. (eds.), *Whatever Happened to the Soul?,* pp. 149-73. Minneapolis: Fortress Press, 1998.

Green, R. L., and W. Hooper. *C. S. Lewis: A Biography.* New York: Harcourt Brace Jovanovich, 1974.

Greenfield, Susan. "Soul, Brain and Mind." In M. James C. Crabbe (ed.), *From Soul to Self,* pp. 108-25. London: Routledge, 1999.

Gregory of Nazianzus. "The Theological Orations" and "Letters on the Apollinarian Controversy." In E. R. Hardy (ed.), *Christology of the Later Fathers,* pp. 128-216. Philadelphia: Westminster Press, 1954.

Gregory, Richard L. "Phrenology." In R. L. Gregory (ed.), *The Oxford Companion to the Mind,* pp. 618-20. Oxford: Oxford University Press, 1987.

Grenz, Stanley J. *The Social God and the Relational Self.* Louisville: Westminster John Knox, 2001.

Griffin, David Ray. "Process Theology and the Christian Good News." In John B. Cobb Jr. and Clark H. Pinnock (eds.), *Searching for an Adequate God,* pp. 1-38. Grand Rapids: Eerdmans, 2000.

247

————. *Religion and Scientific Naturalism: Overcoming the Conflicts.* Albany, NY: State University of New York Press, 2000.

————. *Unsnarling the World-Knot: Consciousness, Freedom, and the Mind-Body Problem.* Berkeley: University of California Press, 1998.

Grillmeier, Aloys, S.J. "Die anthropologisch-christologische Sprache des Leontius von Byzanz und ihre Beziehung zu den Symmikta *Zētēmata* des Neuplatonikers Porphyrius." In H. Eisenberger (ed.), *Hermeneumata: Festschrift für Hadwig Horner,* pp. 61-72. Heidelberg: Carl Winter Universitätsverlag, 1990.

————. *Christ in Christian Tradition.* Trans. by O. C. Dean. Louisville: Westminster John Knox, 1996.

————. "The Understanding of the Christological Definitions of Both (Oriental Orthodox and Roman Catholic) Traditions in the Light of the Post-Chalcedonian Theology (Analysis of Terminologies in a Conceptual Framework)." In P. Fries and Tiran Nersoyan (eds.), *Christ in East and West,* pp. 65-82. Macon, GA: Mercer University Press, 1987.

Gundry, Robert. *Sōma in Biblical Theology.* Cambridge: Cambridge University Press, 1976.

Gunton, Colin. *The One, The Three and the Many: God, Creation and the Culture of Modernity.* Cambridge: Cambridge University Press, 1993.

————. "Trinity, Ontology and Anthropology." In C. Schwöbel and C. Gunton (eds.), *Persons: Divine and Human,* pp. 47-61. Edinburgh: T&T Clark, 1991.

Gutiérrez, Gustavo. *A Theology of Liberation.* Trans. by Sister Caridad Inda and John Eagleson. Maryknoll, NY: Orbis Books, 1988.

Habermas, Gary, and J. P. Moreland. *Beyond Death: Exploring the Evidence for Immortality.* Wheaton, IL: Crossway, 1998.

Hall, Douglas John. *Imaging God: Dominion as Stewardship.* Grand Rapids: Eerdmans, 1986.

Hauerwas, Stanley, and L. Gregory Jones (eds.). *Why Narrative? Readings in Narrative Theology.* Grand Rapids: Eerdmans, 1989.

Haught, John. *God after Darwin: A Theology of Evolution.* Boulder, CO: Westview Press, 2000.

Hefner, Philip. *The Human Factor: Evolution, Culture and Religion.* Minneapolis: Fortress Press, 1993.

Hegel. *Hegel's Science of Logic.* Trans. by A. V. Miller, edited by H. D. Lewis. Amherst, NY: Humanity Books, 1999.

————. *Phenomenology of Spirit.* Trans. by A. V. Miller. Oxford: Oxford University Press, 1977.

Heidegger, Martin. *Being and Time.* Trans. by J. Macquarrie and E. Robinson. San Francisco: HarperCollins, 1962.

Heil, John. *Philosophy of Mind: A Contemporary Introduction.* London: Routledge, 1998.

Helm, Paul. *Faith and Understanding.* Grand Rapids: Eerdmans, 1997.

Henriksen, Jan-Olav. "Body, Nature and Norm: An Essay Exploring Ways of

Understanding the Integrity of Creation." *Irish Theological Quarterly* 62 (1996): 308-23.

Heppe, Heinrich. *Reformed Dogmatics: Set Out and Illustrated from the Sources.* Revised and edited by Ernst Bizer, trans. by G. T. Thomson. London: George Allen & Unwin, 1950.

Hinlicky, Paul R. "Theological Anthropology: Toward Integrating *Theosis* and Justification of Faith." *Journal of Ecumenical Studies* 34/1 (Winter 1997): 38-73.

Hoitenga, Dewey, Jr. *John Calvin and the Will: A Critique and Corrective.* Grand Rapids: Baker, 1997.

Holbrook, Clyde A. "Jonathan Edwards Addresses Some 'Modern Critics' of Original Sin." *The Journal of Religion* 63/3 (July 1983): 211-30.

Hughes, Philip Edgcumbe. *The True Image: The Origin and Destiny of Man in Christ.* Grand Rapids: Eerdmans, 1989.

Hull, John M. *What Prevents Christian Adults from Learning?* Philadelphia: Trinity Press, 1991.

Humphrey, Nicholas. *A History of the Mind: Evolution and the Birth of Consciousness.* New York: Simon and Schuster, 1992.

Hunsinger, George. *How to Read Karl Barth: The Shape of His Theology.* Oxford: Oxford University Press, 1991.

Hutchinson, George P. *The Problem of Original Sin in American Presbyterian Theology.* New Jersey: Presbyterian and Reformed Publishing Co., 1972.

James, Susan. *Passion and Action: The Emotions in Seventeenth Century Philosophy.* Oxford: Clarendon Press, 1997.

Jenson, Robert. *Systematic Theology,* 2 vols. Oxford: Oxford University Press, 1997, 1999.

Jewett, Paul K. *Man as Male and Female.* Grand Rapids: Eerdmans, 1975.

———. *Who We Are: Our Dignity as Human — A Neo-Evangelical Theology.* With Marguerite Shuster. Grand Rapids: Eerdmans, 1996.

Johnson, William Stacy, and John H. Leith (eds). *Reformed Reader: A Sourcebook in Christian Theology,* Vol. 1. Louisville: Westminster John Knox, 1993.

Jones, Stanley L. "A Constructive Relationship for Religion with the Science and Profession of Psychology." *American Psychologist* 49/3 (1994): 184-99.

Jónsson, Gunnlaugur. *The Image of God: Genesis 1:26-28 in a Century of Old Testament Research.* Lund, Sweden: Almqvist & Wiksell International, 1988.

Jüngel, Eberhard. *God's Being Is in Becoming: The Trinitarian Being of God in the Theology of Karl Barth.* Trans. by John Webster. Grand Rapids: Eerdmans, 2001.

Junker-Kenny, M. "Schleiermacher's Transcendental Turn: Shifts in Argumentation between the First and Second Editions of the *Glaubenslehre.*" *New Atheneum/Neues Atheneum* 3 (1992): 21-41.

Kafatos, Menas, and Robert Nadeau. *The Conscious Universe: Part and Whole in Modern Physical Theory.* New York: Springer-Verlag, 1990.

Kahn, Charles H. "Discovering the Will: From Aristotle to Augustine." In J. M.

249

Dillon and A. A. Long (eds.), *The Question of "Eclecticism": Studies in Later Greek Philosophy*, pp. 234-59. Berkeley: University of California Press, 1988.

Kant, Immanuel. *Critique of Pure Reason.* Trans. by Norman Kemp Smith. New York: St. Martin's Press, 1965.

Karlberg, Mark W. "The Original State of Adam: Tensions within Reformed Theology." *Evangelical Quarterly* 87/4 (1987): 291-309.

Kaufman, Peter Iver. "Augustine, Evil and Donatism: Sin and Sanctity before the Pelagian Controversy." *Theological Studies* 51 (1990): 115-26.

Kegan, Robert. *The Evolving Self: Problem and Process in Human Development.* Cambridge, MA: Harvard University Press, 1982.

—————. *In over Our Heads: The Mental Demands of Modern Life.* Cambridge, MA: Harvard University Press, 1994.

Kelly, Anthony. *The Trinity of Love: A Theology of the Christian God.* Wilmington, DE: Glazier, 1989.

Kelly, J. N. D. *Early Christian Doctrines.* Revised edition. San Francisco: Harper & Row, 1978.

Kenny, Anthony. "Body, Soul, and Intellect in Aquinas." In M. James C. Crabbe (ed.), *From Soul to Self,* pp. 33-48. London: Routledge, 1999.

Kierkegaard, Søren. *The Sickness Unto Death.* Trans. by Howard V. and Edna H. Hong. Princeton University Press, 1980.

Korsmeyer, Jerry. *Evolution & Eden: Balancing Original Sin and Contemporary Science.* New York: Paulist Press, 1998.

Kraus, C. Norman. *Jesus Christ our Lord.* Scottsdale, PA: Herald Press, 1987.

LaCugna, Catherine M. *God for Us: The Trinity and Christian Life.* San Francisco: HarperCollins, 1991.

Lash, Nicholas. "Production and Prospect: Reflections on Christian Hope and Original Sin." In E. McMullin (ed.), *Evolution and Creation,* pp. 273-89. Notre Dame, IN: University of Notre Dame Press, 1985.

Lee, Sang Hyun. *The Philosophical Theology of Jonathan Edwards.* Expanded edition. Princeton, NJ: Princeton University Press, 1988.

Leith, John. *Introduction to the Reformed Tradition.* Atlanta: John Knox Press, 1981.

Levinas, Emmanuel. "God and Philosophy." In A. T. Peperzak et al. (eds.), *Emmanuel Levinas: Basic Philosophical Writings.* Bloomington: Indiana University Press, 1996.

—————. *Otherwise than Being or Beyond Essence.* Trans. by Alphonso Lingis. Pittsburgh: Duquesne University Press, 1981.

—————. *Totality and Infinity: An Essay on Exteriority.* Trans. by Alphonso Lingis. Pittsburgh: Duquesne University Press, 1969.

Levine, Joseph. *Purple Haze: The Puzzle of Consciousness.* Oxford: Oxford University Press, 2001.

Lévi-Strauss, Claude. *The Story of Lynx.* Trans. by C. Tihanyi. Chicago: University of Chicago Press, 1995.

—————. *Structural Anthropology.* Trans. by C. Jacobson and B. G. Schoepf. San Francisco: Basic Books, 1963.

Lewis, Gordon, and Bruce Demarest. *Integrative Theology.* Grand Rapids: Zondervan, 1996.

Loder, James. "Barth, Bohr and Dialectic." In W. Mark Richardson and Wesley J. Wildman (eds.), *Religion & Science: History, Method, Dialogue*, pp. 271-89. New York: Routledge, 1996.

———. *The Logic of the Spirit: Human Development in Theological Perspective.* San Francisco: Jossey-Bass, 1998.

———. "Negation and Transformation: A Study in Theology and Human Development." In C. Brusselmans et al. (eds.), *Toward Moral and Religious Maturity*, pp. 165-92. Morristown, NJ: Silver Burdett, 1980.

———. "The Place of Science in Practical Theology: The Human Factor." *International Journal of Practical Theology* 4 (2000): 22-41.

———. "Practical Theology and Interdisciplinary Method." Paper presented at the International Academy of Practical Theology. Bern, Switzerland, 1995.

———. *Religious Pathology and Christian Faith.* Philadelphia: Westminster Press, 1966.

Loder, James, and W. Jim Neidhardt. *The Knight's Move: The Relational Logic of the Spirit in Theology and Science.* Colorado Springs, CO: Helmers & Howard, 1992.

Lonergan, Bernard J. F. *Insight: A Study of Human Understanding.* New York: Harper and Row, 1978.

———. *Method in Theology.* University of Toronto Press, 1971.

Longman, Tremper, III. "Reading the Bible Postmodernly." *Mars Hill Review* 12 (Fall 1998): 23-30.

Loofs, Friedrich. "Leontius von Byzanz und die gleichnamigen Schriftsteller der griechischen Kirke." In O. Von Gebhardt and A. Harnack (eds.), *Texte und Untersuchungen*, vol. 3, pp. 1-317. Leipzig, 1887.

Lossky, Vladimir. *In the Image and Likeness of God.* Crestwood, NY: St. Vladimir's Seminary Press, 1974.

———. *Orthodox Theology: An Introduction.* Trans. by Ian and Ihita Kesarcodi-Watson. Crestwood, NY: St. Vladimir's Seminary Press, 1978.

Luther, Martin. *Lectures on Romans.* Edited and trans. by Wilhelm Pauck. Philadelphia: Westminster Press, 1961.

Lynch, John J. "Leontius of Byzantium: A Cyrillian Christology." *Theological Studies* 36 (1975): 455-71.

Lynch, William, S.J. *Images of Hope: Imagination as Healer of the Hopeless.* Notre Dame, IN: University of Notre Dame Press, 1965.

Macken, John, S.J. *The Autonomy Theme in the "Church Dogmatics."* New York: Cambridge University Press, 1990.

MacIntyre, Alasdair. *Whose Justice? Which Rationality?* Notre Dame, IN: University of Notre Dame Press, 1988.

MacKinnon, D. M. "Aristotle's Conception of Substance." In Renford Bambrough (ed.), *New Essays on Plato and Aristotle*, pp. 97-119. New York: The Humanities Press, 1965.

Magee, John. *Boethius on Signification and Mind.* Leiden: E. J. Brill, 1989.

Maranda, Elli and Pierre. *Structural Models in Folklore and Transformational Essays.* The Hague: Mouton, 1971.

Marcel, Richard. "Léonce et Pamphile." *Revue des sciences philosophiques et theologiques* 27 (1938): 27-52.

Martin, Robert K. "Congregational Studies and Critical Pedagogy in Theological Perspective." *Theological Education* 33/2 (1997): 121-46.

Matuštík, Martin J., and Merold Westphal (eds.). *Kierkegaard in Post/Modernity.* Bloomington: Indiana University Press, 1995.

McClendon, James. *Ethics: Systematic Theology,* vol. I. Nashville: Abingdon Press, 1986.

McCormack, Bruce. *Karl Barth's Critically Realistic Dialectical Theology.* Oxford: Clarendon Press, 1995.

McElway, Alexander. "Perichoretic Possibilities in Barth's Doctrine of Male and Female." *Princeton Seminary Bulletin* (1986): 231-43.

McFadyen, Alistair. *Bound to Sin: Abuse, Holocaust and the Christian Doctrine of Sin.* Cambridge: Cambridge University Press, 2000.

―――. *The Call to Personhood: A Christian Theory of the Individual in Social Relationships.* Cambridge: Cambridge University Press, 1990.

McFarlane, Graham. *Christ and the Spirit: The Doctrine of the Incarnation according to Edward Irving.* Carlisle: Paternoster Press, 1996.

McLean, Stuart. "Creation and Anthropology." In John Thompson (ed.), *Theology beyond Christendom: Essays on the Centenary of the Birth of Karl Barth,* pp. 111-42. Allison Park, PA: Pickwick, 1986.

McLeod, Frederick G., S.J. *The Image of God in the Antiochene Tradition.* Washington, DC: Catholic University of America Press, 1999.

Mendieta, E. "Metaphysics of Subjectivity and the Theology of Subjectivity: Schleiermacher's Anthropological Theology." *Philosophy and Theology* 6/3 (1992): 276-89.

Merriam, Sharan B., and Rosemary S. Caffarella. *Learning in Adulthood.* San Francisco: Jossey-Bass, 1991.

Merton, Thomas. *New Seeds of Contemplation.* New York: New Directions, 1961.

Meyendorff, John. *Byzantine Theology: Historical Trends and Doctrinal Themes.* New York: Fordham University Press, 1974.

Mezirow, Jack. *Transformative Dimensions of Adult Learning.* San Francisco: Jossey-Bass, 1991.

Midgley, Mary. "Consciousness, Fatalism and Science." In N. H. Gregersen et al. (eds.), *The Human Person in Science and Theology.* Edinburgh: T&T Clark, 2000.

―――. *Science as Salvation: A Modern Myth and Its Meaning.* New York: Routledge, 1992.

Migliore, Daniel. *Faith Seeking Understanding: An Introduction to Christian Theology.* Grand Rapids: Eerdmans, 1991.

Miller, Kenneth. *Finding Darwin's God: A Scientist's Search for Common Ground between God and Evolution.* New York: HarperCollins, 1999.

Minns, Dennis, O.P. "Traditional Doctrine and the Antique World-View: Two Case Studies, the Virgin Birth and Original Sin." In Victor Pfitzner and Hilary Regan (eds.), *The Task of Theology Today,* pp. 139-62. Grand Rapids: Eerdmans, 1998.

Mitchell, Stephen A. *Relationality: From Attachment to Intersubjectivity.* Hillsdale, NJ: Analytic Press, 2000.

Mithen, Steven. *The Prehistory of the Mind: The Cognitive Origins of Art, Religion and Science.* London: Thames & Hudson, 1996.

Moltmann, Jürgen. *God in Creation: A New Theology of Creation and the Spirit of God.* Trans. by Margaret Kohl. San Francisco: Harper and Row, 1985.

————. "Theologia Reformata et Semper Reformanda." In David Willis and Michael Welker (eds.), *Toward the Future of Reformed Theology: Tasks, Topics, Traditions,* pp. 120-35. Grand Rapids: Eerdmans, 1999.

————. *The Trinity and the Kingdom.* Trans. by Margaret Kohl. Minneapolis: Fortress Press, 1993.

Moo, Douglas. *The Epistle to the Romans.* Grand Rapids: Eerdmans, 1996.

Moreland, J. P., and Scott B. Rae. *Body & Soul: Human Nature and the Crisis in Ethics.* Downers Grove, IL: InterVarsity Press, 2000.

Muller, Richard. "The Christological Problem as Addressed by Friedrich Schleiermacher: A Dogmatic Query." In M. Shuster and R. Muller (eds.), *Perspectives on Christology: Essays in Honor of Paul K. Jewett,* pp. 141-62. Grand Rapids: Zondervan, 1991.

Murphy, Nancey. "Darwin, Social Theory, and the Sociology of Scientific Knowledge." *Zygon* 34/4 (Dec. 1999): 573-600.

Murray, John. *The Imputation of Adam's Sin.* Grand Rapids: Eerdmans, 1959.

Murray, Michael. "Intellect, Will, and Freedom: Leibniz and His Precursors." *Leibniz Society Review* 6 (1996): 25-59.

Nealeigh, M. "The Epistemology of Friedrich Schleiermacher from a Dipolar Perspective." In R. D. Richardson (ed.), *Schleiermacher in Context,* pp. 174-202. Lewiston, NY: Edwin Mellen Press, 1991.

Nellas, Panayiotis. *Deification in Christ: The Nature of the Human Person.* Trans. by Norman Russell. Crestwood, NY: St. Vladimir's Seminary Press, 1987.

Neville, Robert. *Creativity and God: A Challenge to Process Theology.* Albany: State University of New York Press, 1995.

————. *Eternity and Time's Flow.* Albany: State University of New York Press, 1993.

Nicholas of Cusa. *Nicholas of Cusa on God as Not-other: A Translation and an Appraisal of De Li Non Aliud* by Jasper Hopkins. Minneapolis: University of Minnesota Press, 1979.

Niebuhr, Reinhold. *The Nature and Destiny of Man,* vol. I. New York: Scribner's, 1943.

Niebuhr, Richard. "Christ, Nature and Consciousness: Reflections on Schleiermacher in the Light of Barth's Early Criticisms." In J. O. Duke and R. F. Streetman (eds.), *Barth and Schleiermacher: Beyond the Impasse?*, pp. 23-42. Atlanta: Scholars Press, 1988.

———. *Schleiermacher on Christ and Religion*. New York: Scribner's, 1964.

Nnamdi, Reginald. *Offenbarung und Geschichte: Zur hermeneutischen Bestimmung der Theologie Wolfhart Pannenbergs*. Frankfurt am Main: Peter Lang, 1993.

Nouwen, Henri J. M. *Reaching Out: The Three Movements of the Spiritual Life*. New York: Image, 1975.

Numbers, Ronald. *The Creationists*. Berkeley: University of California Press, 1993.

———. *Darwin Comes to America*. Cambridge, MA: Harvard University Press, 1998.

O'Hara, M. L. (ed.). *Substances and Things: Aristotle's Doctrine of Physical Substance in Recent Essays*. Washington, D.C.: University Press of America, 1982.

Otto, S. *Person und Subsistenz: Die philosophische Anthropologie des Leontios von Byzanz; Ein Beitrag zur spätantiken Geistesgeschichte*. Munich: Wilhelm Fink, 1968.

Padgett, Alan G. "The Body in Resurrection: Science and Scripture on the 'Spiritual Body' (1 Cor 15:35-38)." In *Word and World* 22/2 (Spring 2002): 155-63.

Pannenberg, Wolfhart. *Anthropology in Theological Perspective*. Trans. by Matthew J. O'Connell. Philadelphia: Westminster Press, 1985.

———. *Grundfragen systematischer Theologie*, Band 2. Göttingen: Vandenhoeck & Ruprecht, 1980.

———. *The Idea of God and Human Freedom*. Trans. by R. A. Wilson. Philadelphia: Westminster Press, 1971.

———. *Jesus — God and Man*, 2nd ed. Trans. by L. Wilkins and D. Priebe. Philadelphia: Westminster Press, 1977.

———. *Metaphysics and the Idea of God*. Trans. by Philip Clayton. Edinburgh: T&T Clark, 1990.

———. "Eine philosophisch-historische Hermeneutik des Christentums." In P. Neuner and H. Wagner (eds.), *Verantwortung für den Glauben*, pp. 35-46. Freiberg: Herder, 1992.

———. *Problemgeschichte der neueren evangelischen Theologie in Deutschland*. Göttingen: Vandenhoeck & Ruprecht, 1997.

———. "Die Rationalität der Theologie." In M. Kessler, W. Pannenberg, and H. J. Pottmeyer (eds.), *Fides quaerens Intellectum: Beiträge zur Fundamentaltheologie*, pp. 533-44. Tübingen: Francke, 1992.

———. *Systematic Theology*. 3 vols. Trans. by G. W. Bromiley. Grand Rapids: Eerdmans, 1991, 1994, 1997.

———. "Theological Appropriation of Scientific Understandings." In C. R. Albright and J. Haugen (eds.), *Beginning with the End: God, Science and Wolfhart Pannenberg*, pp. 427-43. Chicago: Open Court, 1997.

———. *Theologie und Philosophie*. Göttingen: Vandenhoeck & Ruprecht, 1996.

————. *Theology and the Kingdom of God.* Philadelphia: Westminster Press, 1969.

————. *Theology and the Philosophy of Science.* Trans. by Francis McDonagh. Philadelphia: Westminster Press, 1976.

————. *What Is Man?* Trans. by Duane Priebe. Philadelphia: Fortress Press, 1970.

Park, Andrew Sun. *The Wounded Heart of God: The Asian Concept of Han and the Christian Doctrine of Sin.* Nashville: Abingdon Press, 1993.

Parker, David. "Original Sin: A Study in Evangelical Theology." *The Evangelical Quarterly* 61/1 (Jan. 1989): 51-69.

Peacocke, Arthur. "Biology and a Theology of Evolution." *Zygon* 34/4 (Dec. 1999): 695-712.

————. *Paths from Science toward God.* Oxford: Oxford University Press, 2001.

————. *Theology for a Scientific Age: Being and Becoming — Natural, Divine and Human.* Minneapolis: Fortress Press, 1993.

Peirce, Charles Sanders. *The Essential Peirce, Volumes I and II.* Edited by Nathan Houser, Christian Kloesel, and the Peirce Edition Project. Bloomington: Indiana University Press, 1992, 1998.

Pelikan, Jaroslav. *The Emergence of the Catholic Tradition (100-600).* Chicago: University of Chicago Press, 1971.

Pénoukou, Efoé Julien. "Christology in the Village." In Robert J. Schreiter (ed.), *Faces of Jesus in Africa,* pp. 24-51. Maryknoll, NY: Orbis, 1991.

Perinbanayagam, R. S. *The Presence of Self.* New York: Rowman & Littlefield, 2000.

Peters, Ted. *God as Trinity: Relationality and Temporality in Divine Life.* Louisville: Westminster John Knox Press, 1993.

————. "Resurrection of the Very Embodied Soul?" In *The Neurosciences and Perspectives on Divine Action,* pp. 305-26. Berkeley, CA: Center for Theology and the Natural Sciences, 1999.

Peterson, Gregory R. "The Evolution of Consciousness and the Theology of Nature." *Zygon* 34/2 (June 1999): 283-305.

Phan, Peter C. *Grace and the Human Condition.* Wilmington, DE: Glazier, 1988.

Philo. *De Opificio Mundi* (Part XXIII.69 in Loeb Classical Library, *Philo,* vol. 1). Trans. by F. H. Colson and G. H. Whittaker. London: Heinemann, 1929.

Pieper, Josef. *The Concept of Sin.* Trans. by Edward T. Oakes. South Bend, IN: St. Augustine's Press, 2001.

Plantinga, Cornelius, Jr. *Not the Way It's Supposed to Be: A Breviary of Sin.* Grand Rapids: Eerdmans, 1995.

Plato. *Complete Works.* Edited by John M. Cooper. Indianapolis, IN: Hackett Publishing Co., 1997.

Plotinus. *The Enneads.* Trans. by Stephen MacKenna. New edition. Burdett, NY: Larson Publications, 1992.

Popper, Karl, and John C. Eccles. *The Self and Its Brain.* London: Routledge, 1977.

Prigogine, Ilya, and Isabelle Stengers. *Order out of Chaos: Man's New Dialogue with Nature.* New York: Bantam, 1984.

Pröpper, Thomas. "Schleiermachers Bestimmung des Christentums und der Erlösung: Zur Problematik der transzendental-anthropologischen Hermeneutik des Glaubens." *Theologische Quartalschrift* 168/3 (1988): 193-214.

Rakestraw, Robert. "Becoming Like God: An Evangelical Doctrine of Theosis." *Journal of the Evangelical Theological Society* 40/2 (June 1997): 257-70.

Rapinchuk, Mark. "Universal Sin and Salvation in Romans 5:12-21." *Journal of the Evangelical Theological Society* 42/3 (Sept. 1999): 427-41.

Reid, Duncan. *Energies of the Spirit: Trinitarian Models in Eastern Orthodox and Western Theology.* Atlanta: Scholars Press, 1997.

Ricoeur, Paul. "Original Sin: A Study in Meaning." In *The Conflict of Interpretations,* pp. 269-86. Evanston, IL: Northwestern University Press, 1974.

Robinson, J. A. T. *The Body: A Study in Pauline Theology.* London: SCM Press, 1952.

Rohls, Jan. "Frömmigkeit als Gefühl schlechthinniger Abhängigkeit: Zu Schleiermachers Religionstheorie in der Glaubenslehre." In K.-V. Selge (ed.), *Internationaler Schleiermacher-Kongress Berlin 1984,* pp. 211-52. Schleiermacher-Archiv, vol. 1,1. Berlin: Walter de Gruyter, 1985.

Rolston, Holmes, III. *Genes, Genesis and God.* Cambridge: Cambridge University Press, 1999.

Rondet, Henri, S.J. *Original Sin: The Patristic and Theological Background.* Trans. by Cajetan Finegan, O.P. New York: Alba House, 1972.

Rosato, Philip J., S.J. *The Spirit as Lord: The Pneumatology of Karl Barth.* Edinburgh: T&T Clark, 1981.

Rue, Loyal. *Everybody's Story: Wising Up to the Epic of Evolution.* Albany: State University of New York Press, 2000.

Sappington, A. A. "Psychology for the Practice of the Presence of God: Putting Psychology at the Service of the Church." *Journal of Psychology and Christianity* 13/1 (1994): 5-16.

Sartre, Jean-Paul. *Being and Nothingness.* Trans. by by Hazel E. Barnes. New York: Philosophical Library, 1956.

Schleiermacher, Friedrich. *The Christian Faith.* 2 vols. Trans. by H. R. Macintosh and J. S. Stewart. Edinburgh: T&T Clark, 1989.

―――. *On the Glaubenslehre: Two Letters to Dr. Lücke.* Trans. by J. Duke and F. Fiorenza Atlanta: Scholars Press, 1981.

―――. *On Religion: Speeches to Its Cultured Despisers.* Trans. and edited by Richard Crouter. Cambridge: Cambridge University Press, 1996.

Schmid, Heinrich. *The Doctrinal Theology of the Evangelical Lutheran Church.* Reprint edition. Trans. by C. A. Hay and H. E. Jacobs. Minneapolis: Augsburg Press, 1961.

Schnelle, Udo. *The Human Condition: Anthropology in the Teachings of Jesus, Paul, and John.* Trans. by O. C. Dean, Jr. Minneapolis: Fortress Press, 1996.

Schoonenberg, Piet. *The Christ.* Trans. by Della Cooling. New York: Herder and Herder, 1971.

Schrag, Calvin. *The Self after Postmodernity*. New Haven, CT: Yale University Press, 1997.

Scott, Peter. "Imaging God: Creatureliness and Technology." *New Blackfriars* 29 (1998): 260-74.

Seils, Martin. "Luther's Significance for Contemporary Theological Anthropology." In Peter Manns and Harding Meyer (eds.), *Luther's Ecumenical Significance*, pp. 183-202. Minneapolis: Fortress Press, 1984.

Sellers, R. V. *The Council of Chalcedon*. London: SPCK Press, 1961.

Shedd, William G. T. *Dogmatic Theology*. 3 vols. Nashville: Thomas Nelson, 1980.

Sheridan, Sybil. "Judaism." In J. Holm (ed.), *Human Nature and Destiny*, pp. 116-43. London: Pinter, 1994.

Shults, F. LeRon. *The Postfoundationalist Task of Theology*. Grand Rapids: Eerdmans, 1999.

———. "Sharing in the Divine Nature: Transformation, *Koinōnia* and the Doctrine of God." In Todd Speidell (ed.), *On Being Christian . . . and Human*, pp. 87-127. Eugene, OR: Wipf and Stock, 2002.

Shults, F. LeRon, and Steven J. Sandage. *The Faces of Forgiveness: Searching for Wholeness and Salvation*. Grand Rapids: Baker Academic, 2003.

Skinner, B. F. *Beyond Freedom and Dignity*. New York: Alfred Knopf, 1971.

Smith, H. Shelton. *Changing Conceptions of Original Sin: A Study in American Theology since 1750*. New York: Charles Scribner's Sons, 1955.

Smith, Roger. *The Norton History of the Human Sciences*. New York: W. W. Norton, 1997.

Sokolowski, Robert. *Introduction to Phenomenology*. Cambridge: Cambridge University Press, 2000.

Sorabji, Richard. "Soul and Self in Ancient Philosophy." In J. Crabbe (ed.), *From Soul to Self*, pp. 8-32. New York: Routledge, 1999.

Sorrentino, S. "Schleiermachers Philosophie und der Ansatz der transzendentalen Philosophie." In R. D. Richardson (ed.), *Schleiermacher in Context*, pp. 227-41. Lewiston, NY: Edwin Mellen Press, 1991.

Spiegler, G. "Theological Tensions in Schleiermacher's *Dialektik*." In R. W. Funk (ed.), *Schleiermacher as Contemporary*, pp. 13-40. New York: Herder and Herder, 1970.

Sprigge, Timothy. "Internal and External Properties." *Mind* 71 (1962): 197-212.

Snyder, C. R. "Conceptualizing, Measuring and Nurturing Hope." *Journal of Counseling and Development* 73 (1995): 355-60.

———. "The Past and Possible Futures of Hope." *Journal of Social and Clinical Psychology* 19/1 (2000): 11-28.

Steiner, H. G. "Relation." In Joachim Ritter and Karlfried Gründer (eds.), *Historisches Wörterbuch der Philosophie*, vol. 8, pp. 578-611. Basel: Schwabe & Co., 1992.

Steiner, George. *Real Presences*. University of Chicago Press, 1989.

Stickelberger, Hans. "Substanz und Akzidens bei Leontius von Byzanz." *Theologische Zeitschrift* 36 (1980): 153-61.

Storms, C. Samuel. *Tragedy in Eden: Original Sin in the Theology of Jonathan Edwards*. New York: University Press of America, 1985.

Stroble, Paul E. *The Social Ontology of Karl Barth*. San Francisco: Christian Universities Press, 1994.

Strong, Augustus. *Systematic Theology*. Philadelphia: The Judson Press, 1907.

Suchocki, Marjorie Hewett. *The Fall to Violence: Original Sin in Relational Theology*. New York: Continuum, 1994.

Sullivan, John Edward, O.P. *The Image of God: The Doctrine of St. Augustine and Its Influence*. Dubuque, IA: The Priority Press, 1963.

Tambasco, Anthony J. *A Theology of Atonement and Paul's Vision of Christianity*. Collegeville, MN: The Liturgical Press, 1991.

Tamburello, Dennis E. *Union with Christ: John Calvin and the Mysticism of St. Bernard*. Louisville: Westminster John Knox, 1994.

Taylor, Charles. *Sources of the Self: The Making of Modern Identity*. Cambridge, MA: Harvard University Press, 1989.

Thandeka. "Schleiermacher's Dialektik: The Discovery of the Self That Kant Lost." *Harvard Theological Review* 85 (1992): 433-52.

Thielicke, Helmut. *Being Human . . . Becoming Human: An Essay in Christian Anthropology*. Trans. by G. W. Bromiley. Garden City, NY: Doubleday & Co., 1984.

Thiselton, Anthony. "Human Being, Relationality and Time in Hebrews, I Corinthians and the Western Tradition." *Ex Auditu* 13 (1997): 76-95.

Thomas Aquinas. *Summa Theologiae*. Blackfriars edition. New York: McGraw-Hill, 1964.

———. *On the Unity of the Intellect against the Averroists*. Trans. by B. H. Zedler. Milwaukee: Marquette University Press, 1968.

Tice, Terrence. "Editor's Postscript." In Schleiermacher, *Brief Outline of Theology as a Field of Study*, pp. 173-210. Trans. with notes by T. Tice. Lewiston, NY: Edwin Mellen Press, 1990.

Tillich, Paul. *Systematic Theology*. University of Chicago Press, 1957.

Torrance, T. F. *Theological Science*. Oxford: Oxford University Press, 1969.

Towner, W. Sibley. "Interpretations and Reinterpretations of the Fall." In Francis A. Eigo, O.S.A. (ed.), *Modern Biblical Scholarship*, pp. 53-85. Villanova, PA: Villanova University Press, 1984.

Urs von Balthasar, Hans. *A Theological Anthropology*. New York: Sheed and Ward, 1967.

van der Ven, Johannes, "Practical Theology as Critical-Empirical Theology." In Adrian Visscher (ed.), *Les Etudes Pastorales à l'Université*, pp. 238-62. Paris: Les Presses de l'Université d'Ottawa, 1990.

———. *Practical Theology: An Empirical Approach*. Kampen, The Netherlands: Kok Pharos, 1993.

———. "Unterwegs zu einer empirischen Theologie." In O. Fuchs (ed.), *Theologie und Handeln: Beiträge zur Fundierung der Praktischen Theologie als Handlungstheorie*. Düsseldorf: Patmos, 1984.

258

Vandervelde, G. *Original Sin: Two Major Trends in Contemporary Roman Catholic Reinterpretation.* Amsterdam: Rodopi, 1975.

van Huyssteen, J. Wentzel. *Duet or Duel? Theology and Science in a Postmodern World.* Harrisburg, PA: Trinity Press International, 1998.

————. *Essays in Postfoundationalist Theology.* Grand Rapids: Eerdmans, 1997.

————. *The Shaping of Rationality: Toward Interdisciplinarity in Theology and Science.* Grand Rapids: Eerdmans, 1999.

Vance, R. "Sin and Consciousness of Sin in Schleiermacher." *Perspectives in Religious Studies* 13/3 (1986): 241-62.

Van Niekerk, A. A. "To Follow a Rule or to Rule What Should Follow? Rationality and Judgement in the Human Sciences." In J. Mouton and D. Joubert (eds.), *Knowledge and Method in the Human Sciences,* pp. 179-194. Pretoria: HSRC, 1990.

von Rad, Gerhard. *Genesis: A Commentary.* Revised edition. Trans. by John H. Marks. Philadelphia: Westminster Press, 1972.

————. *Old Testament Theology.* 2 vols. Trans. by D. M. G. Stalker. Louisville: Westminster John Knox, 2001.

Waltke, Bruce. "The Literary Genre of Genesis, Chapter One." *Crux* 27/4 (Dec. 1991): 2-10.

Ward, Keith. *Religion and Human Nature.* Oxford: Oxford University Press, 1998.

Ware, Kallistos. "The Soul in Greek Christianity." In M. James C. Crabbe (ed.), *From Soul to Self,* pp. 49-69. London: Routledge, 1999.

Watts, Fraser. "The Multifaceted Nature of Human Personhood: Psychological and Theological Perspectives." In Niels Gregersen et al. (eds.), *The Human Person in Science and Theology,* pp. 41-63. Grand Rapids: Eerdmans, 2000.

Weaver, David. "The Exegesis of Romans 5:12 among the Greek Fathers and Its Implications for the Doctrine of Original Sin: The 5th-12th Centuries." *St. Vladimir's Theological Quarterly* 29/2 (1985): 133-59 [Part II] and 29/3 (1985): 231-57 [Part III].

————. "From Paul to Augustine: Romans 5:12 in Early Christian Exegesis." *St. Vladimir's Theological Quarterly* 27/3 (1983): 187-206. [Part I.]

Welker, Michael. *Creation and Reality.* Minneapolis: Fortress Press, 1999.

Welton, Michael. "Seeing the Light: Christian Conversion and Conscientization." In P. Jarvis and N. Walters (eds.), *Adult Education and Theological Interpretations,* pp. 105-23. Malabar, FL: Krieger, 1993.

Wesche, K. P. "Mind and Self in the Christology of Saint Gregory the Theologian: Saint Gregory's Contribution to Christology and Christian Anthropology." *The Greek Orthodox Theological Review* 39/1 (1994): 33-61.

Westermann, Claus. *Creation.* Trans. by John J. Scullion, S.J. Philadelphia: Fortress Press, 1974.

Whitehead, Alfred North. *Modes of Thought.* New York: Capricorn Books, 1938.

————. *Process and Reality.* Corrected edition, edited by David Ray Griffin and Donald W. Sherburne. New York: Free Press, 1978.

Widmer, Gilbert. "L'homme créé à l'image de Dieu chez Calvin et Barth." In

Holderegger et al. (eds.), *De dignitate hominis,* pp. 227-42. Wien: Freiburg, 1987.

Williams, N. P. *The Ideas of the Fall and Original Sin.* New York: Longmans, 1927.

Williams, Patricia A. *Doing without Adam and Eve: Sociobiology and Original Sin.* Minneapolis: Fortress Press, 2001.

Williams, Robert R. "Hegel and Schleiermacher on Theological Truth." In L. S. Rouner (ed.), *Meaning, Truth and God,* pp. 52-69. University of Notre Dame Press, 1982.

————. "Schleiermacher, Hegel and the Problem of Concrete Universality." *Journal of the American Academy of Religion* 56 (1988): 473-96.

————. *Schleiermacher the Theologian: The Construction of the Doctrine of God.* Philadelphia: Fortress Press, 1978.

————. "Sin and Evil." In Peter C. Hodgson and Robert H. King (eds.), *Christian Theology: An Introduction to Its Traditions and Tasks,* pp. 194-221. Philadelphia: Fortress Press, 1985.

Wils, Jean-Pierre. *Sittlichkeit und Subjektivität: Zur Ortsbestimmung der Ethik im Strukturalismus, in der Subjektivitätsphilosophie und bei Schleiermacher.* Freiburg: Herder, 1987.

Wingren, Gustaf. *Man and the Incarnation: A Study in the Biblical Theology of Irenaeus.* Trans. by Ross Mackenzie. Philadelphia: Muhlenberg, 1959.

Wolff, Hans Walter. *Anthropology of the Old Testament.* Trans. by Margaret Kohl. Philadelphia: Fortress Press, 1974.

Woodfin, Yandell. "The Futurity of Beauty." *Theologische Zeitschrift* 29 (July-Aug. 1973): 256-79.

Worthing, Mark W. *Foundations and Functions of Theology as Universal Science: Theological Method and Apologetic Praxis in Wolfhart Pannenberg and Karl Rahner.* Frankfurt am Main: Peter Lang, 1996.

Worthington, Everett L. "A Blueprint for Intradisciplinary Integration." *Journal of Psychology and Theology* 22/2 (1994): 79-86.

Wright, N. T. *The New Testament and the People of God.* Minneapolis: Fortress Press, 1992.

Young, Davis A. *The Biblical Flood: A Case Study of the Church's Response to Extrabiblical Evidence.* Grand Rapids: Eerdmans, 1995.

Index

Aesthetics, 22, 66, 69, 219. *See also*
  Beauty
Anesthesia, educational, 69-70; theological, 74
Anselm, 197
Anxiety, 1, 2, 8, 11, 29, 36, 63-64, 92-93;
  epistemic, 6, 163, 191-92, 215-16; ethical, 6, 163, 191-92, 215-16; ontological,
  6, 163, 217-18, 241
Aristotle, 2, 6, 12ff., 19ff., 27, 29, 32, 34,
  152-53, 165ff., 170ff., 183n.5, 188, 223,
  226, 229
Athanasius, 223, 236
Augustine, 6, 16n.16, 167-68, 170-71,
  173n.22, 191ff., 224-25, 227; attitude
  toward science, 207; and
  Manicheanism, 194ff., 203; and
  Pelagianism, 194ff., 206; theory of
  inherited sin, 191-212

Barbour, Ian, 18n.9, 50, 209n.55
Barth, Karl, 5, 35, 56-57, 97, 99n.8,
  114n.28, 117ff., 140ff., 199, 234; and
  analogia relationis, 35, 127
Beauty, 6, 74, 163, 196, 218-19
Berkouwer, G. C., 128, 135, 211n.61,
  230n.35
Body, 18, 29, 72, 121, 130-31, 132, 145ff.,
  152, 159, 172, 173n.22, 184, 224n.23,
  227, 229, 230n.35, 238n.60, 240; res-

urrection of, 178, 184, 216; and soul,
  5-6, 130ff., 145ff., 159, 165ff., 177ff.
  See also Embodied; Soul
Boethius, 16, 31, 168, 172, 225
Bonhoeffer, D., 124
Brunner, Emil, 119, 128, 233-34
Buber, Martin, 31, 118, 129n.25, 233
Bultmann, Rudolf, 177-78

Calvin, John, 1, 3, 5-6, 19, 39, 85, 169,
  172, 185, 198, 227, 229. *See also* Reformed theology
Causality, 21-22, 170n.14, 174, 200n.30
Chalcedon, 56-57, 84-85, 144-45
Christology, 5, 35, 56, 77, 81, 93, 97ff.,
  109, 113ff., 139, 140ff., 168, 172, 189,
  197; Alexandrian and Antiochene,
  84-85, 169
Church, 4, 62, 68, 75, 115, 130-31, 139,
  158-59, 193-94, 222, 241
Class, xiii, 82, 86. *See also* Oppression;
  Liberation theology
Community, 2, 4, 22, 31, 42, 47, 69, 75,
  77, 135ff., 165, 178, 181, 213, 241-42
Consciousness, 20, 25, 28, 39, 51, 68,
  81, 103, 109, 130, 164-65, 179n.43,
  181ff., 235; orders of, 43ff.; self-
  consciousness, 24, 31, 34, 47, 79,
  97ff., 136, 139n.48, 240
Cultural anthropology, 3, 78ff.

Made in the USA
Charleston, SC
06 January 2012